Longitudinal Interactional Histories

"Institutions, writing, vocations, passions, languages, relationships, literacies, modalities—these are the makings of Kibler's longitudinal accounts of immigrant youth. Applying a "longitudinal interactional histories approach" to the experiences of youth as they move from high school into higher education and adulthood, Kibler introduces us to Jaime, Ana, Diego, Fabiola, and Maria and reveals how they negotiate the complexities of everyday life alongside policies, institutions, and practices that offer both possibilities and challenges.

Kibler has expertly accepted the challenge to use longitudinal methods as a means to document trajectories of becoming that too often limit possibilities for talented youth. However, Kibler, does not stop there. The accounts of Jaime, Ana, Diego, Fabiola, and Maria present spaces of possibility that promise to inspire educators and suggest possibilities for educators at all levels.

Kibler's stories of youth offer not only opportunities to learn and understand, but also spaces of possibility that invite us to re-conceptualize and re-imagine possibilities for youth in schools and communities."
—Catherine Compton-Lilly, *John C. Hungerpiller Chair of Education, University of South Carolina, USA*

"With an equal amount of exactness, patience, and affection, Amanda Kibler followed the same multilingual youth over 8 years and documented their literacy development through high school, college, and beyond. A true longitudinal feat that few of us have managed."
—Yasuko Kanno, *Associate Professor of Language Education, Boston University, USA*

"In this rigorously researched and beautifully written book, Amanda Kibler offers us a unique look at how five Mexican immigrant-origin youth developed bilingual and biliterate expertise over time and in the face of significant obstacles. Through rich and detailed cases, Kibler paints a vivid portrait of the triumphs and struggles these youth encountered. Her work challenges us to do better in our efforts to serve immigrant-origin youth, and it invites us to look beyond temporal, institutional, and ideological constraints in order to perceive how language and literacy develop across the lifespan."
—Ramón Antonio Martínez, *Assistant Professor, Graduate School of Education and Center for Comparative Studies in Race and Ethnicity, Stanford University, USA*

Amanda K. Kibler

Longitudinal Interactional Histories

Bilingual and Biliterate Journeys of Mexican Immigrant-origin Youth

Amanda K. Kibler
College of Education
Oregon State University
Corvallis, OR, USA

ISBN 978-3-319-98814-6   ISBN 978-3-319-98815-3   (eBook)
https://doi.org/10.1007/978-3-319-98815-3

Library of Congress Control Number: 2018955431

This Palgrave Macmillan imprint is published by the registered company Springer Nature Switzerland AG
The registered company address is: Gewerbestrasse 11, 6330 Cham, Switzerland

Foreword

As I write this foreword, I am in the process of destroying a data set from a five-year study of Latinx youth that I collected years ago. In truth, I probably held onto it too long, but parting with it has felt a bit like losing an old friend. My office feels barren without the bins full of student work samples I collected over the years, each evoking particular students, teachers, schools, and communities.

So I'm especially mindful at the moment about the nature of the work we do as longitudinal case study researchers working with multilingual youth. Amanda Kibler worked on the study featured here for eight years, which represents about a quarter of an average academic career. Practically an eon in the age of impact factors, when studies are considered antiquated after their first year in publication. While most scholars pay lip service to the desirability of longitudinal studies, few actually carry them out. Longitudinal qualitative research of the sort featured in this book is an investment (and a gamble) of the researcher's funds, time, and patience. It's an act of faith, starting off on what may be a wandering journey with unexpected twists and turns, while counting on a broad curiosity (and perhaps serendipity) to eventually yield intelligible results.

Perhaps just as importantly, it's also an emotional investment. As Kibler notes, longitudinal research ultimately requires building a particular sort of mutual trust between the researcher and the researched. It's a deeply interpersonal enterprise. It is also an especially tricky one when dealing with adolescents, who are often guarded in their relationships with adults. It's a tribute to Kibler that she was able to build such a strong bond with her participants, one that survived geographic scattering and life transitions.

And then once one has the data, we longitudinal researchers are left with the privilege and challenge of trying to represent the experience of multilingual youth in ways that will help others understand the very real consequences of theory and policy in individuals' lives. This is harder than it may look. Longitudinal studies tend to yield large and unwieldy data sets that can be paralyzing or make it difficult to see beyond the particular. Moreover, even the adolescents themselves who are the subjects of our studies tend to find their lives and literacy practices unremarkable, if not boring. Youth are often bemused by the eccentric researcher who finds their essays, text messages, Facebook pages, and doodles so endlessly fascinating. I must also confess that some of my own early attempts to portray the intricacies and significance of longitudinal case study research to colleagues at conferences put more than one audience member asleep.

In this book, Kibler has done an artful job of distilling years of data into compelling and usable portraits of her research participants. This wide-ranging tale shows how seemingly mundane high school and college literacy practices such as persuasive essays are interconnected with so many other things: students' previous schooling histories; multilingual peer interactions; intersectional identities and the roles of religiosity and gender; district, state, and national curriculum standards and regimes of standardized testing; the pernicious effects of tracking and segregation for English learners; enduring tensions between notions of academic language as process versus product; histories of Mexican American immigration and transnationalism; discrimination and disparate schooling outcomes; English-only ideologies; and digital affordances and divides.

Kibler makes these connections through what she has dubbed a "longitudinal interactional histories approach" (LIHA). It includes meticulous ethnographic documentation and analysis of key literacy events in students' lives. Kibler's LIHA allows her to see beyond the surface of a written product or classroom events and to examine how students' literacy practices and written texts are shaped by their life experiences, literacy histories, and multiple layers of social context. As a result, she is able to show how policies and practices at the institutional and societal level are manifested in individual experiences with literacies that change over time.

There is an inherent optimism in this work. The book builds compassionate, sympathetic portraits of youth while not shying away from their human fallibilities. Students forget things, attend selectively, and misunderstand or disregard information or deadlines that might be important to their schooling or career ambitions. Undocumented or remedialized status drags on their goals and ambitions, rendering them less than stellar or cooperative students. A case study participant unexpectedly stops communicating. The book addresses these issues but doesn't dwell on them, and ultimately what comes through is Kibler's successful achievement of "seeking goodness."

Along the way, this book delivers many important messages, among them that multilingual youth literacy practices can be profoundly multilingual, interactional, and socially constructed even when written products are single-authored and monolingual; that migration and documentation status are nowhere near as simple or straightforward as "build the wall" adherents might suggest; and that even youth from the same ethnolinguistic background and community who at first glance seem fairly homogeneous may over time be revealed as widely differing in their schooling and career paths.

The book's Mexican-origin adolescent focus is an especially important one given an age of increasingly overt stereotyping and discrimination toward immigrants. Yet despite its social and historic specificity, these students' experiences are pertinent far beyond one particular classroom or set of individuals. The issues addressed here should be of interest to all of us given the growing ethnolinguistic diversity to be found throughout much of the United States. In these student narratives, Kibler conveys the normalcy and quotidian nature of migration, transnationalism, and multilingualism among contemporary American youth. As such, the book makes a significant contribution to on-going national and international dialogue among educators about how we can best recognize and support multilingual students' academic strengths and needs while avoiding the pitfalls of labels, impoverished curricula, or low academic expectations.

University of Georgia   Linda Harklau
Athens, GA, USA
August, 2018

Acknowledgments

The research upon which this book is based spans eight years (2006–2014), nine educational institutions, five youth and the many people in their lives, hundreds of interviews and observations, thousands of pages of data, notes from countless articles and books, and the lifetimes of two audio/video recorders and three different laptops. As someone invested in understanding the stories behind texts, I recognize that my own book presents its own formidable set of interactional histories, and as a result there are a number of important acknowledgments I would like to make.

This work began while I was a PhD student at Stanford University (2005–2009), where funding as a Stanford Graduate Fellow supported me in pursuing research at South Sierra High School starting in 2006. This first phase of the study would not have been possible without the guidance and support of my advisor, Guadalupe Valdés, whose work continues to inspire me to conduct rigorous research, critically evaluate theory, and imbue everything I do with an unwavering commitment to social justice. I am also greatly indebted to the sage advice and valuable feedback provided by my dissertation committee members Kenji Hakuta, Andrea Lunsford, and Rachel Lotan in support of this project, as well as by colleagues Martha Castellón and Sarah Capitelli, among many others.

I continued this study as a postdoctoral researcher at Stanford (2009–2010) and an assistant professor at the University of Virginia, where I began working in 2010. In both contexts, colleagues were unfailing in their encouragement, and supervisors and department chairs provided me with time and resources necessary to undertake the data collection, analysis, and writing that formed this long-term endeavor.

I also thank the many colleagues who read and responded to portions of this book and/or commented upon it as discussants over the years, as well as the reviewers and editors whose feedback helped shape the articles and book chapters I published on this data along the way. Among the editors whom I particularly wish to thank are Heidi Byrnes, Kerri Ann Enright, Dana Ferris, Guillaume Gentil, Christina Ortmeier-Hooper, Lee Indrisano, Icy Lee, Ilona Leki, George Kamberelis, Luciana de Oliveria, Todd Ruecker, and Tony Silva. I am also very grateful for feedback from study participant Fabiola, who meticulously read and commented on several drafts of the article upon which Chap. 7 is based. This book also owes much to the colleagues and former students with whom I have co-authored using various portions of the data gathered for this study and who have been invaluable in developing my thinking for this book, including Elena Andrei, Christine Hardigree, Natasha Heny, Natalia Palacios, and April Salerno. I also thank students in my Discourse Analysis and Writing Research graduate seminars for their responses to various versions of this work. Finally, I extend my gratitude to Yasuko Kanno and anonymous Palgrave reviewers for their invaluable comments and responses on the full draft of this book, as well as to Linda Harklau for writing the foreword, and Cathy Scott, Beth Farrow, and the Palgrave editorial team for their support.

Family and friends have also been critical to this endeavor, and in particular I thank my husband Jeremy for his ongoing support and the many different forms it took: discussing and reading drafts, serving as a practice audience for presentations, attending the graduations and weddings of young people in the study, helping me set aside the time I needed to write, and encouraging me to take the time off I needed to recharge.

Most profoundly, I thank Jaime, Ana, Diego, Fabiola, and Maria—as well as their families, schools, and teachers—for opening their lives to me over the many years of this study. This book would simply not have been possible without their willingness to share so much of their experiences and their writing with me. It is my hope that this book does justice to the "goodness" of their language and literacy journeys while also presenting meaningful lessons to guide the development of more equitable educational opportunities for linguistically minoritized and immigrant-origin youth.

Contents

List of Figures

List of Tables

1

Starting the Journey: Introducing the Study, Youth, and Their Stories

Diego leans over his paper and reads aloud the beginning of a new sentence he is writing, "When your factory…" In Spanish, he begins to ask Zulema, who is sitting next to him, how to say something ("*cómo se*/how do you"), but before he can finish his question, she leans over and reads what he wrote aloud to herself. As she reads, Diego jumps in with a suggestion for a next word: "come." Zulema, eyes still on the paper, quickly rephrases it to the past tense, saying "came," and Diego nods in agreement. He then suggests additional wording, and together they animatedly discuss whether "came to my land," "came to the land," or "came to our land" would be the best option. They eventually agree that the last version would be most suitable, with Zulema noting, "OUR land, yeah, *suena mejor*/it sounds better." Diego nods and writes this new phrase on his paper. (Observation, 7 February 2008)

I watched many in- and out-of-class writing sessions such as this one, in which bilingual youth acted as co-authors, tutors, and editors, often interlacing their conversations about what they were writing with jokes, gossip, and comments about the latest photos they had posted online. Yet these were not the only interactions through which young people created texts. In both English and Spanish, they engaged with adults, orally and

© The Author(s) 2019
A. K. Kibler, *Longitudinal Interactional Histories*,
https://doi.org/10.1007/978-3-319-98815-3_1

in writing, and they drew from other written and multimodal texts, often using various digital technologies to do so. They also interacted with less tangible but often quite impactful policies, practices, and discourses in ways that shaped their opportunities to create texts and the texts themselves.

Their stories tell of the successes, difficulties, compromises, strategies, and struggles involved in developing bilingual and biliterate repertoires both inside and outside of schooling. By following these youth through adolescence and into early adulthood, I was able to witness their language and literacy journeys across multiple contexts and years. Doing so allowed me to better understand how a range of discourses, governmental and institutional policies and practices, individuals, texts, and technologies served to facilitate and/or hinder the development of their bilingual and biliterate expertise. *Longitudinal Interactional Histories: Bilingual and Biliterate Journeys of Mexican Immigrant-Origin Youth* aims to provide insight into patterns of language and literacy development as they occur in and across multiple and diverse settings during linguistically minoritized youth's adolescence and young adulthood.

This book analyzes the experiences of five young people: Jaime, Ana, Diego, Fabiola, and Maria. As immigrant-origin individuals from Spanish-speaking homes who were classified by their school system as "English learners," they are part of a large and growing demographic in the United States, one that tends to be discussed as a problem to be fixed in schools rather than as the foundation of our increasingly multilingual[1] society. While theories of language acquisition and development have arguably experienced a multilingual turn (May, 2014) in recent years through increasing recognition of the fundamental role of *all* languages in individuals' repertoires, the contexts in which the youth in this study developed language and literacy expertise varied in their support for multilingualism. A better understanding of the promises and contradictions inherent in such settings and their implications for language and literacy development has much to offer the fields of education, rhetoric and composition, applied linguistics, and sociolinguistics.

This study draws upon eight years of data collection, which started when youth began ninth grade at South Sierra High School, a small charter school in the Northern California community of South Sierra, and extended four years after their high school graduation.[2] All five were assessed to be at beginning or intermediate English language proficiency overall and in writing when they began high school, according to standardized English language proficiency test results, had lived in Mexico for at least some of their school-aged years, and spoke Spanish as a dominant home language[3] (see Kibler, 2009). They all graduated on time, four from South Sierra High School and one from neighboring West Hills High School. After graduation, the participants dispersed geographically, with Maria moving to the East Coast of the United States, Diego to Southern California, and Fabiola to a different part of Northern California. Ana and Jaime remained in the South Sierra community and lived with family there. The academic and vocational paths they pursued also differed: Maria undertook Catholic religious training, Diego and Fabiola went to universities, Jamie took classes at community college, and Ana enrolled in a cosmetology program. As they progressed through and beyond these institutions, the language and literacy practices in which they engaged became increasingly diverse.

Youth's languages and literacies are described and analyzed as social practices, ones that take place in social, cultural, and historical contexts that are embedded within each other (Ivanič, 2004) and across time. I also take a critical-sociocultural orientation to language and literacy development, recognizing the power relationships that are visible in individuals' experiences and the ways in which institutional and social forces shape language and literacy practices (Moje & Lewis, 2007). From this perspective, it is imperative to counter the predominant deficit-oriented discourses[4] that tend to linguistically minoritize the capacities and assets of multilingual youth from immigrant backgrounds by devaluing or ignoring their home and community language and literacy resources. In response to these concerns, this book is dedicated to *seeking goodness*, which Lawrence-Lightfoot and Davis (1997) described as "an intentionally generous and eclectic process that begins by searching for what is good and healthy and assumes that the expression of goodness will always be laced with imperfections" (p. 9).

I use writing in particular as a lens through which to explore language and literacy practices over time for several reasons. First, written texts are deeply enmeshed with other multimodal practices. As individuals write, they are often doing so in response to other texts they have read or seen and conversations they have had with other people, both in the moment of a literacy event and in the days, weeks, months, and years preceding it. In this sense, writing not only demonstrates a multivocality that is of interest to many scholars but also offers a valuable means of understanding how various aspects of an individual's language and literacy expertise work together within a given social context. Second, while many aspects of language and literacy practices can be—and often are—treated as "products" to be measured and assessed within the context of educational institutions and research, writing in particular tends to be viewed in this manner and to be used as a gatekeeper to accessing educational opportunities. Such a trend disadvantages many immigrant-origin multilingual writers, whose strengths and expertise can easily be overlooked when only considering the texts they produce rather than both the complex (and often multilingual) processes through which they create texts and the minoritizing discourses they may encounter as they do so, particularly in educational settings. Third, I focus on writing because of its potential to be a powerful means of both communication and reflection: As Jaime explains in Chap. 4, writers "express something, a point of view that you really have. I mean, it's something I could go back to later on and reflect on, like it's a permanent point of view for myself" (Interview, 24 May 2014).

To tell the stories of these young people, I have used what I call a "longitudinal interactional histories approach" (LIHA) to qualitative data analysis. It draws upon interviews and samples of youth's writing over time, along with ethnographic observations during their early high school careers, to understand three key phenomena: the interactions individuals had with discourses, governmental and institutional policies and practices, individuals, texts, and technologies while creating their own texts in and out of school; how those interactions shaped their texts; and how their texts (and the processes through which they were created) changed over time. While each young person's story is necessarily unique, I argue that their language and literacy journeys reflect larger trends among multilinguals from immigrant backgrounds in the United States in three key respects. First, non-English resources tended to be marginalized by academic and institutional policies and practices, but bilingual and biliterate expertise was often key to academic and professional activities and identities. Second, success within institutions depended not only on young people's literacy expertise and development but also on having a range of mutually reinforcing and supportive interactions with discourses, governmental and institutional policies and practices, individuals, texts, and technologies. Third, even in the most promising situations, youth had relatively few opportunities to develop robust biliterate repertoires within traditional educational settings.

A Rationale

While this book addresses issues of language and literacy through the lenses of multilingualism and immigration in ways that are applicable to many individuals, the focus on youth of Mexican origin[5] in the United States is a purposeful one. The imperative for improving educational opportunities for this group has never been more urgent. As Gándara (2015) argued, "Poverty, unequal K-12 schooling opportunities, low parental education, and low expectations of Mexican-origin youth's abilities and educational prospects remain endemic" (p. ix). Such inequitable circumstances have had dramatic impacts. Recent census data suggest that individuals of Mexican origin—who comprise 64.1% of the Latinx[6] population in the United States, or 34.6 million people—have higher average levels of poverty and lower levels of academic achievement and advancement relative to the overall Latinx and US populations (López & Patten, 2015; see also Jensen & Sawyer, 2013).[7]

Another reason I focus on Mexican-origin youth in particular is that educational and other discourses tend to "essentialize the Hispanic/ Latino category, erasing the experiences of Mexican American men and women" (Zambrana & Hurtado, 2015, p. 78). Indeed, research itself often fails to disaggregate Latinx populations by country of origin, a trend that is reflected in the studies I reference throughout this book. Yet, census data suggest that individuals of Mexican heritage, like those from other Latinx groups, tend to self-identify according to their country of origin rather than pan-ethnic labels (López & Patten, 2015). There are also sociohistorical circumstances that make the experiences of people of Mexican origin unique, in that parts of what is now the United States were formerly part of Mexico itself. Because of this history and ongoing patterns of migration, this population has had a longer history of discrimination and segregation than those of many other contemporary immigrant groups (Caldera, Velez-Gomez, & Lindsey, 2015). Further, the economic and geographic ties between the United States and Mexico have helped forge stronger transnational connections and communication among populations on both sides of the border than have taken place in many other immigrant populations (Gándara & García, 2013). Mexican-origin youth are also an important part of current debates on immigration in the United States, in that they comprise the majority of the well-known DREAMer[8] population of immigrant-origin young people who arrived in childhood without authorization/documentation (American Immigration Council, 2012). They also comprise over 70% of all individuals under age 18 in the United States who had at least one unauthorized/undocumented parent as of 2010 (Passel & Cohn, 2011). Given these varied circumstances, making Mexican-origin youth a focus of study can contribute to a better understanding of the range of intersecting economic, linguistic, social, and legal factors that can disadvantage immigrant-origin children and youth from all backgrounds. Such a focus also highlights the ways in which the unique circumstances and cultural strengths of communities of Mexican heritage (Jensen & Sawyer, 2013) can influence those processes.

At the same time, however, Mexican-origin populations in the United States must be understood as diverse and multidimensional. Communities of origin in Mexico and those of reception in the United States vary according to geography, urbanity/rurality, educational opportunities, and cultural and linguistic characteristics and traditions. Individual variations are also present in terms of generational and socioeconomic status, educational background, gender, acculturation/enculturation, cultural and linguistic affiliation, proficiency in and use of different varieties of Spanish and/or English (and at times indigenous languages), and indigenous and/or European ancestry, among other features (Caldera et al., 2015). Reese (2013) argued that this situation is yet more complex because cultural practices are dynamic rather than static, in that cultural models in both United States and Mexico are changing as individuals and families respond to new contexts, a situation that problematizes generalizations that are often made about Mexican-origin individuals and communities. This book seeks to explore such dynamic circumstances through attending carefully to the particular interactions influencing Mexican immigrant-origin youth's language and literacy development.

Situating the Study

Here I describe the community and institutional contexts in which I first met Jaime, Ana, Diego, Fabiola, and Maria and conducted the initial ethnographic fieldwork for this study. In a broad sense, the location of the South Sierra community in California is significant. The land that currently comprises the state has long played an important role in the global migration flows shaping the contemporary United States, dating from movements of native peoples and European colonization and extending through multiple waves of immigration to the present day (Starr, 2005). California is currently the most populous state in the United States, according to results of the American Community Survey; as of 2016, its more than 39 million people accounted for over 10% of the national population.[9] Latinx is the single largest race/ethnicity in the state at 38.9% of the total, the third highest statewide percentage in the country after New Mexico and Texas, and more than twice the national average. Further, although immigrants from Latin America are increasingly settling in a range of new destinations in the United States, the Latinx population in California includes 35% of all individuals in the United States who report being of Mexican origin, more than 12 million people in total (López & Patten, 2015). In terms of linguistic diversity, 43.9% of persons aged 5 or older in California are estimated to speak a language other than English at home, the highest percentage in the nation and again more than twice the national average.

At South Sierra High School and in the local community, the presence of Mexican-origin and multilingual individuals was even greater. For example, in Mr. Smith's class, which was profiled at the beginning of this chapter and which I observed during the ethnographic phase of this study, all but 2 of the 23 students spoke a home language other than or in addition to English. With the exception of one Tongan and one Fijian youth, the rest of the bilingual students in the class identified as both Mexican and Spanish-speaking. Similar demographic patterns existed (and continue today) at the school and in the South Sierra community, with the addition of small numbers of speakers of Samoan, Hindi, Mandarin, and other languages. At the time of the study, most families of South Sierra High School students also had at least one member who was in the country without authorization/documentation, and fear of *la migra* (the Immigration and Customs Enforcement Agency), possible deportation, and family separation were concerns that touched almost every student.[10] And although the South Sierra community today is increasingly known for the rapid gentrification it has experienced, most of the students at South Sierra High School during this study came from families in which parents worked multiple jobs and typically had less than a high school education, either in the United States or abroad. For these young people, such a situation meant that they had relatively less access to the academic enrichment activities typical in middle- and upper-class households, unless they were provided by schools, and they also relied heavily (or entirely) on scholarships or other forms of assistance if they chose to pursue postsecondary schooling. Those students without authorization/documentation had to cope with additional anxieties about their legal status as well as greater barriers to further education.[11] For example, although at the time of this study they were eligible by state law to receive in-state tuition at postsecondary institutions (rather than the far more expensive international student rate), government-sponsored financial aid and many private scholarships required citizenship or other forms of documentation.

Like many charter schools, South Sierra High School was far smaller than nearby traditional comprehensive high schools, enrolling just 300 students across grades 9–12. Teachers and administrators encountered the range of institutional challenges faced by many charter schools: They served socioeconomically disadvantaged students who had been poorly educated for years before arriving at their door, but they had to do so with insufficient financial resources, limited physical space, and high staff turnover. During the study, the school was also repeatedly under threat of various federal sanctions due to multiple years of failing to meet annual yearly progress benchmarks on English-medium standardized assessments. State-level restrictions in place at the time also meant that few, if any, students had been able to take part in bilingual or dual-language education programs during elementary or middle school.

This school was unique, however, in multiple regards. First, following a strict no-tracking policy that is quite rare in US secondary schools (Callahan, Wilkinson, & Muller, 2010; Umansky, 2016), the school placed students at all academic and linguistic proficiency levels in general education courses (rather than remedial ones), offering students potential access to grade-level curriculum but also forcing teachers to face the challenge of designing instruction for a wide range of students. The curriculum was designed to be rigorous; for example, students' annual humanities courses, through which they learned both English and social studies, were centered on a philosophy of teaching challenging texts. According to one of the school's founding teachers, students in those courses needed to read several "thick, important books" a year. However, many teachers struggled to teach these texts in ways that were accessible to all students. Second, the school was also distinctive in its attempts to navigate several of the gaps between the monolingual orientations of school policies and the realities of its multilingual students and families. While there was no formal bilingual program at South Sierra High School, students could enroll in a bilingual humanities course for incoming ninth graders as well as Spanish-for-Native-Speakers courses, the latter of which were also offered at West Hills High School, the school to which Jaime transferred in tenth grade. Several teachers and other adults at South Sierra High School spoke Spanish (with six of them having grown up speaking Spanish at home), students regularly used Spanish in hallways and classrooms, and in some classes, students were exposed to literature written by Latinx, African American, and other authors of color. Although teachers' Spanish use and the bilingual humanities course were clearly transitional in nature, those efforts alongside the Spanish courses and the use of multicultural literature can be seen as attempts to maintain and enhance students' existing linguistic and cultural resources.

As the stories of Jaime, Ana, Diego, Fabiola, and Maria presented in this book suggest, although they shared many of the same experiences as members of the South Sierra community and students at South Sierra High School (or West Hills High School for Jaime, explored in more detail in Chap. 4), they developed very different interactional histories with languages and literacies during those years. As they progressed through adolescence and into young adulthood, their language and literacy practices became even more distinct as the contexts in which they lived, studied, and worked changed as well.

Researching Bilingual and Biliterate Lives: My Positioning and Repositioning

One day in a biology class I was observing, Diego, dressed in pressed khakis and a polo shirt, was chatting animatedly with a classmate at his assigned table. As Ms. Morales, their teacher, began to explain the genetics lesson for the day, I placed an audio recorder between the two boys, inadvertently interrupting their conversation. The classmate, who had just returned to school after a month-long trip to Mexico, asked Diego what the recorder was for. Diego, already used to having the recorder around, shrugged, smiled, and said, "*Es para ver como son*/It's to see how things are."[12] Diego was well versed in the particular purposes of my research project, which I had dutifully explained to him and his classmates in keeping with the dictates of my university's research review board, but the simple response he offered revealed much about my aims while conducting research. It was my sincere hope that the data I was collecting would eventually allow me to offer an analysis of "how things are" for young people from Mexican immigrant families who were in relatively early stages of developing English language and literacy expertise as they began high school, one that would highlight their voices, experiences, and perspectives as they moved through adolescence and into adulthood. Doing justice to these stories, however, required attention to not only the participants in this research but also my own role in the process.

During the eight years of this study, I played multiple roles: an instructional coach for South Sierra High School teachers, someone just "hanging out," an informal tutor, and an interviewer, among others. My lack of a formal teacher role, my use of Spanish with students, and my ongoing communication with them across settings and years helped me to earn their trust and gain access to their experiences inside and outside of school. However, as an English-dominant White woman in her 30s, my age, ethnicity, Spanish language expertise (developed as an adult), middle-class socioeconomic position, and professional identity marked me as an outsider in the South Sierra community, although one with privileges often denied to minoritized immigrant youth and their families. These differences in privilege and background inevitably shaped my interactions with the young people in the study, and throughout data collection and analysis I strove to "listen" carefully—to both what they told me and what they did not—in efforts to better understand their perspectives and experiences. As I describe further in the Methodological Appendix and throughout the book, these identities and positionalities influenced our relationships and shifted over time in different ways that reflected such complexities.

Introducing Youth and Looking Ahead

This book is organized into three main sections in order to contextualize the research study, highlight the richness and complexity of each young person's language and literacy journey over time, and draw conclusions about similarities among their experiences and implications for research and practice. Chapter 2 provides readers with an overview of the language and literacy theories from which I draw to understand the stories of the young people in this study, along with a brief background on what is known empirically about multilingual immigrant-origin adolescents and young adults' language and literacy practices and patterns of development over time, with an emphasis on writing in particular. This chapter closes with an exploration of the minoritizing discourses that often impact these students and their experiences inside and outside educational settings. Chapter 3 focuses on methodology, specifically the longitudinal qualitative case study and ethnographic traditions I drew upon in conducting this research. It addresses the overall design of the study and the approaches to data collection as well as the longitudinal interactional histories approach (LIHA) to qualitative analysis described earlier, including both the theoretical under-pinnings and the methodological implications of each step of this approach.

The next section of the book (Chaps. 4, 5, 6, 7, and 8) presents the individual stories of Jaime, Ana, Diego, Fabiola, and Maria and explores the ways their language and literacy journeys unfolded through various "turning points" over the eight years of the study. The order in which these chapters are presented reflects the prominence of certain institutional pathways among multilingual and Latinx populations in the United States. Research has shown that multilingual, English-learner classified, and Latinx students who attend postsecondary schooling tend to enroll in community colleges[13] more often than four-year postsecond-ary institutions (Kanno & Cromley, 2015; Krogstad, 2016; Núñez & Sparks, 2012). For this reason, I first present the experiences of Jaime and Ana, who both attended community colleges, although Ana's choice to pursue a vocational rather than an academic track was unique. I then turn to experiences at four-year universities, where graduation rates for Latinx populations have grown since 2002 but still trail behind those of White students (NCES, 2016). In that context, I explore the journeys of Diego, who began university studies but did not complete them, and Fabiola, who successfully finished her coursework and earned a bachelor's degree. The last chapter in this section focuses on Maria, who chose to pursue religious studies outside of traditional postsecondary institutions, a journey in which she engaged in language and literacy practices that were very different from those of many multilingual and Latinx youth in the United States.

The following are brief descriptions of each young person in the study:

- Jaime attended school in Mexico until arriving in the United States in third grade. Jaime's relatively small physical stature—which often led people to think he was younger than he was—belied a big personality. An outgoing, affable movie buff quick to use humor in English or Spanish, Jaime was a favorite of several of his teachers despite his usual reluctance to engage in writing or reading tasks. Jaime left South Sierra High School in the spring of his tenth-grade year to attend a nearby comprehensive high school, West Hills, where he was placed in remedial-track or English-learner-only classes and at times struggled academically. He had limited access to financial aid for postsecondary schooling because of his authorization/documentation status, but with the help of a benefactor from the community, he enrolled in a local community college the fall after his high school graduation. Despite successful engagement with writing tasks and support from teachers and others, Jaime grew frustrated with the required remedial class sequence and eventually stopped taking courses at the community college, instead working full-time in jobs where he often acted as a language broker for colleagues. His language and literacy journey is analyzed in Chap. 4.

- Ana came from Mexico in fifth grade and attended schools in the South Sierra community from that time onward. When I met her, she was a passionate, loyal teenager fiercely dedicated to her friends but ambivalent about school. Always knowledgeable about the latest fashions, Ana appeared at high school perfectly put-together every morning, her make-up carefully applied, her clothing painstakingly selected, and her short, straight hair impeccably styled. During her high school years, she spent time at home caring for her younger siblings, playing on a club soccer team, and hanging out with friends. Ana used English and Spanish orally with a variety of fellow students and teachers, but I often observed that she only grudgingly read or wrote in either language for school-based tasks. In 12th grade, an inspirational Mexican-origin Latina role model and an interest in pursuing cosmetology propelled Ana through her last year of high school, and she spoke excitedly about her plans for the future. She successfully completed a cosmetology program with the help of a loan from a former teacher, but because of then-current immigration policies was not eligible to obtain a state cosmetology license. Ana at first worked at a small neighborhood salon run by a Spanish-dominant boss, where she was regularly given all the English-speaking clients because her English was considered the strongest. She later ran her own salon from her family's home, using a range of resources to keep current on the latest styles for her bilingual clients. Her language and literacy journey is analyzed in Chap. 5.
- Diego was born in the South Sierra community and attended school until first grade. He then moved to Mexico with his family and lived with them on a remote *rancho* for several years without attending school.

He returned to South Sierra and to formal education at age 12. Tall and athletic, Diego could often be found playing pick-up games of volleyball on the asphalt schoolyard at his high school or showing his friends the latest photos he had taken on his digital camera. Despite having an interrupted education, he excelled in mathematics and developed a reputation among teachers as a hardworking student. He prided himself on speaking to his teachers in English, although in the first two years of high school he often relied on his peers[14] to explain teachers' lectures and on both teachers and classmates to help him complete written work in English. By his last year of high school, however, Diego had successfully developed an identity as an increasingly competent English user who met his school's criteria for academic success. He earned a competitive scholarship and began university studies, but once there quickly came to believe he "didn't know the basics," especially in writing. At Ocean College, he was placed in a sequence of remedial and introductory classes—rather than the business courses he was looking forward to—and, despite supportive interactions with some of his teachers and the mentor provided through his scholarship, struggled to pass several of them. His language and literacy journey is analyzed in Chap. 6.

- Fabiola was born in the United States but moved to Mexico with her family as a preschooler. She returned to the United States and began ninth grade at South Sierra High School after completing schooling in Mexico through *secundaria* (grades 7–9). Fabiola participated in Student Council, finished her homework regularly, and earned high grades in her classes, all the while also working 20 hours a week at a local convenience store. For the first two years of high school, she very reluctantly used spoken English in class, although by 12th grade she joked that her teachers couldn't get her to *stop* talking in either English or Spanish. Fabiola earned a scholarship to a top-tier state university, where she eventually majored in Gender and Women's Studies. Through writing experiences in her major, she developed a multifaceted identity as a "Mexican feminist" but had limited opportunities to assert a legitimate language learner identity or biliterate expertise in support of her disciplinary or more general writerly identities. Her language and literacy journey is analyzed in Chap. 7.

- Zulema was born in the South Sierra community, but at age five she moved to Mexico with her family because of the illness of a grandparent there. She attended a local elementary school in Mexico and returned to South Sierra in sixth grade, where she went on to excel academically at her middle and high schools. A motivated and sociable student, she was always in contact with her friends, in person, by phone, or online, in conversations that revolved around music, school, and social events. Although Zulema moved easily between English and Spanish in conversations with her teachers and classmates in high school, she often worried that she could not express herself in English as well as she would like, either orally or in writing. Comments about university peppered her assignments and discussions with others throughout high school, and so her choice upon high school graduation to become a novice, or prospective member of a Catholic convent, surprised many in her school community who had assumed that she would go to one of the universities to which she had already been accepted. She completed the novitiate program—where she took on a new name, Maria—and two subsequent years of study at a Catholic institution of Latin American origin she called the Institute. While at the Institute, she took on a range of duties there and in local parishes, including religious teaching. She then studied for a final year in Rome. In these postsecondary experiences, Maria's bilingual and biliterate expertise played a significant role in her formal studies and her role as a teacher of children and youth. Her language and literacy journey is analyzed in Chap. 8.

These brief portraits suggest some of the many ways in which these young people grew to hold a range of different social, linguistic, and literate identities: language broker, bilingual stylist, hardworking English user, Mexican feminist, and Catholic sister, among others. These intersectional identities were developed through the varied language and literacy practices in which they engaged over time and across settings, which made each individual's journey unique.

The third and final section of the book is Chap. 8, which synthesizes Jaime, Ana, Diego, Fabiola, and Maria's experiences in efforts to explore key patterns in youth's language and literacy development; the influence of key interactions with discourses, governmental and institutional policies and practices, individuals, texts, and technologies; and the roles played by bilingual and biliterate practices both inside and outside of formal educational settings. In doing so, I focus on the deep contradictions faced by Spanish-English speakers in the United States whose bilingual and biliterate expertise play key roles in many of their journeys, despite limited institutional support or recognition. I then turn to implications for policymakers, educators, and researchers related to facilitating the success of minoritized multilingual youth in today's secondary and postsecondary schools and understanding the complexity of language and literacy practices that occur both across languages and over the lifespan.

Notes

1. As described in Chap. 2, I use the term *bilingual* in reference to individuals or communities who consider themselves users of two societally defined languages, or studies, programs, or policies that describe such contexts. *Multilingual*, as I use it, is a broader and more inclusive term with less focus on a particular number of languages but with an emphasis on more than one language in use.
2. All individual, institutional, and local place names in this book are pseudonyms, and any relationship to actual names is purely coincidental. In the US educational system, ninth graders are typically 14–15 years old. South Sierra High School enrolled students in grades 9–12, which is a common pattern nationwide. In some US school districts, however, ninth grade is included as part of lower secondary schooling, which is typically referred to as junior high school or middle school.
3. Indigenous languages are spoken in many Mexican-origin households, but none of the young people in this study reported using any languages other than Spanish and English. They described using primarily Spanish with parents and adult family/community members but both English and Spanish with siblings, younger relatives, and friends. These patterns were fairly consistent over time, although all youth used somewhat more English with the latter group as they grew older.

4. Throughout this book, I use the term "discourse" in the sense of the social and historical identities and ideologies that are enacted through language and other means, in keeping with Gee's (2014) notion of "big D Discourse."

5. My use of the term "Mexican origin" includes individuals who were born in Mexico or who are descendants of those who were, without any attempts to define generational status. In contrast, I use "immigrant origin" to refer to individuals who are immigrants themselves or the children of immigrants, following other scholars' use of these terms (Suárez-Orozco, Abo-Zena, & Marks, 2015).

6. This book was written at a time in which the term "Latinx" was becoming increasingly common as part of a larger emphasis on gender inclusivity in language use. The data for this study was collected before this movement gained traction, however, when "Latino" or "Latina" were more common terms in general, and "Latin@" was employed in certain academic circumstances. In this book, I employ "Latinx"— currently the most inclusive term—in reference to larger demographic populations previously defined using the terms Latino and/or Hispanic, but in all other instances retain original terminology (as used in the research setting) to reflect how students, teachers, or other institutional stakeholders spoke or wrote about themselves or this group.

7. It should be noted that the Mexican-origin population is slightly above (or below) averages for these indicators, rather than at the extremes of highest poverty or lowest educational attainment among Latinx populations. Such patterns are nevertheless troubling, particularly given the relative size of the Mexican-origin population and number of youth whom this encompasses.

8. "DREAMers" refers to those individuals who would meet requirements of the proposed Development, Relief, and Education for Alien Minors (DREAM) Act. More details regarding this act and its fate are provided later in the book. See also Gonzales and Raphael (2017) for a detailed analysis of policies shaping immigrants' legal status from the mid-twentieth century onward.

9. Except where noted, demographic data in this paragraph was drawn from the U.S. Census Bureau's American Community Survey (ACS) and Puerto Rico Community Survey (PRCS) 5-Year Estimates and retrieved from https://www.census.gov/quickfacts.

10. Having family members without authorization/documentation can also have educational implications: Bean, Brown, and Bachmeier (2013) and

Bean, Brown, Leach, Bachmeier, and Tafoya-Estrada (2015) found that a lack of parental authorization/documentation is associated with lower educational outcomes for Mexican-origin children. Bean et al. (2013) hypothesized that this trend is driven by work imperatives and familial economic decisions due to immigration status, greater levels of stress and anxiety (see also Potochnick & Perreira, 2010), and discrimination.

11. Gonzales (2011) argued that unauthorized/undocumented adolescents' coming of age coincides with increased legal barriers as they begin to enter adult roles—like getting a driver's license or applying for college—that require legal status. This process often involves frustration and uncertainty that can lead to a lack of academic motivation and withdrawal from support networks in later years of high school (Gonzales, 2011, 2016), as well as lower educational expectations than those of youth from similar backgrounds who have authorization/documentation (Perreira & Spees, 2015). Research has also found greater levels of anxiety among immigrant adolescents and young adults who lack legal status than among those who are authorized/documented (Gonzales, Suárez-Orozco, & Dedios-Sanguineti, 2013; Teranishi, Suárez-Orozco, & Suárez-Orozco, 2015). For further exploration of the implications of unauthorized/undocumented status on youth development, see Yoshikawa, Suárez-Orozco, and Gonzales (2017).

12. Throughout this book, I italicize uses of Spanish and provide a translation immediately after, either using a slash mark (/) or placing it underneath the original.

13. I use the term community college to refer to postsecondary institutions which primarily offer two-year degrees and coursework across a range of fields that include traditional academic disciplines as well as more workforce-related areas. I use the term university to refer to postsecondary institutions that grant four-year bachelor's degrees. It should be noted, however, that some four-year institutions in the United States are named as a "college," like "Ocean College" that Diego attended.

14. I have argued elsewhere that who a "peer" is can only be defined relative to particular social or institutional contexts, and with attention to both similarity and difference (Kibler, 2017). In this study, the term "peer" applies primarily to individuals who are fellow classmates in the various educational institutions youth attended. Shared placement in a class does not imply that peers necessarily had similar language and literacy repertoires: those varied quite widely—even in highly tracked classes—and played important roles in what students learned from and taught one another.

References

American Immigration Council. (2012). *Who and where the DREAMers are, revised estimates*. Washington, DC: American Immigration Council. Retrieved from https://www.americanimmigrationcouncil.org/research/who-and-where-dreamers-are-revised-estimates

Bean, F. D., Brown, S. K., & Bachmeier, J. D. (2015). *Parents without papers: The progress and pitfalls of Mexican American integration*. New York: Russell Sage Foundation.

Bean, F. D., Brown, S. K., Leach, M. A., Bachmeier, J. D., & Tafoya-Estrada, R. (2013). Unauthorized migration and its implications for Mexican American educational incorporation. In B. Jensen & A. Sawyer (Eds.), *Regarding educación: Mexican-American schooling, immigration, and bi-national improvement* (pp. 43–65). New York: Teachers College Press.

Caldera, Y. M., Velez-Gomez, P., & Lindsey, E. W. (2015). Who are Mexican Americans? An overview of history, immigration, and cultural values. In Y. M. Caldera & E. W. Lindsey (Eds.), *Mexican American children and families: Multidisciplinary perspectives* (pp. 3–12). New York: Routledge.

Callahan, R., Wilkinson, L., & Muller, C. (2010). Academic achievement and course taking among language minority students in U.S. schools: Effects of ESL placement. *Educational Evaluation and Policy Analysis, 32*(1), 84–117. http://epa.sagepub.com/content/32/1/84.short. https://doi.org/10.3102/0162373709359805.

Gándara, P. (2015). Foreword. In R. E. Zambrana & S. Hurtado (Eds.), *The magic key: The educational journey of Mexican Americans from K-12 to college and beyond* (pp. ix–xiv). Austin: The University of Texas Press.

Gándara, P., & García, E. (2013). Foreword. In B. Jensen & A. Sawyer (Eds.), *Regarding educación: Mexican-American schooling, immigration, and bi-national improvement* (pp. ix–xi). New York: Teachers College Press.

Gee, J. P. (2014). *An introduction to discourse analysis: Theory and method* (4th ed.). Oxon, UK: Routledge.

Gonzales, R. G. (2011). Learning to be illegal: Undocumented youth and shifting legal contexts in the transition to adulthood. *American Sociological Review, 76*(4), 602–619. https://doi.org/10.1177/0003122411411901.

Gonzales, R. G., Suárez-Orozco, C., & Dedios-Sanguineti, M. C. (2013). No place to belong: Contextualizing concepts of mental health among undocumented immigrant youth in the United States. *American Behavioral Scientist, 57*(8), 1174–1199.https://doi.org/10.1177/0002764213487349.

Gonzales, R. G. (2016). *Lives in limbo: Undocumented and coming of age in America*. Berkeley: University of California Press.

Gonzales, R. G., & Raphael, S. (2017). Illegality: A contemporary portrait of immigration. *RSF: The Russell Sage Foundation Journal of the Social Sciences, 3*(4), 1–17. http://www.jstor.org/stable/10.7758/rsf.2017.3.4.01.

Ivanič, R. (2004). Discourses of writing and learning to write. *Language and Education, 18*(3), 220–245. https://doi.org/10.1080/09500780408666877.

Jensen, B., & Sawyer, A. (2013). Regarding *educación*: A vision for school improvement. In B. Jensen & A. Sawyer (Eds.), *Regarding educación: Mexican-American schooling, immigration, and bi-national improvement* (pp. 1–24). New York: Teachers College Press.

Kanno, Y., & Cromley, J. G. (2015). English language learners' pathways to four-year colleges. *Teachers College Record, 117*(12), 1–44.

Kibler, A. K. (2009). *Talking writing: Adolescent English learners in the content areas* (Unpublished doctoral dissertation). Stanford, CA: Stanford University.

Kibler, A. K. (2017). Peer interaction and learning in multilingual settings from a sociocultural perspective: Theoretical insights. *International Multilingual Research Journal, 11*(3), 199–203. https://doi.org/10.1080/19313152.2017.1328970.

Krogstad, J. M. (2016). *5 facts about Latinos and education*. Washington, DC: Pew Research Center. Retrieved from: http://www.pewresearch.org/fact-tank/2016/07/28/5-facts-about-latinos-and-education/

Lawrence-Lightfoot, S., & Davis, J. H. (1997). *The art and science of portraiture*. San Francisco: Jossey-Bass Publishers.

López, G., & Patten, E. (2015). *The impact of slowing immigration: Foreign-born share falls among 14 largest U.S. Hispanic groups*. Washington, DC: Pew Research Center. Retrieved from: http://www.pewhispanic.org/2015/09/15/the-impact-of-slowing-immigration-foreign-born-share-fallsamong-14-largest-us-hispanic-origin-groups/

May, S. (Ed.). (2014). *The multilingual turn: Implications for SLA, TESOL and bilingual education*. New York: Routledge.

Moje, E. B., & Lewis, C. (2007). Examining opportunities to learn literacy: The role of critical sociocultural literacy research. In C. Lewis, P. Enciso, & E. B. Moje (Eds.), *Reframing sociocultural research on literacy: Identity, agency, and power* (pp. 15–48). Mahwah, NJ: Erlbaum.

National Center for Education Statistics. (2016). *Digest of Education Statistics, Table 326.10. Graduation rate from first institution attended for first-time, full-time bachelor's degree-seeking students at 4-year postsecondary institutions, by race/ethnicity, time to completion, sex, control of institution, and acceptance rate: Selected cohort entry years, 1996 through 2009*. Washington, DC: National

Center for Education Statistics. Retrieved from: https://nces.ed.gov/pro-grams/digest/d16/tables/dt16_326.10.asp

Núñez, A. M., & Sparks, P. J. (2012). Who are linguistic minority students in higher education? An analysis of the Beginning Postsecondary Students Study 2004. In Y. Kanno & L. Harklau (Eds.), *Linguistic minority students go to college: Preparation, access, and persistence* (pp. 110–129). New York: Routledge.

Passel, J., & Cohn, D. (2011). *Unauthorized immigrant population: National and state trends, 2010*. Washington, DC: Pew Research Center. Retrieved from: http://www.pewhispanic.org/2011/02/01/unauthorized-immigrant-population-brnational-and-state-trends-2010/

Perreira, K. M., & Spees, L. (2015). Foiled aspirations: The influence of unauthorized status on the educational expectations of Latino immigrant youth. *Population Research and Policy Review, 34*(5), 641–664. https://doi.org/10.1007/s11113-015-9356-y.

Potochnick, S. R., & Perreira, K. M. (2010). Depression and anxiety among first-generation immigrant Latino youth: Key correlates and implications for future research. *Journal of Nervous and Mental Disease, 198*(7), 470–477. https://doi.org/10.1097/NMD.0b013e3181e4ce24.

Reese, L. (2013). Cultural change and continuity in U.S. and Mexican settings. In B. Jensen & A. Sawyer (Eds.), *Regarding educación: Mexican-American schooling, immigration, and bi-national improvement* (pp. 213–233). New York: Teachers College Press.

Starr, K. (2005). *California: A history*. New York: Penguin Random House.

Suárez-Orozco, C., Abo-Zena, M. M., & Marks, A. K. (2015). *Transitions: The development of children of immigrants*. New York: New York University Press.

Teranishi, T., Suárez-Orozco, C., & Suárez-Orozco, M. (2015). *In the shadows of the ivory tower: Undocumented undergraduates and the luminal state of immigration reform*. Los Angeles: Institute for Immigration, Globalization, and Education, UCLA.

Umansky, I. M. (2016). Leveled and exclusionary tracking: English learners' access to academic content in middle school. *American Educational Research Journal, 53*(6), 1792–1833. https://doi.org/10.3102/0002831216675404.

Yoshikawa, H., Suárez-Orozco, C., & Gonzales, R. G. (2017). Unauthorized status and youth development in the United States: Consensus statement of the society for research on adolescence. *Journal of Research on Adolescence, 27*(1), 4–19. https://doi.org/10.1111/jora.12272.

Zambrana, R. E., & Hurtado, S. (2015). An intersectional lens: Theorizing an educational paradigm of success. In R. E. Zambrana & S. Hurtado (Eds.), *The magic key: The educational journey of Mexican Americans from K-12 to college and beyond* (pp. 77–99). Austin: The University of Texas Press.

2

Understanding Languages and Literacies of Immigrant-Origin Multilingual Youth: Insights from Theory and Research

In this chapter, I first discuss the conceptualizations of languages and literacies that are relevant to understanding the stories of youth in this study. Next, I provide an overview of current findings in the literature regarding immigrant-origin multilingual youth's language and literacy practices, with a particular focus on adolescents from Spanish-dominant families and communities in the United States. This is followed by an analysis of recent research documenting development in these practices over time, especially in relation to writing. Finally, I describe a range of minoritizing discourses that often impact multilingual young people from immigrant backgrounds and some of the ways that research can counter such portrayals.

Situating Language and Literacy Practices and Development

Patterns of language and literacy use and development can be understood from an ecological perspective as interrelated, complex, and fluid (Hornberger, 2003; Hornberger & Link, 2012). A recent publication by

© The Author(s) 2019
A. K. Kibler, *Longitudinal Interactional Histories*,
https://doi.org/10.1007/978-3-319-98815-3_2

the Douglas Fir Group for the centennial edition of the *Modern Language Journal* (2016), for example, described language learning and teaching as nested not only in the micro level of activity (which includes both cognitive and social aspects of learning) but also in the meso-level sociocultural contexts of institutions and communities and in macro-level ideological structures. In a similar vein, Cumming and Geva (2012) conceptualized literacy learning as composed of cognitive, sociocultural, and macro-societal processes, which operate in tandem but often remain distinct in research. Because this study is qualitative and ethnographic, it sheds more light on the social aspects of these models (at micro, meso, and macro levels), and as such, it is vital to explain key theories that align with these aspects of language and literacy practices and development.

A Critical Sociocultural Orientation This study is framed by a critical sociocultural orientation that takes into consideration the complex ecologies in which language and literacy repertoires are developed and used. According to the writings of Vygotsky (1978), whose work forms the basis of many contemporary sociocultural theories, learning begins in social activity. In essence, knowledge is acquired interpersonally before it becomes internalized, at which point it can be accessed with less overt assistance from other people or visual and linguistic supports (Lantolf, 2000). In this sense, both thinking and action develop through the resources for meaning-making that are available in a given context, which is itself shaped by both cultural and historical factors (Enciso, 2007). Not all resources in an environment are necessarily supportive of language and literacy development, however. Van Lier (2000) drew upon the ecological theory of affordances to explain that for development to occur, there needs to be an adequate fit between what an individual brings to a setting and what an environment provides. Only in such a situation can various resources (or mediational tools, in the words of sociocultural theorists) actually be affordances for language and literacy development. Critical perspectives on sociocultural theory also argue for the importance of carefully considering the ways that power is (re)produced in everyday language and literacy use, and how societal and institutional structures frame—and for many individuals on the receiving end of marginalizing discourses, restrict—access to true affordances for learning (Lewis, Enciso, & Moje, 2007).

Language as Participation Following from a critical sociocultural approach to learning and development, I understand language first and foremost from the perspective of participation, or action (van Lier & Walqui, 2012). In other words, although language clearly encompasses lexical, grammatical, and discourse-level elements, which have been conceptualized and studied from varied perspectives, those features are inadequate on their own to fully explain how we actually communicate. When language is understood as participation, or as Heller and Morek (2015) described it, situated action, the focus of attention is on how actual people navigate the world through the linguistic resources at their disposal. Leung (2014) argued that participation, rather than only the knowledge of a language, is key. Although an understanding of language elements clearly facilitates communication, people can (and often do) communicate without a "requisite level of normative knowledge" (p. 141). What cannot be missing from the equation, however, is participation. Further, related perspectives on language as action— described by scholars as languaging—also emphasize the ways in which language is simultaneously used and transformed through that use (Wei, 2011a). These fluid and dynamic understandings challenge the practices of educational institutions to treat language as an academic subject comprised of a finite body of knowledge and skills that can be sequenced, taught, and assessed, what Valdés (2015) calls the curricularization of language. Viewing language as participation also calls into question some popular (and at times ill-defined) notions of "academic language" and who does, or does not, have mastery of those supposed linguistic registers (Rolstad, 2014).

Literacies as Social Practices Any discussion of language, particularly in relation to schooling, is incomplete without also considering the ways in which literacy-related theories can help explain how individuals engage in communication across various settings over time. Although some scholars understand literacy as a set of concrete reading and writing skills that have universal application and that can be easily defined and measured, those who see literacy as a social practice argue for a broader understanding of both literacy and texts themselves. Barton (2007, 2009) suggested that any investigation of literacy must first look at how people's everyday social practices involve the use of various texts for a range of purposes. Because social practices are embedded in particular contexts, it means that different literacies are appropriate for different contexts (Barton & Hamilton, 2000). In this sense, literacy is better understood in the plural, as literacies. Such an approach allows for a more critical focus on what counts as literacy in any particular time and space and whose literacies are dominant, marginalized, or resisted (New London Group, 1996; Street, 2003, 2012). Further, the term "practices" is often used to encompass not only a particular literacy event, or occasion of interpreting or producing a text, but also the broader cultural and social models, values, and beliefs shaping and shaped by these events (Street, 2003, p. 78).

Texts are embedded in, and I would argue, inextricable from, the contexts in which they were created. In this way, texts make visible the "necessarily dialectic relationship between the individual and the social" described in sociocultural theories of mind (Lantolf, 2005, p. 341). Because scholars working in this tradition have at times been criticized for celebrating the local at the expense of meso- or macro-level trends and influences, it is important to recall that literacy practices are neither wholly dictated from outside nor solely individually or locally created. In this way, it is clear that in schools and classrooms, like any other social setting, individuals develop routinized ways of interpreting and producing texts, but these practices are also created anew as individuals respond to and navigate the particular literacy event in which they are participating (Bourne, 2002; Dias, 2000).

In most of our everyday lives, the written word is omnipresent and increasingly accompanied by visual and auditory messages. Many scholars have likewise come to broaden their definition of literacy to encompass "the process of using reading, writing, and oral language to extract, construct, integrate, and critique meaning through interaction and involvement with multimodal texts in the context of socially situated practices" (Frankel, Becker, Rowe, & Pearson, 2017, p. 7). Such a broadened view also acknowledges that individuals' communicative repertoires (Rymes, 2014) include a wide range of both verbal and non-verbal means of expression. This holistic understanding is useful in understanding literate practices, which in schools include not just reading and writing expertise but also the academic ways of knowing (Zamel & Spack, 1998) that are valued in a classroom or school and the literate behaviors (Blanton, 1994) through which students are expected to demonstrate their learning.

Understanding Languages and Literacies What does it mean to be multilingual in today's schools, workplaces, and communities? Early definitions of bilingualism proposed by researchers focused on native-like control of two languages (e.g., Bloomfield, 1933), but these notions of languages as distinct, autonomous, and parallel entities have gradually given way to a recognition that any individual's repertoire is dynamic and includes varied competences within and across languages. Reflecting these trends, scholars have developed what Marshall and Moore (2018, p. 19) called a "panoply of lingualisms" to describe the various ways that language and literacy resources co-exist and are used at individual and societal levels. Terms include, but are not limited to, bilingualism, multilingualism, polylingualism, metrolingualism, plurilingualism, codeswitching, code-mixing, code-meshing, translanguaging, and translingualism.

While it is outside the scope of this book to provide a review of all these terms and their differing uses by various scholars, here I comment on those I use and how I use them. Bilingual and multilingual are words that I use to refer to both individuals' and societies' uses of languages. I use "bilingual" to maintain the notion of two societally defined languages, in that participants in this study considered themselves speakers of two languages, Spanish and English, and spoke about them in these terms. (I also use bilingual when discussing other studies, programs, or policies focused on other contexts of this sort or that explicitly use the term.) In this same way, I describe literacies whose uses span across both English and Spanish as "biliterate" practices. "Multilingualism," as I use it, is a broader and more inclusive term, with less focus on a particular number of languages or specific context but with an emphasis on multiple languages in use. In addressing literacies used and developed across languages in a general sense, I call these "multilingual literacies" or "literacies across languages" to avoid confusion with the term "multi-literacies" frequently employed in New Literacy Studies in reference to the different types of literate practices in which individuals may engage.

There is agreement among many scholars that named societal languages like "English" and "Spanish" are more sociopolitical idealizations than linguistic realities (e.g., Makoni & Pennycook, 2006). Further, every person's language repertoire is unique, including resources that might be popularly associated with various named languages as well as social languages (Gee, 2014)—a term that encompasses dialects, registers, varieties, or styles—within and at times across particular named languages. At the same time, it is also important to understand linguistic diversity in terms of not just different languages but also different meanings being communicated, which Pennycook (2008) described as glosso-diversity and semiodiversity, respectively.

There are notable differences of opinion at this time among scholars as to whether multilinguals have a single mental system that is undifferentiated across languages, growing from the translanguaging movement (García & Otheguy, 2014; Otheguy, García, & Reed, 2015, in press), or one that includes some level of language-specific differentiation, defined recently as an integrated multilingual model (MacSwan, 2017). However, both perspectives share a holistic view that bilingual individuals are not two separate monolinguals in one (Grosjean, 1982) but rather individuals whose complex, dynamic, and fluid language and literacy repertoires reflect the varied sociolinguistic contexts in which they have lived and developed these resources. Descriptions of the language and literacy journeys presented in this book draw from such a perspective as well as the notion that it is important for both researchers and educators to normalize rather than minoritize these heteroglossic experiences and language practices.

Attention to all languages in multilingual individuals' repertoires has become increasingly common in studies of second-language acquisition and applied linguistics and is considered by many to be evidence of a bi/multi/plurilingual turn in the field (Cenoz & Gorter, 2011; Ortega & Carson, 2010; Polio, 2014). Related trends in composition studies have emphasized semiotic diversity through a focus on translinguality and translingual writing (e.g., Canagarajah, 2013; Horner, 2016). At the same time, Kubota (2016) has warned scholars that such developments must be examined critically, in that they can overlap conceptually with a neoliberal multiculturalism that ignores racism, neoliberal competition, and the global dominance of English. From a slightly different perspective, Paquet-Gauthier and Beaulieu (2016) argued that recent emphases on multilingual pedagogies growing from this conceptual turn may have little staying power as long as monolingual performances are still expected in curricula and assessment. Responses to such critiques are ongoing, reflecting continuing scholarly debate about this notable shift in the field.

Youth's Multilingual Language and Literacy Practices

Multilinguals participate in a range of complex language and literacy practices, phenomena that can be found in speakers of any age. Certain trends, however, are particularly notable among adolescents and young adults, the focus of this book. For example, they often engage in language brokering, or translating/interpreting for family and other community members, a practice that demonstrates and develops linguistic flexibility and metalinguistic awareness (Orellana, 2009, Valdés, 2003). Adolescents' skillful use of languages for a range of other social purposes is also well-established, particularly in the case of Spanish/English bilinguals (Martínez, 2013; Martínez & Morales, 2014; Rosa, 2015, 2016). Such practices, however, are not immune from local and more distant ideologies, influences, and tensions (Lee & Marshall, 2012). For example, bilingual adolescents may hold ideologies that at once valorize and denigrate language practices such as so-called Spanglish (Martínez, 2013). These trends highlight the demands many Spanish-speaking young people face to be able to both speak "unaccented" English and demonstrate their community and cultural membership through an intimate knowledge of Spanish (Rosa, 2015). Multilingualism also plays a key role in immigrant-origin adolescents and young adults' voluntary reading and writing practices, particularly in digital spaces (de la Piedra, 2010; Lam, 2009; Lee, 2006; Yi, 2007).

Because English-medium classrooms remain the most common educational setting for immigrant-origin multilingual secondary and postsecondary students in the United States, non-English aspects of their language and literacy repertoires often remain hidden from educators (Jørgensen & Quist, 2007; Wei, 2011b). This is an especially notable trend for Mexican-origin and other Latinx adolescents (Bruna, 2007; de la Piedra, 2010; García, 1999; Martínez & Morales, 2014; Villalva, 2006; see Escamilla, Butvilofsky, & Hopewell, 2018, for similar trends in elementary school settings). Further, monolingual orientations and discourses often devalue multilingualism in the classroom even when laws and policies allow for the use of non-English languages. In these contexts, students who use those languages orally or in writing may be seen as less proficient in English than those who do not (Canagarajah, 2011; Kiramba, 2017).

Language and Literacy Development Over Time for Multilingual Youth

The development of language and literacy expertise is far from a linear or sequential process. To capture the complexity of change across time and space in relation to writing in particular, Compton-Lilly (2014) referred to the phenomenon as a "long-term trajectory of becoming" (p. 399), a process that is influenced by individuals' dispositions and their transitions across various fields. Such descriptions are apt for multilingual youth as well: As research with younger learners has shown, the development of language and literacy repertoires is shaped by both the amount and quality of opportunities provided and taken across all languages (McCarthey, Guo, & Cummins, 2005), both inside and outside of school. Longitudinal studies—while few in number—have found varied patterns of change over time in multilingual youth's language and literacy practices across settings, particularly in relation to writing. In a year-long examination of eight adolescents and adults in French and Chinese immersion programs in Australia (de Courcy, 2002), for example, both groups gradually relied less on translation as a writing strategy but continued to draw upon bilingual texts to support their writing in English.

Such patterns echo more general findings about writing processes, suggesting "multicompetent writers are likely to use both (or all) their languages to aid themselves" (Ortega & Carson, 2010, p. 50), even at advanced proficiency levels. Related patterns were also noted in a setting where late-elementary, middle, and high school immigrant students in the United States were allowed and encouraged to use any of their languages in their written texts (Fu, 2009). These writers demonstrated notable but nonlinear growth in English writing, shifting back and forth among languages, depending on academic content, complexity, audience, purpose, and genre. Further, in a two-year study of Spanish-speaking immigrant middle school students, Valdés (1999) and Valdés and Sanders (1998) found varied growth in English writing development in terms of communicative tasks performed, organization, and mechanics. Such patterns depended on students' instructional settings and exposure to English outside of school, among other factors.

At the university level, growth has also been documented among multilingual writers as they progress into and through their degrees. Based on a four-year study of students who began university studies in an entry-level English as a Second Language (ESL)[1] writing class, Leki (2007) concluded that writing and disciplinary growth developed in tandem as a result of time spent writing and focusing in-depth on topics, and that the development of reading and writing expertise were mutually supportive. The socio-academic relationships students in her study had with peers and instructors were also key to their overall success, and likely the most important factor in improving their writing was their willingness to seek out feedback and revise. In Sternglass' (1997) longitudinal study of university students (many of whom were multilingual) originally placed in remedial or basic-level English courses, their writing development was a nonlinear and multiple-year process that was dependent upon not only instruction in writing but also discipline-specific courses focused on critical thinking and writing. Spack (1997) came to similar conclusions in her three-year study of a Japanese student who came to the United States to attend university. Most notably, reading and writing improved in tandem, alongside the development of productive strategies to complete the tasks and a willingness to discuss assignments with instructors outside of class.

In her ten-year study of diverse K-12 youth, Compton-Lilly (2014, 2017) argued that literacy practices are deeply intertwined with the dispositions that students develop over the many years of schooling. Drawing upon Bordieau's notion of habitus, she explained that the process of becoming a writer for one of her focal students was not simply about the writing instruction he received: It was inextricable from dispositions toward being good at school (and being recognized as such) as well as relationships with others based on the literacy practices in which he engaged (Compton-Lilly, 2014). When youth do not hold such dispositions toward school-based literacy practices, Compton-Lilly (2017) argued that these instances should be considered as potentially more than simple "disaffection from school" (p. 63), in that students may in fact have rich literacy repertoires but are instead responding to marginalizing institutional or societal discourses about race, class, and gender, among other factors.

Such patterns are also visible as young people transition into and through postsecondary education. Research on Francophone youth in Canada has suggested that students' self-conceptions of linguistic and cultural identity can shift, although unpredictably, while attending university (Lamoureux, 2011), and immigrant students' socialization into multiple and sometimes contradictory sociolinguistic and cultural identities during this time can influence their academic performance and aspirations (Kim & Duff, 2012). Multilingual immigrant students' agency and self-assertiveness have been noted as important elements that allow them to succeed in meeting the language and literacy expectations of postsecondary schooling over time, even though such actions at times can also lead to marginalization from peers or institutional communities (Fuentes, 2012; Riazantseva, 2012; Varghese, 2012).

Uncovering and Undermining Marginalizing Discourses

Multilingual adolescents and young adults from immigrant backgrounds experience a range of educational and sociopolitical discourses that often "minoritize" (Flores, Kleyn, & Menken, 2015; Flores & Rosa, 2015) non-English languages and their speakers in the United States. I purposefully return to this notion of minoritizing throughout the book to call attention to the ways that discourses and institutional policies and practices often devalue or ignore immigrant-origin youth's home/community language resources. Drawing on Nasir's (2011) work on racialized identities, I contend that the term language minority (like race) is not simply a descriptive category. Rather, discourses actively minoritize language groups and their speakers by positioning these individuals and their resources as non-normative and less valuable. Flores and Rosa (2015) described these processes in terms of raciolinguistic ideologies, in that linguistically minoritized speakers share a racial positioning in which their language practices are seen as linguistically deficient "regardless of how closely they follow supposed rules of appropriateness" (p. 149; see also Rosa & Flores, 2017). Such positionalities are multifaceted, including dimensions of language and race as well as immigration, poverty, and negative stereotypes, according to research on Mexican-origin adolescents' varied experiences with discrimination (Edwards & Romero, 2008).

These discourses can have powerful influences on students' experiences inside and outside of institutions, and, in turn, on their language and literacy development. Harklau (1999) argued, for example, that universities and community colleges' judgments of multilingual students as either needing remedial or ESL classes may come from a desire to help those individuals whom they think are underprepared or need language support but nonetheless isolate and marginalize these young people, sending the message that they deviate from "normal" postsecondary students (see also Marshall, 2010; Ortmeier-Hooper, 2008). Ruecker (2015) likewise contended that such practices both shift the blame for potential failure from institutions to students themselves and fail to recognize the larger marginalizing discourses that students and their families have experienced, sometimes for multiple generations. Individual teachers may hold restrictive beliefs as well: Harklau (2000) found that while adolescents from immigrant backgrounds educated in the United States may be seen as struggling but determined and inspirational by teachers and others in high school, once in postsecondary settings they may be labeled as having the "worst of American habits" (p. 52) and a range of cultural or academic deficits.

Language-related discourses that impact immigrant-origin multilinguals are inextricable from discourses about immigration itself. Waves of pro- and anti-immigrant sentiment in the United States date from the earliest days of European settlement and Native American displacement and extermination (Banks, Suárez-Orozco, & Ben-Peretz, 2016). They continue into the present, contributing in part to varied contexts of reception (Portes & Rumbaut, 2001, 2006) that strongly influence immigrants' and their children's experiences. Although this study took place before the most recent heightened polarization around immigration dating from the 2016 presidential election in the United States, such discourses most definitely influenced youth's lives as well as their educational and professional aspirations. The ways in which adolescents or young adults of immigrant origin understand and interpret exclusionary/inclusionary discourses of immigration vary considerably, however (Dabach, Fones, Merchant, & Kim, 2017), suggesting diverse rather than monolithic responses to such social and political messages.

Marginalizing discourses about multilingual and other minoritized students can also be seen in language and literacy research itself (Gutiérrez & Orellana, 2006; Orellana & Gutiérrez, 2006). One long-standing and prominent example is the ongoing research focus on a so-called language gap, in which children in families with low socioeconomic status (and often in immigrant-origin and other communities of color) are argued to know fewer words at certain developmental points and therefore have impoverished language skills and greater likelihood of later educational failure. Although this work has been subsequently criticized on both methodological and conceptual grounds, research and educational interventions in the language gap tradition have continued to grow.[2] Another recent discussion of linguistically minoritizing discourses can be found in debates surrounding the label "long-term English learner," used to describe non-English-background students who do not meet benchmarks for English language proficiency in US schools in a certain number of years. This learner label has been subsequently criticized because of the ways in which assumptions about normative development are applied to students who have highly varied educational and linguistic backgrounds and at times insufficient instructional experiences (Brooks, 2015, 2016; Flores et al., 2015; Kibler et al., in press; Menken, 2013; Menken & Kleyn, 2010; Thompson, 2015). Such a term can also minimize the range of intersecting discourses and mechanisms that shape constructions of learners in schools (Kibler & Valdés, 2016).

Efforts to dismantle deficit-oriented discourses prominent in studies of English-learner-classified students and other minoritized multilingual populations are clearly important scholarly undertakings (Orellana & Gutiérrez, 2006). One perspective that holds particular promise in this regard is that of Lawrence-Lightfoot and Davis (1997), who argued that educational research is too dominated by the documentation of failure and should instead explicitly strive to seek goodness. This can be done, they explained, by privileging participants' voices and their perspectives, knowledge, and authority while also acknowledging the complexities and contradictions inherent in their experiences. The larger goal of this process is authenticity: a search for universality through the details of an individual's experiences. As Lawrence-Lightfoot (2005) explained, "The more specific the description, the more likely it is to evoke identification" (p. 13). These identifications, it is hoped, can lead readers to question taken-for-granted assumptions and beliefs, leading to positive change at a number of levels.

One aspect of seeking goodness in Mexican-origin and other Latinx youth is valuing their cross-national experiences as well as their cultural assets and developmental competencies, prominent among them being cultural values like *educación* (Reese, Balzano, Gallimore, & Goldenberg, 1995; Valdés, 1996), which encompasses family and group loyalty, cooperative behaviors, respect for authority, personal goodness, and politeness (see also Jensen & Sawyer, 2013). Research can also work to seek goodness and undermine existing marginalizing discourses through understanding multilingual young people as necessarily using language and literacy practices that cross the boundaries of named languages. What is key to this perspective is that each individual is seen as having a complete language repertoire, although there may be more or fewer features associated with particular named languages. In this sense, multilingual youth are viewed on their own terms—using what García and Otheguy (2014) called a "speaker-centered view" as part of a "heteroglossic ideology"

(p. 639)—rather than being compared to idealized monolingual Spanish or English speakers. From this perspective, it is also easier to see multilingual practices as encompassing both creativity and criticality (Wei, 2011b) rather than as flawed in some way because they do not conform to monolingual expectations.

Marginalizing discourses can also be contested through attention to youth's intersectional identities. In this sense, language is one of many factors—including but not limited to race/ethnicity, age, class, nationality, sexuality, and (dis)ability—around which individuals construct and negotiate their identities and for which they may experience privilege, marginalization, or both (Núñez, 2014; Shields, 2008). Such a perspective is particularly important for this study; as Ruiz-Alvarado and Hurtado (2015) have argued:

> The intersectionality lens suggests that Mexican Americans cannot and do not experience the world through race and ethnicity alone, but rather through a combination of those and the other social identities coconstructed through dimensions of difference, making it problematic to homogenize all students into one category and overlook the effect of various interactions of these identities. (p. 186: see also Zambrana & Hurtado, 2015)

Compton-Lilly, Papoi, Venegas, Hamman, and Schwabenbauer (2017) contended that such intersectional perspectives are useful in understanding not only individuals' social identities but also the "networks of self" (p. 122) that children create through their language and literacy practices across home, school, and community contexts. In this book, I endeavor to present participants' identities and language and literacy practices as intersectional and actively negotiated, highlighting rather than minimizing complexity, agency, and power dynamics.

Conclusion

Minoritized multilingual youth's language and literacy practices are conceptualized in this book as social practices that are best understood as forms of participation in sociocultural contexts that are locally situated but also influenced by cultural-historical factors as well as institutional and instructional dynamics and larger societal discourses. Multilingual language and literacy repertoires are complex, dynamic, and fluid, reflecting the range of circumstances in which individuals have lived and learned. Research suggests that immigrant-origin multilingual young people are confronted with institutional circumstances and varied discourses that at times are well-intentioned efforts to support their academic and linguistic development but often serve to minoritize their non-English-language expertise and hinder their bilingual and biliterate growth and school-based success. Understanding ways in which researchers can seek goodness and understand the complexities of youth's intersectional identities is an important step in normalizing rather than minoritizing their experiences while also exposing practices and discourses that impede the development of their language and literacy repertoires.

Notes

1. English as a Second Language (ESL) and English for Speakers of Other Languages (ESOL) are often used interchangeably in the literature to describe such classes, although they do have different connotations. English language development (ELD) is the term that was most commonly used in K-12 settings at the time of this study in California, where data collection took place.
2. See Kibler, Palacios, Simpson Baird, Bergey, and Yoder (2016) for further discussion of these issues.

References

Banks, J. A., Suárez-Orozco, M. M., & Ben-Peretz, M. (Eds.). (2016). *Global migration, diversity, and civic education: Improving policy and practice.* New York: Teachers College Press.

Barton, D. (2007). *Literacy: An introduction to the ecology of written language* (2nd ed.). Oxford, UK: Wiley-Blackwell.

Barton, D. (2009). Understanding textual practices in a changing world. In M. Baynham & M. Prinsloo (Eds.), *The future of literacy studies* (pp. 38–53). Basingstoke, UK: Palgrave Macmillan.

Barton, D., & Hamilton, M. (2000). Literacy practices. In D. Barton, M. Hamilton, & R. Ivanič (Eds.), *Situated literacies: Reading and writing in context* (pp. 7–15). London: Routledge.

Blanton, L. L. (1994). Discourse, artifacts, and the Ozarks: Understanding academic literacy. *Journal of Second Language Writing, 3*(1), 1–16. https://doi.org/10.1016/1060-3743(94)90002-7.

Bloomfield, L. (1933). *Language.* New York: Holt, Rinehart and Winston.

Bourne, J. (2002). "Oh, what will miss say!": Constructing texts and identities on the discursive processes of classroom writing. *Language and Education, 16*(4), 241–259. https://doi.org/10.1080/09500780208666830.

Brooks, M. D. (2015). "It's like a script": Long-term English learners' experiences with and ideas about academic reading. *Research in the Teaching of English, 49*(4), 383–406.

Brooks, M. D. (2016). Notes and talk: An examination of a long-term English learner reading-to-learn in a high school biology classroom. *Language and Education, 30*(3), 235–251. https://doi.org/10.1080/09500782.2015.1102275.

Bruna, K. R. (2007). Traveling tags: The informal literacies of Mexican newcomers in and out of the classroom. *Linguistics and Education, 18*(3–4), 232–257. https://doi.org/10.1016/j.linged.2007.07.008.

Canagarajah, A. S. (2011). Codemeshing in academic writing: Identifying teachable strategies of translanguaging. *The Modern Language Journal, 95*(3), 401–417. https://doi.org/10.1111/j.1540-4781.2011.01207.x.

Canagarajah, A. S. (Ed.). (2013). *Literacy as translingual practice: Between communities and classrooms.* New York: Routledge.

Cenoz, J., & Gorter, D. (2011). A holistic approach to multilingual education: Introduction. *Modern Language Journal, 95*(3), 339–343. https://doi.org/10.1111/j.1540-4781.2011.01204.x.

Compton-Lilly, C. (2014). The development of writing habitus: A ten-year case study of a young writer. *Written Communication, 31*(4), 371–403. https://doi.org/10.1177/0741088314549539.

Compton-Lilly, C. (2017). *Reading students' lives: Literacy learning across time.* New York: Routledge.

Compton-Lilly, C., Papoi, K., Venegas, P., Hamman, L., & Schwabenbauer, B. (2017). Intersectional identity negotiation: The case of young immigrant children. *Journal of Literacy Research, 49*(1), 115–140. https://doi.org/10.11 77/1086296X16683421.

Cumming, A. H., & Geva, E. (2012). Purpose and approach. In A. H. Cumming (Ed.), *Adolescent literacies in a multicultural context* (pp. 1–22). New York: Routledge.

Dabach, D. B., Fones, A., Merchant, N. H., & Kim, M. J. (2017). Discourses of exclusion: Immigrant-origin youth responses to immigration debates in an election year. *Journal of Language, Identity, and Education, 16*(1), 1–16. https://doi.org/10.1080/15348458.2016.1239538.

de Courcy, M. (2002). *Learners' experiences of immersion education: Case studies of French and Chinese.* Bristol, UK: Multilingual Matters.

de la Piedra, M. T. (2010). Adolescent worlds and literacy practices on the United States–Mexico border. *Journal of Adolescent and Adult Literacy, 53*(7), 575–584. https://doi.org/10.1598/JAAL.53.7.5.

Dias, P. (2000). Writing classrooms as activity systems. In P. Dias & A. Paré (Eds.), *Transitions: Writing in academic and workplace settings* (pp. 11–29). Cresskill, NJ: Hampton Press.

Douglas Fir Group. (2016). A transdisciplinary framework for SLA in a multilingual world. *The Modern Language Journal, 100*(S1), 19–47. https://doi. org/10.1111/modl.12301.

Edwards, L. M., & Romero, A. J. (2008). Coping with discrimination among Mexican descent adolescents. *Hispanic Journal of Behavioral Sciences, 30*(1), 24–39. https://doi.org/10.1177/0739986307311431.

Enciso, P. (2007). Reframing history in sociocultural theories: Toward an expansive vision. In C. Lewis, P. Enciso, & E. B. Moje (Eds.), *Reframing sociocultural research on literacy: Identity, agency, and power* (pp. 49–74). Mahwah, NJ: Lawrence Erlbaum.

Escamilla, K., Butvilofsky, S., & Hopewell, S. (2018). What gets lost when English-only writing assessment is used to assess writing proficiency in Spanish-English emerging bilingual learners? *International Multilingual Research Journal, 12*(4), 221–236. https://doi.org/10.1080/19313152.2016. 1273740.

Flores, N., Kleyn, T., & Menken, K. (2015). Looking holistically in a climate of partiality: Identities of students labeled long-term English language learners. *Journal of Language, Identity and Education, 14*(2), 113–132. https://doi.org /10.1080/15348458.2015.1019787.

Flores, N., & Rosa, J. (2015). Undoing appropriateness: Raciolinguistic ideologies and language diversity in education. *Harvard Educational Review, 85*(2), 149–171. https://doi.org/10.17763/0017-8055.85.2.149.

Frankel, K. K., Becker, B. L. C., Rowe, M. W., & Pearson, P. D. (2017). From "what is reading?" to what is literacy? *Journal of Education, 196*(3), 7–17.

Fu, D. (2009). *Writing between languages: How English language learners make the transition to fluency*. Portsmouth, NH: Heinemann-Boynton/Cook.

Fuentes, R. (2012). Benefits and costs of exercising agency: A case study of an English learner navigating a four-year university. In Y. Kanno & L. Harklau (Eds.), *Linguistic minority students go to college: Preparation, access, and persistence* (pp. 220–237). New York: Routledge.

García, O. (1999). Educating Latino high school students with little formal schooling. In C. Faltis & P. Wolfe (Eds.), *So much to say: Adolescents, bilingualism, and ESL in the secondary school* (pp. 61–82). New York: Teachers College Press.

García, O., & Otheguy, R. (2014). Spanish and Hispanic bilingualism. In M. Lacorte (Ed.), *The Routledge handbook of Hispanic applied linguistics* (pp. 639–658). New York: Routledge.

Gee, J. P. (2014). *An introduction to discourse analysis: Theory and method* (4th ed.). Oxon, UK: Routledge.

Grosjean, F. (1982). *Life with two languages: An introduction to bilingualism*. Cambridge, MA: Harvard University Press.

Gutiérrez, K. D., & Orellana, M. F. (2006). The "problem" of English learners: Constructing genres of difference. *Research in the Teaching of English, 40*(4), 502–507.

Harklau, L. (1999). Representations of immigrant language minorities in US higher education. *Race Ethnicity and Education, 2*(2), 257–279. https://doi.org/10.1080/1361332990020206.

Harklau, L. (2000). From the "good kids" to the "worst": Representations of English language learners across educational settings. *TESOL Quarterly, 34*(1), 35–67. https://doi.org/10.2307/3588096.

Heller, V., & Morek, M. (2015). Academic discourse as situated practice: An introduction. *Linguistics and Education, 31*, 174–186. https://doi.org/10.1016/j.linged.2014.01.008.

Hornberger, N. H. (2003). Continua of biliteracy. In N. H. Hornberger (Ed.), *Continua of biliteracy: An ecological framework for educational policy, research, and practice in multilingual settings* (pp. 3–34). Clevedon, UK: Multilingual Matters.

Hornberger, N. H., & Link, H. (2012). Translanguagig and transnational literacies in multilingual classrooms: A biliteracy lens. *International Journal of Bilingual Education and Bilingualism, 15*(3), 261–278. https://doi.org/10.1080/136700 50.2012.658016.

Horner, B. (2016). *Rewriting composition: Terms of exchange.* Carbondale: Southern Illinois University Press.

Jensen, B., & Sawyer, A. (2013). Regarding *educación:* A vision for school improvement. In B. Jensen & A. Sawyer (Eds.), *Regarding educación: Mexican-American schooling, immigration, and bi-national improvement* (pp. 1–24). New York: Teachers College Press.

Jørgensen, J. N., & Quist, P. (2007). Bilingual children in monolingual schools. In P. Auer & W. Li (Eds.), *Handbook of multilingualism and multilingual communication* (pp. 155–174). Berlin, Germany: Mouton de Gruyter.

Kibler, A. K., Karam, F., Futch Ehrlich, V., Bergey, R., Wang, C., & Molloy Elreda, L. (in press). Who are long-term English learners? Deconstructing a manufactured learner label. *Applied Linguistics.* https://doi.org/10.1093/applin/amw039.

Kibler, A. K., Palacios, N., Simpson Baird, A., Bergey, R., & Yoder, M. (2016). Bilingual Latin@ children's exposure to language and literacy practices through older siblings in immigrant families. *Linguistics and Education, 35,* 63–77. https://doi.org/10.1016/j.linged.2016.06.001.

Kibler, A. K., & Valdés, G. (2016). Conceptualizing language learners: Socio-institutional mechanisms and their consequences. *Modern Language Journal, 100*(S1), 96–116. https://doi.org/10.1111/modl.12310.

Kim, J., & Duff, P. A. (2012). The language socialization and identity negotiations of generation 1.5 Korean-Canadian university students. *TESL Canada Journal, 29*(6), 81–102. https://doi.org/10.18806/tesl.v29i0.1111.

Kiramba, L. K. (2017). Translanguaging in the writing of emergent multilinguals. *International Multilingual Research Journal, 11*(2), 115–130. http://doi.org/10.1080/19313152.2016.1239457.

Kubota, R. (2016). The multi/plural turn, postcolonial theory, and neoliberal multiculturalism: Complicities and implications for applied linguistics. *Applied Linguistics, 37*(4), 474–494. https://doi.org/10.1093/applin/amu045.

Lam, W. S. E. (2009). Multiliteracies on instant messaging in negotiating local, translocal, and transnational affiliations: A case of an adolescent immigrant. *Reading Research Quarterly, 44*(4), 377–397. https://doi.org/10.1598/RRQ.44.4.5.

Lamoureux, S. A. (2011). D'élève à étudiant: Identité et competences linguistiques et experiences de transition de jeunes francophones en milieu minoritaire en Ontario (Canada) [From high school to college student: Identity and linguistic competencies and the transitional experiences of francophone minority youth in Ontario (Canada)]. *Bulletin Suisse de Linguistique Appliquée* [Swiss Bulletin of Applied Linguistics], *94*, 153–165.

Lantolf, J. P. (2000). Introducing sociocultural theory. In J. P. Lantolf (Ed.), *Sociocultural theory and second language learning* (pp. 1–26). Oxford, UK: Oxford University Press.

Lantolf, J. P. (2005). Sociocultural and second language learning research: An exegesis. In E. Hinkel (Ed.), *Handbook of research in second language teaching and learning* (pp. 335–354). Mahwah, NJ: Erlbaum.

Lawrence-Lightfoot, S. (2005). Reflections on portraiture: A dialogue between art and science. *Qualitative Inquiry, 11*(1), 3–15. https://doi.org/10.1177/1077800404270955.

Lawrence-Lightfoot, S., & Davis, J. H. (1997). *The art and science of portraiture.* San Francisco: Jossey-Bass Publishers.

Lee, J. S. (2006). Exploring the relationship between electronic literacy and heritage language maintenance. *Language, Learning, and Technology, 10*(2), 93–113. http://dx.doi.org/10125/44063.

Lee, E., & Marshall, S. (2012). Multilingualism and English language usage in 'weird' and 'funny' times: A case study of transnational youth in Vancouver. *International Journal of Multilingualism, 9*(1), 65–82. https://doi.org/10.1080/14790718.2011.595795.

Leki, I. (2007). *Undergraduates in a second language: Challenges and complexities of academic literacy development.* Mahwah, NJ: Lawrence Erlbaum.

Leung, C. (2014). Communication and participatory involvement in linguistically diverse classrooms. In S. May (Ed.), *The multilingual turn: Implications for SLA, TESOL and bilingual education* (pp. 123–146). New York: Routledge.

Lewis, C., Enciso, P., & Moje, E. B. (2007). Introduction: Reframing sociocultural research on literacy. In C. Lewis, P. Enciso, & E. B. Moje (Eds.), *Reframing sociocultural research on literacy: Identity, agency, and power* (pp. 1–14). Mahwah, NJ: Lawrence Erlbaum.

MacSwan, J. (2017). A multilingual perspective on translanguaging. *American Educational Research Journal, 54*(1), 167–201. https://doi.org/10.3102/0002831216683935.

Makoni, S., & Pennycook, A. (Eds.). (2006). *Disinventing and reconstituting languages.* Clevedon, UK: Multilingual Matters.

Marshall, S. (2010). Re-becoming ESL: Multilingual university students and a deficit identity. *Language and Education, 24*(1), 41–56. https://doi.org/10.1080/09500780903194044.

Marshall, S., & Moore, D. (2018). Plurilingualism amid the panoply of lingualisms: Addressing critiques and misconceptions in education. *International*

Journal of Multilingualism, 15(1), 19–34. https://doi.org/10.1080/14790718.2016.1253699.

Martínez, R. (2013). Reading the world in *Spanglish*: Hybrid language practices and ideological contestation in a sixth-grade English language arts classroom. *Linguistics and Education, 24*(3), 276–288. https://doi.org/10.1016/j.linged.2013.03.007.

Martínez, R. A., & Morales, P. Z. (2014). *¿Puras groserías?*: Rethinking the role of profanity and graphic humor in Latin@ students' bilingual wordplay. *Anthropology and Education Quarterly, 45*(4), 337–354. https://doi.org/10.1111/aeq.12074.

McCarthey, S. J., Guo, Y.-H., & Cummins, S. (2005). Understanding changes in elementary Mandarin students' L1 and L2 writing. *Journal of Second Language Writing, 14*(2), 71–104. https://doi.org/10.1016/j.jslw.2005.05.003.

Menken, K. (2013). Emergent bilingual students in secondary school: Along the academic language and literacy continuum. *Language Teaching, 46*(4), 438–476. https://doi.org/10.1017/S0261444813000281.

Menken, K., & Kleyn, T. (2010). The long-term impact of subtractive schooling in the educational experiences of secondary English language learners. *International Journal of Bilingual Education and Bilingualism, 13*(4), 399–417. https://doi.org/10.1080/13670050903370143.

Nasir, N. S. (2011). *Racialized identities: Race and achievement among African American youth*. Stanford, CA: Stanford University Press.

New London Group. (1996). A pedagogy of multiliteracies: Designing social futures. *Harvard Educational Review, 66*(1), 60–93. https://doi.org/10.17763/haer.66.1.17370n67v22j160u.

Núñez, A. M. (2014). Advancing an intersectionality framework in higher education: Power and Latino postsecondary opportunity. In M. Paulsen (Ed.), *Higher education: Handbook of theory and research* (Vol. 29 pp. 33–92). Dordrecht, The Netherlands: Springer. https://doi.org/10.1007/978-94-017-8005-6_2.

Orellana, M. F. (2009). *Translating childhoods: Immigrant youth, language, and culture*. New Brunswick, NJ: Rutgers University Press.

Orellana, M. F., & Gutiérrez, K. D. (2006). What's the problem? Constructing different genres for the study of English learners. *Research in the Teaching of English, 41*(1), 118–123.

Ortega, L., & Carson, J. (2010). Multicompetence, social context, and L2 writing research praxis. In P. K. Matsuda & T. Silva (Eds.), *Practicing theory in second language writing* (pp. 48–71). West Lafayette, IN: Parlor Press.

Ortmeier-Hooper, C. (2008). English may be my second language, but I'm not "ESL". *College Composition and Communication, 59*(3), 389–419. http://www.jstor.org/stable/20457011.

Otheguy, R., García, O., & Reid, W. (2015). Clarifying translanguaging and deconstructing named languages: A perspective from linguistics. *Applied Linguistics Review, 6*(3), 281–307. https://doi.org/10.1515/applirev-2015-0014.

Otheguy, R., García, O., & Reid, W. (in press). A translanguaging view of the linguistic system of bilinguals. *Applied Linguistics Review.* https://doi.org/10.1515/applirev-2018-0020.

Paquet-Gauthier, M., & Beaulieu, S. (2016). Can language classrooms take the multilingual turn? *Journal of Multilingual and Multicultural Development, 37*(2), 167–183. https://doi.org/10.1080/01434632.2015.1049180.

Pennycook, A. (2008). English as a language always in translation. *European Journal of English Studies, 12*(1), 33–47. https://doi.org/10.1080/13825570801900521.

Polio, C. (2014). Editor's introduction. *Annual Review of Applied Linguistics, 34*, v–vi. https://doi.org/10.1017/S0267190514000117.

Portes, A., & Rumbaut, R. G. (2001). *Legacies: The story of the immigrant second generation.* Berkeley: University of California Press.

Portes, A., & Rumbaut, R. G. (2006). *Immigrant America: A portrait* (3rd ed.). Berkeley: University of California Press.

Reese, L., Balzano, S., Gallimore, R., & Goldenberg, C. (1995). The concept of *educación:* Latino family values and American schooling. *International Journal of Educational Research, 23*(1), 57–81. https://doi.org/10.1016/0883-0355(95)93535-4.

Riazantseva, A. (2012). "I ain't changing anything": A case study of successful generation 1.5 immigrant college students' writing. *Journal of English for Academic Purposes, 11*(3), 184–193. https://doi.org/10.1016/j.jeap.2012.04.007.

Rolstad, K. (Ed.). (2014). Introduction: Rethinking language at school. *International Multilingual Research Journal, 8*(1), 1–8. https://doi.org/10.1080/19313152.2014.852423.

Rosa, J. (2015). Nuevo Chicago? Language, diaspora, and Latino/a panethnic formations. In R. M. Reiter & L. M. Rojo (Eds.), *A sociolinguistics of diaspora: Latino practices, identities, and ideologies* (pp. 31–47). New York: Routledge.

Rosa, J. (2016). From mock Spanish to inverted Spanglish: Language ideologies and the racialization of Mexican and Puerto Rican youth in the United States. In H. S. Alim, J. R. Rickford, & A. F. Ball (Eds.), *Raciolinguistics: How language shapes our ideas about race* (pp. 65–80). Oxford, UK: Oxford University Press.

Rosa, J., & Flores, N. (2017). Unsettling race and language: Toward a raciolinguistic perspective. *Language in Society, 46*(5), 621–647. https://doi.org/10.1017/S0047404517000562.

Ruecker, T. (2015). *Transiciones: Pathways of Latinas and Latinos writing in high school and college.* Logan: Utah State University Press.

Ruiz-Alvarado, A., & Hurtado, S. (2015). Campus climate, intersecting identities, and institutional support among Mexican American college students. In R. E. Zambrana & S. Hurtado (Eds.), *The magic key: The educational journey of Mexican Americans from K-12 to college and beyond* (pp. 168–189). Austin: The University of Texas Press.

Rymes, B. (2014). *Communicating beyond language: Everyday encounters with diversity.* New York: Routledge.

Shields, S. A. (2008). Gender: An intersectionality perspective. *Sex Roles, 59*(5-6), 301–311. https://doi.org/10.1007/s11199-008-9501-8.

Spack, R. (1997). The acquisition of academic literacy in a second language. *Written Communication, 14*(1), 3–62. https://doi.org/10.1177/0741088397 014001001.

Sternglass, M. S. (1997). *Time to know them: A longitudinal study of writing and learning at the college level.* Mahwah, NJ: Lawrence Erlbaum.

Street, B. (2003). What's "new" in new literacy studies? Critical approaches to literacy in theory and practice. *Current Issues in Comparative Education, 5*(2), 77–91.

Street, B. (2012). New literacy studies. In M. Grenfell, D. Bloome, C. Hardy, K. Pahl, J. Rowsell, & B. Street (Eds.), *Language, ethnography, and education: Bridging new literacy studies and Bourdieu* (pp. 27–49). New York: Routledge.

Thompson, K. D. (2015). Questioning the long-term English learner label: How categorization can blind us to students' abilities. *Teachers College Record, 117*(12), 1–50.

Valdés, G. (1996). *Con respeto: Bridging the distances between culturally diverse families and schools: An ethnographic portrait.* New York: Teachers College Press.

Valdés, G. (1999). Incipient bilingualism and the development of English language writing abilities in the secondary school. In C. J. Faltis & P. Wolfe (Eds.), *So much to say: Adolescents, bilingualism, & ESL in the secondary school* (pp. 138–175). New York: Teachers College Press.

Valdés, G. (2003). *Expanding definitions of giftedness: The case of young interpreters from immigrant communities.* Mahwah, NH: Lawrence Erlbaum.

Valdés, G. (2015). Latin@s and the intergenerational continuity of Spanish: The challenges of curricularizing language. *International Multilingual Research Journal, 9*(4), 253–273. https://doi.org/10.1080/19313152.2015.1086625.

Valdés, G., & Sanders, P. A. (1998). Latino ESL students and the development of writing abilities. In C. R. Cooper & L. Odell (Eds.), *Evaluating writing: The role of teachers' knowledge about text, learning, and culture* (pp. 249–278). Urbana, IL: National Council of Teachers of English.

van Lier, L. (2000). From input to affordance: Social-interactive learning from an ecological perspective. In J. P. Lantolf (Ed.), *Sociocultural theory and second language learning* (pp. 245–260). Oxford, UK: Oxford University Press.

van Lier, L., & Walqui, A. (2012). *Language and the common core standards.* Stanford, CA: Understanding Language. Retrieved from: http://ell.stanford.edu/papers/language

Varghese, M. M. (2012). A linguistic minority student's discursive framing of agency and structure. In Y. Kanno & L. Harklau (Eds.), *Linguistic minority students go to college: Preparation, access, and persistence* (pp. 148–162). New York: Routledge.

Villalva, K. E. (2006). Hidden literacies and inquiry approaches of bilingual high school writers. *Written Communication, 23*(1), 91–129. https://doi.org/10.1177/0741088305283929.

Vygotsky, L. S. (1978). *Mind in society: The development of higher psychological processes.* Harvard, MA: Harvard University Press.

Wei, L. (2011a). Moment analysis and translanguaging space: Discursive construction of identities by multilingual Chinese youth in Britain. *Journal of Pragmatics, 43*(2), 1222–1235. https://doi.org/10.1016/j.pragma.2010.07.035.

Wei, L. (2011b). Multilinguality, multimodality, and multicompetence: Code- and modeswitching by minority ethnic children in complementary schools. *Modern Language Journal, 95*(3), 370–384. https://doi.org/10.1111/j.1540-4781.2011.01209.x.

Yi, Y. (2007). Engaging literacy: A biliterate student's composing practices beyond school. *Journal of Second Language Writing, 16*(1), 23–39. https://doi.org/10.1016/j.jslw.2007.03.001.

Zambrana, R. E., & Hurtado, S. (2015). An intersectional lens: Theorizing an educational paradigm of success. In R. E. Zambrana & S. Hurtado (Eds.), *The magic key: The educational journey of Mexican Americans from K-12 to college and beyond* (pp. 77–99). Austin: The University of Texas Press.

Zamel, V., & Spack, R. (1998). Preface. In V. Zamel & R. Spack (Eds.), *Negotiating academic literacies: Teaching and learning across languages and cultures* (pp. ix–xviii). Mahwah, NJ: Lawrence Erlbaum.

3

Developing Understandings Over Time and Across Contexts

The longitudinal qualitative case studies in this book were created in keeping with rich traditions in applied linguistics to engage in "naturalistic, long-term, intensive documentation of processes of second language acquisition in a small number of language learners in context" (Harklau, 2013, p. 26; see also Duff, 2008, 2014; Harklau, 2008; van Lier, 2005). Below I explore several important elements of this type of research as I enacted it: selecting and defining cases, attending to depth and complexity, utilizing breadth to connect macro/meso/micro contexts, and incorporating an ethnographic perspective. I then describe the data collection procedures used in this study. Lastly, I explain data analysis processes in terms of both the longitudinal interactional histories approach (LIHA) I used and the ways I identified turning points and selected literacy events to illustrate each young person's language and literacy journey.

Selecting and Defining Cases

Perhaps one of the most important decisions in case study research is deciding what counts as a case (Flyvbjerg, 2011; Stake, 2000). And because many (although not all) scholars argue that it is the cases—rather

© The Author(s) 2019
A. K. Kibler, *Longitudinal Interactional Histories*,
https://doi.org/10.1007/978-3-319-98815-3_3

than any particular types of data collection or analysis used—that are the defining mark of case study research, it is important to explain how my selection of the five individuals introduced in Chap. 1 fit into the parameters of case study research more generally. My initial choice regarding cases involved the selection of South Sierra High School. While my work as an instructional coach at the school influenced this decision, in that I had built relationships with many students and teachers, I was also drawn to the rich opportunities the demographics of the school offered for the study of language and literacy development among Mexican immigrant-origin multilingual youth. I began observations of two different ninth-grade classrooms in the 2006–7 school year as part of my instructional coaching work, and in youth's tenth-grade year—when the ethnographic phase of the data collection began—I selected student-level cases. Throughout the study, I was aware of the implicit frame that any choice would impose by highlighting the experiences of some young people while excluding those of others, which Gutiérrez and Orellana (2006) identified as a potential pitfall of research when studying English-learner classified students. As a result, I selected students along particular criteria that would maximize opportunities to see both similarity and difference within Mexican immigrant-origin youth who were assessed to be in early stages of English language development when beginning high school. I therefore selected among students who met the following criteria:

1. They scored at the two lowest (of five) proficiency levels in writing on the standardized state English language proficiency assessment in ninth grade.
2. They were enrolled by teacher recommendation in the ninth-grade English language development (ELD) course and/or bilingual humanities (combined English and social studies) course[1] where I had conducted classroom observations.
3. The school had collected assessment data and writing samples for these students since ninth grade as part of a related research project in which I was engaged.
4. A group of at least five such students was placed in the same tenth-grade humanities class, which allowed for a deeper exploration of classroom context.

Two sets of students met these criteria, those in Ms. Connor's and Mr. Smith's humanities classes. Because of certain challenges Ms. Connor was experiencing that year, I chose to observe in Mr. Smith's class and focused on all five of his students who met these criteria. Although specific findings would have necessarily been different had Ms. Connor's students been selected for the study, the issues arising from Jaime, Ana, Diego, Fabiola, and Maria's experiences have resonance far beyond one particular classroom or set of individuals.

These youth at first represented what Flyvbjerg (2011) called "critical cases" (p. 307), in that their assessed levels of English proficiency seemed to position them as particularly likely to experience difficulties in the context of school-based literacy events and the language and literacy expectations of English-medium schooling overall. Over time, however, they became cases of "maximum variation" (p. 307) because their experiences during and after high school differed so dramatically from each other. In this way, their early high school setting was a "starting place from which connections [were] traced outwards" (Hamilton, 2015, p. 112) rather than an isolated site of study. Divergence was also inevitable because although I observed, interviewed, and collected documents for all five students who met the aforementioned requirements, the data were not spread neatly and evenly among them, due to logistical factors, changing circumstances, and the different relationships I developed with youth. (See the Methodological Appendix for an exploration of changes in my positioning as a researcher over the course of the study.) I have argued elsewhere (Kibler, 2017b) that such variation is inherent to the work of longitudinal qualitative research, and to impose uniformity or evenness—or an expectation of it—would distort participants' stories and our roles as researchers in them.

Jaime, Ana, Diego, Fabiola, and Maria comprise the main cases, or units of analysis for this study, and shared contexts and experiences clearly connected these young people in important ways. For this reason, the term "collective case study" (Stake, 2000, p. 437) is a useful means of understanding the instrumental reason for which these students were selected: to understand the challenges and successes encountered in the language and literacy journeys of Mexican immigrant-origin youth who were considered to be in the early stages of developing English language and literacy expertise as they began high school.

Engaging with Depth and Complexity

Another key element of longitudinal qualitative case studies is the depth and richness they can provide through extended and intensive naturalistic inquiry into individual cases. Contexts in which multiple languages and literacies are employed are inherently complex (Duff, 2008)—particularly when juxtaposed against monolingual assumptions embedded in educational and other institutions—and this type of research is one means of doing justice to such settings. Harklau (2013) is well known for working in this tradition with multilingual adolescents and young adults in the United States, and she argued that the insights available through long-term "portraits of human experience in all its complexities and contradictions" (p. 10) are unique, in that they cannot necessarily be gleaned from larger-scale studies.

Although attention to these complexities often confounds educational stakeholders who seek "silver bullets" or other singular solutions to inequitable circumstances and outcomes found in schools, it is only through deep engagement over time that we can truly uncover the full extent of the goodness found in the rich and complex lives of multilingual youth from immigrant families. This depth is in part achieved through the collection of multiple sources of data, typically participant observations, documents or other texts used or created by individuals, and interviews with a range of people and across varied contexts over time (Harklau, 2013). Multifaceted information of this type helps researchers understand the phenomena they are witnessing as well as the different possible interpretations of it that individuals may have.

The nature of this data, particularly when collected over a long period of time, also requires researchers to continuously revisit and revise their understandings of what they think is happening and why. This interpretation is done with a careful eye toward the many data sources and an acknowledgment that "data are co-constructed (not simply collected)" (Duff, 2014, p. 239). In this sense, interviews—for example—are not simply a means of giving and receiving the "truth" about what happens in a research context. Rather, they are a context in which both interviewers and interviewees perform (at times multiple) situated social identities (Harklau, 2013; Josselson, 2004; Seale, 1999).

Schools and related institutions tend to create partial (and as a result often deficit-oriented) portraits of minoritized students. Once youth move from ninth to tenth grade, for example, they take new classes, interact with different sets of teachers who often have little or no knowledge of their academic and linguistic growth during the previous year, and usually become part of new cohorts for the purposes of accountability. Compton-Lilly (2017) called this tendency the "horizontal nature of schools" (p. 134), which means that students rarely develop long-term relationships with adults who understand the histories they bring to the classroom. Without such knowledge, it can be difficult for teachers to understand not only where students have been but also where they are (or could be) going, in terms of lives they wish to lead and the people they aspire to be. Longitudinal qualitative case studies, in contrast, offer depth and complexity that help provide more holistic and nuanced understandings.

Maximizing Breadth

Longitudinal qualitative case studies allow us to gain more than depth. They also provide a kind of breadth that is unique, because by looking at individual experiences over time we can more clearly connect micro-level individual contexts with larger institutional and social forces. Neale and Flowerdew (2003) explained that "it is only through time that we gain a better appreciation of how the personal and the social, agency and structure, the micro and macro are interconnected and how they come to be transformed" (p. 190). In this sense, longitudinal study can uncover relationships among factors that—while still complex, or even contradictory—are far more meaningful than the kinds of speculations made in shorter-term research that can only hypothesize about the long-term impact of particular policies or pedagogical approaches.

Longitudinal qualitative case studies therefore bring several empirical strengths, but perhaps the most profound is that they carry with them the breadth and power of narrative. Stories compel us to enter the lives and worlds of others, and in so doing, broaden our perspectives on others' experiences and our own. Understanding individual situated cases in all their complexity and then synthesizing across multiple experiences with different cases—which Flyvbjerg (2011) argued is critical to developing expertise in a field—can therefore help both researchers and educators deepen their understanding and awareness.

Incorporating an Ethnographic Perspective

One aspect of this project that extends beyond traditional case studies is the use of an ethnographic perspective (Green & Bloome, 1997) that is attuned to social groups' daily lives and cultural practices. Such attention can be particularly useful because it helps researchers examine the ways in which context and culture shape the meaning of any utterance, as well as "how discourse shapes both what is available to be learned and what is, in fact, learned" (Gee & Green, 1998, p. 126). Scholars have argued for the importance of these perspectives not only for language in general but for writing in particular, from Grabe and Kaplan's (1996) call for an ethnography of writing ("who writes what to whom, for what purpose, why, when, where, and how?", p. 203) to Lillis' (2013) ethnographic view of academic writing as inextricable from the context of its use and users.

The study described in this book employs elements of what Lillis (2008) considered to be three different approaches to ethnography in writing research. The first, most basic level is that of ethnographic method (examining talk around texts and not simply texts themselves), and the second is ethnographic methodology (use of multiple data sources and sustained, involved fieldwork as texts are produced). I employed both of these in this study, although as described later in the chapter, my observational fieldwork occurred primarily in the second year of the project. My interactions with youth in the other years of the study were regular but less frequent, but the relationships and understandings built during the ethnographic fieldwork were absolutely fundamental in allowing me to pursue ethnographic understandings of these young people's experiences in subsequent years. In this way, I have been able to explore elements of what Lillis (2008) called the third and most involved level of ethnography, that of deep theorizing (citing Blommaert, 2007) that attempts to narrow the gap between text and context by explicitly engaging not only with the immediate circumstances of writing but with the larger social, cultural, and historical contexts in which it occurs and which it may also influence.

Collecting Data

Data collection began in youth's ninth-grade year, when I served as an instructional coach at South Sierra High School, which they attended at that time. Because I worked with the bilingual humanities and ELD teachers for that grade level, I was often in their classrooms taking notes on lessons to discuss with teachers afterward. These observations included attention to students, including Jaime, Ana, Diego, Fabiola, and Maria, all of whom were in one or both of those classrooms. I also collected assessment data and writing samples for students in these classes as part of a related research project, which I was given permission to use for this study as well.

Ethnographic Phase The ethnographic focal point of the study was youth's tenth-grade year (2007–2008), in which I shadowed each individual on a rotating basis in almost all of his or her classes for a total of 80 instructional days, as well as most sessions of a Saturday program some of them attended. I used fieldnote writing and audio recordings to document what occurred. During these observations, I made what Emerson, Fretz, and Shaw (2011) call *jottings* and then expanded these into more complete fieldnotes later in the day that included a full description of what took place as well as initial reflections on what was occurring. I also placed small digital audio recorders with the youth being observed, and reviewed these recordings later in the day to revisit any moments that I had marked in my fieldnotes as especially significant to youth's participation in literacy events. Any new data gained from the recordings was then integrated into the fieldnotes for that day. I did not systemically observe students between classes, before school, after school, or at lunch, but I often walked around the school at these times, watching or talking with Jaime, Ana, Diego, Fabiola, and Maria or other youth at the school. In those cases, I later added insights from those conversations and observations to my fieldnotes for the day. In efforts to engage in initial analysis during the course of data collection, I wrote weekly memos identifying connections among events and emerging patterns and themes.

I collected in-school writing samples on most days I observed as well as all drafts of all extended writing that youth completed and additional out-of-school writing they chose to share with me. I defined "extended writing" tasks in a rough sense as those that typically involved more than a page of writing and were usually completed over multiple class periods, days, or weeks. (Outside of educational institutions, I did not find evidence of the young people in this study engaging in writing of this type during high school.) I also gathered data from the school's cumulative files and databases, which provided information on youth's educational histories, language proficiency classification as assigned by the school, grades, and achievement on standardized state assessments.

I conducted semi-structured interviews with each young person using prepared interview guides (Lofland, Snow, Anderson, & Lofland, 2006). During the ethnographic phase of the study, these included an initial background interview and then up to three stimulated elicitation interviews (Prior, 2004) about different extended writing texts they completed. During these interviews, together we looked at their drafts, teacher handouts, and feedback they received (if available). I asked general questions about the texts, such as what they liked most about their writing or what they would change, as well as more specific questions about the steps they took to complete each task within the larger assignment, feedback they received, and changes they made (or did not make). Teachers of the classes I observed who assigned extended writing tasks were interviewed as well, and questions focused on their assignments and the writing that Jaime, Ana, Diego, Fabiola, and Maria completed for their classes. (See the Methodological Appendix for youth and teacher interview guides and further details on interviews.) During the ethnographic phase, interviews were completed in school locations chosen by youth and teachers themselves, like empty classrooms, the library, the cafeteria, and outdoor spaces, when others were not present.[2] These more formal interviews were supplemented by countless informal conversations throughout the study, which were integrated into fieldnotes. Kibler (2009) provides additional details regarding data collection in the ethnographic phase.

Punctuated Revisits What followed ethnographic data collection can best be considered a series of "punctuated revisits" (Burawoy, 2003, p. 647), a process by which an ethnographer returns to individuals or sites after intensive fieldwork has been completed for purposes of seeing what has changed over time, and why. From youth's last two years of high school (grades 11–12) through their fourth year after high school graduation, I stayed in touch with them in person and via email, text, Skype, phone, and/or mail, as their specific situations required. While they were still in high school, I also visited their schools a few times each year to observe. I collected writing samples from each young person approximately three to four times per year, asking in each instance for them to give me two or three pieces of writing they completed that were most important to them or that they most wanted to talk about. (I asked for both extended writing as well as any other writing they completed in academic/vocational or other contexts.) Shortly after each round of writing sample collection, we then completed interviews following a consistent semi-structured interview guide that included specific questions focused on their writing alongside more general ones designed to elicit broader descriptions of their language and literacy experiences since I had seen them last. (See Methodological Appendix.)

Data collection procedures were adapted as youth's circumstances changed. For example, after their high school graduations, the study participants and I were now spread across the country. This separation meant that although I continued to collect data at least three to four times per year (and kept in touch more frequently through texted and emailed greetings), I sometimes conducted interviews via online video platforms or, in Maria's case, via phone because Internet access at the Institute she attended was very limited. I typically collected writing samples by email and mail, but I also made in-person summertime visits each year to Maria at the Institute and to Jaime, Ana, Diego, and Fabiola in California.

An additional change to data collection was made in the sixth year of the study, by which time Ana had finished her cosmetology program and Jaime had stopped taking community college courses. As a result, they were no longer completing academic/vocational writing tasks and claimed that they "just don't write anymore." I still made contact with them at least three times per year but chose to focus my data collection efforts for them on the in-person interviews I conducted during annual summer visits to California. Face-to-face, it was far easier to untangle the writing they *were* doing (but didn't really consider "writing," as it turned out), obtain samples of that writing, and talk with them about the range of language and literacy practices in which they were engaged.

As the years progressed, semi-structured interviews inevitably became more reflective. Questions that asked about past and future lives drew out richer answers not only because youth had more "life" to reflect upon but also because our relationships had deepened. As Okano (2009) explained in her study of working-class Japanese young women, researchers and participants in longitudinal research have shared histories—what Gordon and Lahelma (2003) called joint memories—that span several years and allow for deeper discussions. "You remember when…" became a frequent refrain in our interview questions and responses, and our joint experiences made it easier for me to probe youth's responses and ask them to extend their ideas.

I also found that interviews became more open-ended, in that we often began with lengthy "catching up" sessions, unbound by formal questions. It was often these casual conversations that revealed important moments in youth's lives and led to further questions that blended into the interview itself. Also, when no longer bound to a school site as a place for interviews, I learned much from visiting young people in their locations of choice. For Diego, for example, this meant seeing the one-bedroom apartment where his family of four lived; or for Maria, the chapel, library, classroom, and shared spaces of the Catholic house in which she lived and studied. I also discovered that Ana's mother was an immaculate housekeeper and cook as well as a full-time caretaker of a young grandson and nephew. For Jaime, although we met in public places, I met his sister and niece and also came to realize that the car he drove to our interviews also brought with it responsibilities to provide transportation for family members. Finally, in Fabiola's apartment during her time at West Coast University, I saw the small but well-used study space where she spent so much of her time.

Although I was often surprised by how responsive youth were to my emails, phone calls, texts, and requests to meet, there was one exception: After the sixth year of data collection, Diego did not respond to me for the remainder of the study, despite my many attempts and efforts. His non-responsiveness to my requests began, in fact, around the same time that he withdrew from his university (which is explored in Chap. 6). I heard through other youth in the study that Diego had later returned home and completed an associate's degree, but he did not contact me again until nearly two years after data collection had ended, and then only for a quick texted greeting and update about what he was doing. In considering why Diego did not continue in the study, it is certainly possible that he saw me as a representative of formal schooling as well as someone who had observed the great hopes many of his high school teachers had for him after graduation. As Sefton-Green (2015a) explained, interviews of the sort I was conducting tend to involve:

> a kind of reflection about the person you were going to be when there appeared to be more possibilities in life. However, if the realities of your life don't quite match up, then I think meeting with ex-teachers and reviewing where you are now and what you might have been, could be a more painful experience. (p. 48)

While this is certainly one possibility, it remains an open question that highlights the complexity of this study as well as longitudinal qualitative research more generally.

Using a Longitudinal Interactional Histories Approach to Data Analysis

The literacy events around which I have framed Jaime, Ana, Diego, Fabiola, and Maria's stories—informed by data from both the extensive ethnographic fieldwork and punctuated revisits—were analyzed according to a longitudinal interactional histories approach to data analysis, which I developed for the purposes of this study (see also Kibler, 2013, 2017a). This approach to language and literacy research has at its core a focus on three key sustaining questions:

1. What interactions do individuals have with discourses, governmental and institutional policies and practices, individuals, texts, and technologies while writing?
2. What impacts do these interactions have on texts they write?
3. How do individuals' texts (and the processes through which they are created) change over time?

These three areas of focus demand attention to the ways in which individuals and communities, as well as local and global concerns, fit together and vary over time. Gutiérrez and Rogoff (2013) contended that this type of analysis is particularly important because "without situating social practices and the histories of participants in particular communities, approaches that attribute style to membership in a group make it difficult to account for variation and change in individuals or their practices" (p. 3). When attention is focused in this way—on how individuals appropriate and use various resources or aspects of them—development is therefore expected to be nonlinear and reflective of the ways in which opportunities and constraints operate at both individual and community levels (Gutiérrez, 2002, p. 210).

While a LIHA analysis has a clear focus on texts, it is not simply a "text analysis." Rather, I sought a deeper understanding of the social practices of writing (Newell, Bloome, & Hirvela, 2015) that were created and developed in and through these literacy events, not just the material circumstances of texts' creation. Further, by drawing upon an ethnographic perspective informed by in-depth observation and interviewing, the longitudinal interactional histories approach I used provided a more comprehensive picture of individuals' experiences over time and across varied contexts. In the following sections I first explain the theories undergirding the aforementioned LIHA questions before describing how I used these questions to analyze each literacy event in the data set.

LIHA Questions 1 and 2: Theories of Interactional Histories Any individual instance of writing, or literacy use more generally, has deep and multiple histories embedded within it. I have argued elsewhere that investigating such histories can tell researchers much more about language use and development than any finished written text (or other literate performance) ever could (Kibler, 2010). This perspective suggests that researchers should attend carefully to both what individuals bring to a literacy event and the details of the actual process of textual creation.

Individuals bring their own histories—which Rogers (2002) has described as "histories of participation" (p. 252)—to any literacy event. Similarly, Burgess and Ivanič (2010) explained that "one powerful influence on how a person responds to a social situation that potentially involves writing is the set of practices, interests, beliefs, allegiances, affiliations, experiences of power relationships, and feelings that she brings to it" (p. 247). These various histories, they argued, are unique to individuals but constrained by what is available in their social worlds. They serve as a medium through which discourses and relationships are brought to the page, including the ways in which writers understand who their audiences are and what they expect from a text. Moje and Lewis (2007) described this process in a slightly different way: Learning "leaves a residue; it makes a mark on the participant" (p. 16), and in this way, it both creates histories and shapes future participation.

The interactional histories described in this book acknowledge these influences while also attending to the complex conditions under which texts are created. Such investigations, which are similar in some ways to what Lillis (2008; see also Lillis & Curry, 2006) called "text histories" (p. 368), can help researchers understand not only why individuals' texts may differ from each other but also how various contextual factors impact the construction and development of a text. These contextual factors—conceptualized in this study as "interactions" with resources or circumstances that individuals bring to or experience during language and literacy events—can be quite diverse. As described earlier, interactions with discourses, governmental and institutional policies and practices, other people, texts, and technologies can all influence what individuals write and how they compose their texts. For example, Diego's tenth-grade experience with essay writing described in Chap. 6 demonstrates how powerful discourses about "hardworking student" identities interacted with institutional policies and practices in which curricula were to include the reading of "thick, important books" regardless of students' levels of English proficiency or literacy expertise. These interactions led to unique resources for Diego's writing. Although he understood relatively little of the assigned book about which he was to write his essay, Diego was successful in enlisting substantial support from various people, including his teacher, and, to somewhat a lesser extent, fellow classmates, to help him complete the writing task during in-class drafting sessions. He often used their language directly in his essay rather than drawing upon the assigned book itself (text) or his own phrasing. His use of technologies[3] included typing into an online word processing program through which his teacher provided feedback (in addition to handwritten notes on an earlier draft), which prompted several further teacher-student interactions during class.

The various resources made available in such interactions are dynamic rather than static or deterministic, in that their use is shaped by the individuals employing them, and they can take on different functions in different situations (Roth & Lee, 2007) in ways that can either hinder or support language and literacy development. As mentioned in the previous chapter, available interactional resources are not necessarily affordances, and any given resources—from course curricula to teacher pedagogies to support from others while writing—can vary in the extent to which they actually help individuals learn new information or expand their language and literacy repertoires. It should also be noted that just as individuals (and the texts they produce) are shaped by their interactions with various resources and circumstances, they may also transform them through use, thereby changing the ecological setting that they or others may experience in the future. Returning to Diego's example, although he had no discernable impact on his school's institutional expectations or the assigned writing task, he did influence his teacher, who felt distinctly uncomfortable that "I was almost writing his essay at one point" (Interview, 18 April 2008). In the remaining months of the school year, I frequently observed this teacher encouraging Diego to first try to write on his own before requesting help.

LIHA Questions 1 and 2: Approaches to Analyzing Interactional Histories To address *question 1* (What interactions do individuals have with discourses, governmental and institutional policies and practices, individuals, texts, and technologies while writing?), I first carefully identified what interactions occurred during each particular literacy event. Because each event and individual were unique, the types of interactions were as well, and as a result, in the chapters that follow, I focused my descriptions on the interactions that were most influential for each event, rather than attempting to present a catalog of each interaction regardless of its significance.

In the ethnographic phase of the study (tenth grade), for each literacy event observed I drew from fieldnotes, weekly memos, writing samples, and other documents collected during classroom observations as well as interviews with youth and teachers to identify interactions. After reading and rereading these materials I engaged in focused coding (Emerson, Fretz, & Shaw, 2011) to identify the specific interactions that occurred during a given literacy event. I then complemented this global analysis with a more local one (Gumperz, 2003), using transcripts of all available audio-recorded observations to understand how interactions between teachers and students or among peers during literacy events unfolded on a turn-by-turn basis. Audio data were analyzed according to the perspective that detailed sequential analyses can illuminate the "local moves and countermoves" of participants in these speech exchanges (Gumperz & Berenz, 1993, p. 95), including the moment to moment changes in alignment that speakers and hearers take toward each other and the content of their talk (Hoyle & Adger, 1998).[4]

In the other years of the study, when observations of writing processes were not possible, I relied upon interviews for global analyses of literacy events, in keeping with the processes described earlier. Although I did not have direct access to the interpersonal interactions that unfolded in order to conduct more local analyses, careful reading of the writing samples youth shared with me, along with my understanding of their previous interactional histories developed through the ethnographic phase of the study, allowed me to ask specific and focused questions about how face-to-face or textual interactions unfolded during the course of literacy events.

To address *question 2* (What impacts do these interactions have on texts they write?), I tracked the actual changes in individuals' texts as they were created, using a process called intertextual analysis (Prior, 2004), which involves looking for relationships between a final written text and (1) initiating texts, like class assignments or other teacher handouts, (2) source texts, like assigned textbooks or novels or lists of websites provided for students to consult, (3) previous versions or drafts of the text, and (4) classroom talk with both teachers and classmates. During the non-ethnographic years of the study when it was not always possible to access initiating texts, multiple drafts, or classroom talk, I relied upon interview questions that asked youth about their interactions and their influence in order to complete the intertextual analysis. After coding both texts and interviews, I wrote integrative memos about each literacy event to synthesize patterns regarding the interactions and their impacts on youth's texts. At this point I was able to make meaningful connections between a given literacy event and the previous experiences and identities that youth brought with them.

LIHA Question 3: Theories of Change Over Time Lemke (2000) is often cited as asking, "How do moments add up to lives?" (p. 273). This question is at the heart of longitudinal research because such studies are not important simply because they occur over a long period of time and take extensive resources to complete: They must also have a "so what" (Sefton-Green, 2015b, p. 9) that cannot be gleaned from research conducted on a shorter timescale. While the years I spent with Jaime, Ana, Diego, Fabiola, and Maria comprised a far more modest span of time than the "lives" Lemke references, the question of change over time is nonetheless a valid one. As described in what follows, I conceptualized change over time in ways that assumed emergence, inextricability from the spaces in which literacy events occur, and visibility at different scales.

Saldaña (2003) argued that in longitudinal qualitative research it is impossible to define change over time other than contextually, and that the nature of any change must emerge over the course of the study. Although the design of my study had particular parameters that defined time rather rigidly—like beginning and ending each of its eight years on the academic calendar—I found that once the young people in this study were no longer restricted by the rhythms and rituals of a high school schedule, lives ran their courses far more fluidly. For example, Ana's shift from a cosmetology student to a hair stylist in a bilingual community happened part-way through her second post–high school year, around the same time that Jaime stopped taking community college classes to work full-time but before Diego left university. Maria, however, undertook novitiate and further religious studies that included various periods and lengths of classes, independent studies, retreats, service trips, work responsibilities, and study abroad. Fabiola's contexts were perhaps the most similar to those under which we began the study, in that she continued in full-time university study through semester-long classes for all four years after graduation. Such differing experiences created unique rhythms to which youth traveled on their varied language and literacy paths. As a result, the significance of their experiences lies more powerfully in the journeys they took than in the end-point at which they arrived four years after graduation. This emphasis on "from-through" rather than "from-to" (Saldaña, 2003, p. 8) is key to understanding change over time. In this sense, even though I use the singular "journey" to describe each individual's experience, it does not imply that these are narrow, unitary, or predictable paths. Following Saldaña (2003), I see any individual journey as a complex set of experiences rather than a linear or singular trajectory.

As these journeys suggest, time cannot be considered in isolation. Space or place must also be considered when trying to understand change. Scholars have drawn upon the notion of "timespace" from a range of perspectives (e.g., Blommaert, 2015; Compton-Lilly, 2017; Sefton-Green, 2015a, 2015b), and Blommaert and De Fina (2017) articulated the concept in a way that is perhaps most relevant to the stories of youth in this study:

> Changes in timespace arrangements trigger complex and sometimes massive shifts in roles, discourses, modes of interaction, dress, codes of conduct and criteria for judgment of appropriate versus inappropriate behavior, and so forth. (p. 4)

This understanding of change accounts for, but moves beyond, what Compton-Lilly (2017) called the "maps and clocks" of space and time (p. 8) to understand the linguistically and socially complex situations in which individuals in my study used and developed language and literacy expertise or at times failed to meet institutional or individual expectations in the context of these events.

Time also operates at different levels, or scales, some of which are uniquely visible in longitudinal research. Cole (1996) proposed a set of timescales that includes micro-genetic (event scale), meso-genetic (extended activity or project scale), onto-genetic (developmental-biographical scale), and historical and evolutionary (what Wortham (2003) calls sociohistorical) scales. Three issues are particularly important when considering how these timescales operate. First, longitudinal research that spans a number of years can engage in micro-genetic, meso-genetic, and even onto-genetic analyses, although as timescales grow, researchers are less and less likely to observe or discover the totality of those experiences. Second, it is often only at the micro-genetic level—individual moments in time—that the relevance, regularity, and influence of larger timescales can be seen (Lemke, 2000; Wortham, 2003). Third, as mentioned earlier in my discussion of interactional histories, language and literacy practices at any given moment are necessarily influenced by previous experiences which may have occurred days, months, and years before, or even exist only as "received wisdom" about what has happened in the past.

LIHA Question 3: Approaches to Analyzing Change Over Time The third and final focus of a LIHA analysis is an emphasis on change over time in youth's written texts and/or the processes through which they were created: How do individuals' texts (and the processes through which they are created) change over time? During the ethnographic phase, I attended primarily to micro-genetic activity and meso-genetic change across a set of related classroom activities within particular literacy events. Gibbons (2006) considered this type of analysis vital in language and literacy research:

> Only by focusing on a sequence of activities…rather than a single lesson or exchange, is it possible to show how the changes in the nature of the discourse, and the differential interactional roles played by the teacher, impacted on students' language and curriculum learning. (p. 271)

During the punctuated revisits that occurred during subsequent years of the study, I was able to attend to change at larger scales, accounting for meso- and onto-genetic changes (and to some extent the sociohistorical contexts that shaped them) over time and across varied contexts. Throughout all phases of the study, however, I also employed an analytic strategy that overtly sought connections among interactions. This search for contiguous relations "segments the data and then *connects* these segments into a relational order within an actual context" (Maxwell & Miller, 2008, p. 468), or in this case, across multiple contexts. Similarly, McLeod (2003) described this type of longitudinal analysis as a process of understanding both continuity and change based upon a rich and comparative "archive of perspectives" (p. 202).

Because question 2 addresses how I attempted to understand micro- and meso-genetic change in individuals' texts within a given literacy event through intertextual analysis, here I explain the ways in which I tried to understand onto-genetic change, the shifts during and across multiple years and settings. At the end of each year of the study, I reread all memos and associated data, looking for both commonalities and differences among youth (similar to Thomson & Holland, 2003). This rereading was important: As Compton-Lilly (2017) suggested, data collected early in a longitudinal study can gain new significance when viewed alongside later data. For example, by comparing Diego's participation in literacy events in high school and university (see Chap. 6), I found that although certain English language and literacy practices were undertaken in more independent ways over time, in university he continued to employ similar teacher-reliance strategies as he did in tenth grade in order to create extended written texts about assigned books. In Jaime's case, however, comparing texts written in similar genres earlier and later in the study helped make clear the notable changes in his written texts as well as in the processes through which they were created (see Chap. 4).

By the sixth year of the study, I found that it was most insightful to begin looking at each young person as an individual case—but still through the lens of interactional histories—because their settings and trajectories had become quite different. This case-by-case approach to analyzing change continued through the remainder of the study and is represented in the organization of this book, which includes separate chapters for Jaime, Ana, Diego, Fabiola, and Maria. The key analytical decision at that point was—after rereading data from all eight years of the study—to attempt to find key moments or decisions that most strongly influenced each young person's language and literacy journey, and to read the data again with that key moment in mind, in efforts to find literacy events leading up to or following from it that best demonstrated key aspects of youth's journeys. I describe this process in the following section.

Presenting Data Through Turning Points

In their ninth-grade year, before I had even started the ethnographic phase of this study, Jaime, Ana, Diego, Fabiola, and Maria wrote and presented "Turning Point" narrative essays as part of a school-wide annual assessment. For this task, they were asked to identify moments in time that had most strongly influenced their lives in school and at home. Little did I know that many years later I would be engaging in a similar process as I tried to make sense of the data I had collected. Notions of time and space are integral to understanding longitudinal qualitative research generally, and interactional histories specifically, and so perhaps the greatest conceptual and methodological challenge in this study was to decide how to identify the defining moments in youth's language and literacy journeys (Kibler, 2017a).

As Neale and Flowerdew (2003) suggested, "the life course, for example, need not be plotted in terms of a linear grid or seen in terms of fixed stages but can be conceptualized in terms of the more fluid and individualized notions of turning points or defining moments" (p. 193). Based on theories that argue time is contextually emergent, inextricable from spaces/places of language literacy use, and visible at several levels, I knew that changes in the purposes, audiences, and uses of literacies across languages in daily and professional/academic lives, as well as changes in individuals' perceptions of them, would be different for each young person in this study. Further, selecting one or more moments, even based on the most meticulous reading of the data, would be necessarily a choice made by me (in consultation with youth but not by them alone) and one that would necessarily exclude other narratives that could have been told.

Both reflective interviewing and multiple data sources helped me make such decisions. In each interview, I asked youth to reflect on what they had done and learned, as well as how they had changed in the previous months, year, or even larger chunks of time. Comparing their responses over time to the texts they shared and/or discussed with me allowed me to see significant changes in their language and literacy use and development. Such shifts were similar to Webster and Mertova's (2007) concept of "critical events" (pp. 73–74) in that they were unique, illustrative of larger issues, confirmable through other similar events, and identified and understood only in retrospect. And although some of these turning points were predictable—such as choices to attend community college or university—others were less so, like Ana's change in motivation and pride in her bilingual and bicultural expertise in her last year of high school, or Maria's decision to enter a bilingual Catholic novitiate program rather than university. Further, defining moments tended to be less about individual moments in time and more about larger decisions that led to shifts in academic or professional spaces.

Because the notion of turning points was one to which the youth and I had been oriented from the beginning of the study, I employ this term to describe these defining moments or critical events. In the chapters that follow, I present LIHA analyses of specific literacy events that occurred both before and after each young person's turning point to explore the interactional histories that students built over time along these varied trajectories. Specifically, I first draw upon the three-question LIHA analysis framework to present each of two literacy events preceding an individual's turning point to demonstrate the ways in which their language and literacy repertoires built toward particular moments of change. I then use the same approach to present LIHA analyses of two literacy events after each turning point that demonstrate the impact of these moments of change on youth's language and literacy journeys. Just as reflective interviewing and multiple data sources helped me determine turning points for each youth, I used these same tools to select literacy events for inclusion that were either (1) representative of repeated literacy events in which youth engaged or (2) distinct from other literacy events but particularly important for youth and/or uniquely insightful in regard to their language and literacy development.

The decision to include LIHA analyses of the same number of literacy events before and after each young person's turning point is clearly arbitrary in some senses, but I chose to rely on this consistent structure to provide accounts that are more comparable across cases. Further, in each chapter I include extensive overviews of youth's more general language and literacy experiences during the study, so that readers can judge for themselves the relationships between the literacy events I chose to profile in-depth and others that took place during the study. The selection of turning points and literacy events were ultimately mine, and so they are inevitably my creations, just as students' essays were theirs. However, youth's accounts and texts guided me toward those moments and events that appeared to have the largest impact and that were most helpful in understanding the interactional influences shaping their complex and nonlinear language and literacy journeys.

Notes

1. There was no bilingual humanities course offered at the tenth grade, and I did not rely on tenth-grade ELD enrollment because class size for that course was cut dramatically due to scheduling issues that year.
2. All spaces carry their own meanings, and school-based interview locations likely evoked different feelings for young people who either did or did not have difficult relationships with the schools and/or its teachers. However, during high school, youth preferred to be interviewed during school hours

rather than before or after them, and I asked them to select which school locations they preferred for the interviews.

3. I recognize that a wide range of tools can be considered "technologies," even writing itself (Ong, 1986). My use of the term in this book emphasizes primarily digital technologies.

4. To conduct this local discourse analysis, I drew from insights in interactional sociolinguistics (IS), and in particular the notion that participants contextualize utterances in light of their previous experiences and language-related knowledge (Gumperz & Cook-Gumperz, 2006). One way of contextualizing what is being said is through "contextualization cues," certain language conventions such as intonation, rhythm, stress, and lexical and stylistic choices that help listeners develop inferences about the interaction in which they are engaged (Gumperz, 1982; Gumperz & Cook-Gumperz, 2006). Although these may be "marginal features" (Schiffrin, 1996, p. 311) that are not as obvious as the propositional content of what is being said, such cues can often play a key role in how participants understand each other.

References

Blommaert, J. (2007). On scope and depth in linguistic ethnography. *Journal of SocioLinguistics, 11*(5), 682–688. https://doi.org/10.1111/j.1467-9841.2007.00346.x.

Blommaert, J. (2015). Chronotopes, scales, and complexity in the study of language in society. *Annual Review of Anthropology, 44*, 105–116. https://doi.org/10.1146/annurev-anthro-102214-014035.

Blommaert, J., & De Fina, A. (2017). Chronotopic identities: On the timespace organization of who we are. In A. De Fina, D. Ikizoglu, & J. Wegner (Eds.), *Diversity and super-diversity: Sociocultural linguistic perspectives* (pp. 1–15). Washington, DC: Georgetown University Press.

Burawoy, M. (2003). Revisits: An outline of a theory of reflexive ethnography. *American Sociological Review, 68*(5), 645–679. https://doi.org/10.2307/1519757.

Burgess, A., & Ivanič, R. (2010). Writing and being written: Issues of identity across timescales. *Written Communication, 27*(2), 228–255. https://doi.org/10.1177/0741088310363447.

Cole, M. (1996). *Cultural psychology.* Cambridge, MA: Harvard University Press.

Compton-Lilly, C. (2017). *Reading students' lives: Literacy learning across time.* New York: Routledge.

Duff, P. (2008). *Case study research in applied linguistics.* New York: Erlbaum/Taylor & Francis.

Duff, P. (2014). Case study research on language learning and use. *Annual Review of Applied Linguistics, 34,* 233–255. https://doi.org/10.1017/S0267190514000051.

Emerson, R. M., Fretz, R. I., & Shaw, L. L. (2011). *Writing ethnographic fieldnotes* (2nd ed.). Chicago: University of Chicago Press.

Flyvbjerg, B. (2011). Case study. In N. K. Denzin & Y. S. Lincoln (Eds.), *The SAGE handbook of qualitative research* (4th ed., pp. 301–316). Los Angeles: SAGE.

Gee, J. P., & Green, J. L. (1998). Discourse analysis, learning, and social practice: A methodological study. *Review of Research in Education, 23*(1), 119–169. https://doi.org/10.3102/0091732X023001119.

Gibbons, P. (2006). *Bridging discourses in the ESL classroom: Students, teachers, and researchers.* London: Continuum.

Gordon, T., & Lahelma, E. (2003). From ethnography to life history: Tracing transitions of school students. *International Journal of Social Research Methodology, 6*(3), 245–254. https://doi.org/10.1080/1364557032000091842.

Grabe, W., & Kaplan, R. B. (1996). *Theory and practice of writing: An applied linguistics perspective.* New York: Longman.

Green, J., & Bloome, D. (1997). Ethnography and ethnographers of and in education: A situated perspective. In J. Flood, S. B. Heath, & D. Lapp (Eds.), *Handbook of research on teaching literacy through the communicative and visual arts* (pp. 181–202). New York: International Reading Association.

Gumperz, J. J. (1982). *Discourse strategies.* Cambridge, UK: Cambridge University Press.

Gumperz, J. J. (2003). Response essay. In S. L. Eerdman, C. L. Prevignano, & P. J. Thibault (Eds.), *Language and interaction: Discussions with John J. Gumperz* (pp. 105–126). Philadelphia, PA: John Benjamins.

Gumperz, J. J., & Berenz, N. (1993). Transcribing conversational exchanges. In J. A. Edwards & M. D. Lampert (Eds.), *Talking data: Transcription and coding in discourse research* (pp. 91–122). Hillsdale, NJ: Erlbaum.

Gumperz, J. J., & Cook-Gumperz, J. (2006). Interactional sociolinguistics in the study of schooling. In J. Cook-Gumperz (Ed.), *The Social construction of literacy* (2nd ed., pp. 50–75). Cambridge, UK: Cambridge University Press.

Gutiérrez, K. D. (2002). Studying cultural practices in urban learning communities. *Human Development, 45*(4), 312–321. https://doi.org/10.1159/000064995.

Gutiérrez, K. D., & Faulstich Orellana, M. (2006). The "problem" of English learners: Constructing genres of difference. *Research in the Teaching of English, 40*(4), 502–507.

Gutiérrez, K. D., & Rogoff, B. (2013). Cultural ways of learning: Individual traits or repertoires of practice. *Educational Researcher, 32*(5), 19–25. https://doi.org/10.3102/0013189X032005019.

Hamilton, M. (2015). The everyday and faraway: Revisiting local literacies. In J. Sefton-Green & J. Rowsell (Eds.), *Learning and literacy over time: Longitudinal perspectives* (pp. 98–115). New York: Routledge.

Harklau, L. (2008). Developing qualitative longitudinal case studies of advanced language learners. In L. Ortega & H. Byrnes (Eds.), *The longitudinal study of advanced L2 capacities* (pp. 23–35). New York: Routledge.

Harklau, L. (2013). Why Izzie didn't go to college: Choosing work over college as Latina feminism. *Teachers College Record, 115*(1), 1–32.

Hoyle, S. M., & Adger, C. T. (1998). Introduction. In S. M. Hoyle & C. T. Adger (Eds.), *Kids talk: Strategic language use in later childhood* (pp. 3–22). New York: Oxford University Press.

Josselson, R. (2004). The hermeneutics of faith and the hermeneutics of suspicion. *Narrative Inquiry, 14*(1), 1–28. https://doi.org/10.1075/ni.14.1.01jos.

Kibler, A. K. (2009). *Talking writing: Adolescent English learners in the content areas* (Unpublished doctoral dissertation). Stanford, CA: Stanford University.

Kibler, A. K. (2010). Writing through two languages: First language expertise in a language minority classroom. *Journal of Second Language Writing, 19*(3), 121–142. https://doi.org/10.1016/j.jslw.2010.04.001.

Kibler, A. K. (2013). "Doing like almost everything wrong": An adolescent multilingual writer's transition from high school to college. In L. C. de Oliveira & T. Silva (Eds.), *L2 writing in secondary classrooms: Student experiences, academic issues, and teacher education* (pp. 44–64). New York: Routledge.

Kibler, A. K. (2017a). Becoming a "Mexican feminist": A minoritized bilingual's development of disciplinary identities through writing. *Journal of Second Language Writing, 38*, 26–41. https://doi.org/10.1016/j.jslw.2017.10.011.

Kibler, A. K. (2017b, March). *Longitudinal insights into interactional histories.* Paper presented at the American Association for Applied Linguistics Annual Conference, Portland, OR.

Lemke, J. L. (2000). Across the scales of time: Artifacts, activities, and meanings in ecosocial systems. *Mind, Culture, and Activity, 7*(4), 273–290. https://doi.org/10.1207/S15327884MCA0704_03.

Lillis, T. (2008). Ethnography as method, methodology, and "deep theorizing": Closing the gap between text and context in academic writing research. *Written Communication, 25*(3), 353–388. https://doi.org/10.1177/0741088308319229.

Lillis, T. (2013). *The sociolinguistics of writing*. Edinburgh, UK: Edinburgh University Press.

Lillis, T., & Curry, M. J. (2006). Professional academic writing by multilingual scholars: Interactions with literacy brokers in the production of English-medium texts. *Written Communication, 23*(1), 3–35. https://doi.org/10.1177/0741088305283754.

Lofland, J., Snow, D., Anderson, L., & Lofland, L. H. (2006). *Analyzing social settings: A guide to qualitative observation and analysis* (4th ed.). Belmont, CA: Wadsworth.

Maxwell, J. A., & Miller, B. A. (2008). Categorizing and connecting strategies in qualitative data analysis. In S. N. Hesse-Biber & P. Leavy (Eds.), *Handbook of emergent methods* (pp. 461–478). New York: Guilford Press.

McLeod, J. (2003). Why we interview now – Reflexivity and perspective in a longitudinal study. *International Journal of Social Research Methodology, 6*(3), 201–211. https://doi.org/10.1080/1364557032000091806.

Moje, E. B., & Lewis, C. (2007). Examining opportunities to learn literacy: The role of critical sociocultural literacy research. In C. Lewis, P. Enciso, & E. B. Moje (Eds.), *Reframing sociocultural research on literacy: Identity, agency, and power* (pp. 15–48). Mahwah, NJ: Lawrence Erlbaum.

Neale, B., & Flowerdew, J. (2003). Time, texture and childhood: The contours of longitudinal qualitative research. *International Journal of Social Research Methodology, 6*(3), 189–199. https://doi.org/10.1080/13645570320000917 98.

Newell, G. E., Bloome, D., & Hirvela, A. (2015). *Teaching and learning argumentative writing in high school English language arts classrooms*. New York: Routledge.

Okano, K. H. (2009). *Young women in Japan: Transitions to adulthood*. New York: Routledge.

Ong, J. S. (1986). Writing is a technology that restructures thought. In G. Baumann (Ed.), *The written word: Literacy in transition* (pp. 23–50). Oxford, UK: Clarendon Press.

Prior, P. (2004). Tracing process: How texts come into being. In C. Bazerman & P. Prior (Eds.), *What writing does and how it does it: An introduction to analyzing texts and textual practice* (pp. 167–200). Mahwah, NJ: Erlbaum.

Rogers, R. (2002). Between contexts: A critical analysis of family literacy, discursive practices, and literate subjectivities. *Reading Research Quarterly, 37*(3), 248–277. https://doi.org/10.1598/RRQ.37.3.1.

Roth, W.-M., & Lee, Y.-J. (2007). "Vygotsky's neglected legacy": Cultural-historical activity theory. *Review of Educational Research, 77*(2), 186–232. https://doi.org/10.3102/0034654306298273.

Saldaña, J. (2003). *Longitudinal qualitative research: Analyzing change through time.* Walnut Creek, CA: Altamira.

Schiffrin, D. (1996). Interactional sociolinguistics. In S. L. McKay & N. H. Hornberger (Eds.), *Sociolinguistics and language teaching* (pp. 307–328). Cambridge, UK: Cambridge University Press.

Seale, C. (1999). *The quality of qualitative research.* London: Sage.

Sefton-Green, J. (2015a). Cultural studies went to school and where did it end up? In J. Sefton-Green & J. Rowsell (Eds.), *Learning and literacy over time: Longitudinal perspectives* (pp. 46–60). New York: Routledge.

Sefton-Green, J. (2015b). Introduction: Making sense of longitudinal perspectives on literacy learning – A revisiting approach. In J. Sefton-Green & J. Rowsell (Eds.), *Learning and literacy over time: Longitudinal perspectives* (pp. 1–15). New York: Routledge.

Stake, R. E. (2000). Case studies. In N. K. Denzin & Y. S. Lincoln (Eds.), *Handbook of qualitative research* (2rd ed., pp. 435–454). Thousand Oaks, CA: Sage.

Thomson, R., & Holland, J. (2003). Hindsight, foresight, and insight: The challenges of longitudinal qualitative research. *International Journal of Social Research Methodology, 6*(3), 233–244. https://doi.org/10.1080/1364557032 000091833.

van Lier, L. (2005). Case study. In E. Hinkel (Ed.), *Handbook of research in second language teaching and learning* (pp. 195–208). Mahwah, NJ: Lawrence Erlbaum Associates.

Webster, L., & Mertova, P. (2007). *Using narrative inquiry as a research method: An introduction to using critical event narrative analysis in research on learning and teaching.* Abingdon, Oxon: Routledge.

Wortham, S. (2003). Curriculum as a resource for the development of social identity. *Sociology of Education, 76*(3), 228–246. https://doi.org/10.2307/3108467.

4

"To Make Something of Myself": Interactional Histories in the Context of Remedial Institutional Practices and Immigration Policies

Jaime was born in a small town in Mexico not far from the Pacific Coast, where he described himself as a "happy kid" who enjoyed school, primarily because of opportunities it provided to connect with friends and play sports. His parents, both of whom had left school in Mexico by third grade, owned a modest two-bedroom home there in which they lived with Jaime and his three siblings. Jaime explained that his father decided to come to the United States because he wanted his family to have better financial and educational possibilities. A few years after leaving—when Jaime was nine—his father earned enough for his wife and children to make the journey to join him in California. Once the family settled into the South Sierra community, Jaime enrolled in third grade at a local school, and while his mother cared for her four young children, his father worked construction jobs. Reunification was difficult, Jaime explained, because of time he had spent away from his father and the strain the separation had put on his parents' marriage. He described feeling nervous when he first started school in the United States, and because he had no

Portions of this chapter draw from data first published in Kibler (2016).

© The Author(s) 2019
A. K. Kibler, *Longitudinal Interactional Histories*,
https://doi.org/10.1007/978-3-319-98815-3_4

exposure to English before that time, initially being lost in class. He attended the same English-medium elementary school as Ana (Chap. 5), but he did not share her experiences with peer conflicts or negative interactions with teachers. Rather, he described making friends with other students, most of whom were Mexican-origin, relatively quickly, and having teachers who "were behind you, telling you what to do, helping you not get behind" (Interview, 10 April 2008).

Jaime began high school at South Sierra, where he had a large and strong network of friends and developed positive relationships with many of his teachers despite his tendency to delay or avoid school-based reading and writing tasks. In the middle of his tenth-grade year, he decided to transfer to a nearby comprehensive school (West Hills High School) via an open-enrollment policy, a decision, he explained, made because of a desire to get away from negative peer influences at South Sierra High School as well as an interest in spending time with friends he already had at West Hills. Through this move, Jaime went from an untracked and majority-Latinx charter school environment to a more demographically and socioeconomically diverse but highly tracked setting in which he "re-be[came]" (Marshall, 2010, p. 41) an English learner (EL) and was placed in increasingly more EL-only classroom settings until his graduation.

The turning point in Jaime's story was his decision to attend community college upon graduation, which he eagerly anticipated and through which he hoped to transfer to a four-year university and specialize in computer technology. Although Jaime experienced higher-quality pedagogy and classroom-based successes in the context of literacy events there than he did in high school, he quickly became disillusioned with community college. He completed only three classes over a year and a half due to enrollment difficulties, an increasingly busy work schedule, and challenges imagining a career for himself without legal authorization/documentation. He received temporary legal status through the Deferred Action for Childhood Arrivals (DACA) program,[1] but only after he had left community college and was working full-time as a restaurant cashier; he chose not to return to school. Throughout his experiences, both during and after school, however, Jaime remained a highly competent "communicator," in his words, across both English and Spanish despite what were often restricted opportunities for literacy development and academic success.

In the following section, I provide an overview of Jaime's language and literacy experiences during this study. I then use LIHA to analyze literacy events before and after his turning point of attending community college (see Table 4.1) in order to understand the impact of this moment in terms of the interactions influencing his production of texts, how they did so, and patterns of change over time.

Overview of Jaime's Language and Literacy Experiences

During High School Jaime completed the first year and a half of high school at South Sierra. There he was placed in bilingual humanities and ELD courses for his ninth-grade year; in keeping with the school's no-tracking policy, he took English-medium classes in math and science that were open to students of all academic levels and language proficiencies. In his tenth-grade year, he was not placed in any specialized courses for language development and took untracked classes for all subjects. Upon his move to West Hills High School, however, he was placed in lower-track classes in English, social studies, math, and science, although counselors and teachers were never able to tell me the rationale for this placement or the criteria used to make this decision. In his last two years at the school, he remained in lower-track math and science and was also placed in SDAIE (specially designed academic instruction in English) track classes, which were designed exclusively for English-learner-classified students, for both English and social studies.[2] According to his school counselor, this was done because he performed poorly on standardized state tests for English language arts at the end of his tenth-grade year, suggesting that such assessments were a key socioinstitutional mechanism (Kibler & Valdés, 2016) in the labeling of Jaime as an English learner. Jaime's weighted[3] grade point average for all four years of high school was a 2.811 out of 4. He typically made Bs and Cs (on an A to F scale), although he failed some of his math, science, and social studies courses on his first attempt at West Hills and had to retake them during the summer.

Table 4.1 Jaime's turning point and literacy events presented through LIHA analysis

	Before the turning point		Turning Point: Attending Community College	After the turning point	
	"To get words to do the same thing"	"Basic skills"		"I put more heart into it"	"Actual reading and writing"
Literacy Event					
Year	Grade 10	Grade 12		Grade 13	Grade 14
Task	Pancho Villa research paper (argumentation[a])	Error correction activity		DREAM Act research paper (argumentation)	Voluntary writing (narration/reflection)
Institutional context (if applicable)	Lower-track high school social studies class	SDAIE high school English class		Remedial community college English class	None

Notes: [a]Genre labels in parentheses are aligned with those originally presented in Kibler (2014), as adapted from Schleppegrell (2004)

The opportunities for language and literacy development provided in his classes at South Sierra and West Hills High Schools were notably different. In the former school, the curricula often focused on "thick, important books" and academic postsecondary preparation for all students (see Chap. 1), although the extent to which teachers and students were able to achieve such a goal varied considerably. Peer learning and collaborative projects were also a frequent feature of courses I observed. West Hills, in contrast, was both highly tracked and highly teacher- and textbook-driven: Teacher lectures, teacher-led homework review, and individual work on textbook questions were the most common activities in classes. There were a few exceptions, however, in which teachers designed their own curriculum rather than relying on textbooks or created somewhat more open-ended assignments and peer learning activities.

In my first observations of Jaime as a tenth grader at West Hills in early 2008, I saw him participate eagerly in his classes, without some of the work avoidance tactics I had seen him practice at South Sierra High School. By the end of the first semester, however, he participated more reluctantly and described school as "boring" (Interview, 13 May 2008), explaining that he would not be able to pass his math or science class that semester. In talking individually with his teachers, each one told me that his grades were low because he did not complete his homework regularly, which Jaime agreed was something he had difficulty motivating himself to do. Multiple times I watched him rush to complete his homework in the few minutes before classes began, and I noted that although he at times struggled with more interpretive or application-based questions, he was generally able to complete the homework without assistance.

By the time Jaime was in grades 11 and 12, he was placed in SDAIE classes for both English and social studies, the only two subjects for which these types of courses were available. These classes were filled completely with Spanish-speaking, English-learner-classified students, demonstrating at a small scale the hyper-segregation of bilingual Latinx youth documented by Carhill-Poza (2017). As one teacher who had previously taught SDAIE classes explained, most of these students were born in the United States or had lived here most of their lives (Interview, 16 May 2008). The teacher went on to describe this system as "broken" and that "the [SDAIE] label has become a death sentence" in terms of academic development and self-image. Youth themselves understood its negative connotations. She recalled, for example, one young man telling her he was upset about his SDAIE course placement because he knew he was "taking the 'beaner' class," using a well-known ethnic/racial slur applied to Mexican-origin people in the United States. While this statement was not made by Jaime himself, it nonetheless suggested the ways in which course placements at West Hills were perceived, at least by some, as reflecting raciolinguistic ideologies (Flores & Rosa, 2015; Rosa & Flores, 2017) and negative social identities related to English-learner and remedial status (Duff, 2002; Ortmeier-Hooper, 2008). In these classes, textbook-driven tasks also dominated the curriculum, and although Jaime's teachers consistently described him as very capable or "much higher" than other students in those classes in terms of his language development, he continued similar patterns of homework non-completion and had to retake two semesters of social studies in summer school to earn a passing grade. Ironically, the courses he retook were untracked (neither SDAIE nor remedial), but he described his teacher as excellent, and earned an A– and a B for them.

These institutional experiences at West Hills tended to highlight academic remediation in English—with the exception of a single Spanish-for-Native-Speakers class, described later—and did not reflect Jaime's perceptions of himself as an English user or the varied uses of languages and literacies in which I saw him engage. Early in his high school career, for example, Jaime understood himself to be a competent user of spoken English. When asked in tenth grade to describe what he could do in English, he explained, "I think I'm kind of fluent, like I'm better than I thought I could be, so I feel like pretty comfortable speaking it, listening to it, and everything" (Interview, 8 April 2008). As he approached high school graduation, he was even more positive, saying, "Since I talk more in English, it's like I feel more confident. I'm not afraid to say something wrong, you know?" (Interview, 6 June 2010). Consistent with Jaime's self-assessment, I observed him using English skillfully with a range of non-Spanish-speaking teachers and fellow students at school, including his English-dominant White (European-

American) girlfriend. With bilingual friends and his siblings, as well as Spanish-speaking adults at school, I likewise saw him engage in a wide range of conversations across both languages, and in particular using humor with friends that featured extensive bilingual wordplay (e.g., Martínez & Morales, 2014). Although I never observed him with other family members, he reported using Spanish orally with his parents and older relatives.

In terms of understanding and producing written texts, Jaime was similarly confident with what he could accomplish in English. In tenth grade, he explained:

> Like in reading, I'm fine. Some words I don't know, they're hard to understand, but I'll like figure them out later, or I go back and I ask someone, what does that mean? I think writing is like, I think it's easy, like well I can write everything I say, like really long words, like really weird words, only if I know I have to, but I can write. (Interview, 8 April 2008)[4]

As mentioned earlier, the time I spent with Jaime convinced me that this self-assessment was largely accurate, and as he alluded to, he typically engaged in school-based practices reluctantly, or "only if I have to." (This complex situation is further explored later in the chapter.) However, he explained feeling that his literacy expertise in Spanish was becoming less developed over time, saying:

> My [spoken] Spanish is very good, but my writing, [only] kind of. I don't have the same skills I had before. I used to be really fast at reading Spanish but now, I'm slower. I get like stuck so I can't read that well. (Interview, 8 April 2008)

I saw this in my school-based observations, particularly in relation to Jaime's participation in his Spanish-for-Native-speakers class at West Hills High School. There, he was a frequent contributor to class discussions but tended to progress through textbook-based literacy tasks more slowly than his peers.

Jaime also skillfully employed English and bilingual literacy expertise in non-academic environments. He was a very frequent communicator on MySpace, the social media platform of the day, creating English, and less commonly, bilingual texts via his posts and emails. He also reported occasionally picking up newspapers on the bus and surprising himself by reading and enjoying *Twilight* (Meyer, 2005), a popular young adult novel. Further, Jaime had significant media savvy: He was always up-to-date on current technology and had a prodigious knowledge of American cinema and the latest soccer news, which he accessed online via English- and Spanish-language sites.

As his high school graduation approached, Jaime acknowledged that reaching this milestone was a significant accomplishment, in part because many of his friends from the South Sierra community did not earn enough credits to graduate. He explained that "I think college is probably [going to] be more challenging for me, but I think I'll handle it if I really put effort into it. I'm not going to let it overcome me" (Interview, 16 June 2010). Jaime hoped to enroll in a community college program to become a computer technician and to also take courses that would eventually allow him to transfer to a four-year university. With the financial help of a family friend (a White community member who had befriended his family years before and who paid Jaime's tuition),[5] he enrolled in a local community college the fall after his high school graduation and explained that, "I look forward for college. I'm like – I don't know – I'm excited" (Interview, 16 June 2010).

During and After Community College   At Mountain Ridge Community College, Jaime was placed in remedial (pre-collegiate) English and Math courses in the fall term as the result of his performance on standardized placement tests. Jaime was well aware that his English class did not carry transfer-level university credit, but in contrast to students who may find ESL courses at tertiary levels to be highly stigmatizing (Ortmeier-Hooper, 2008; Marshall, 2010), Jaime appeared to have a more pragmatic approach to English courses. He said he would have preferred to be in the upper-level ESL class offered by the school because it offered transferable English credits instead of his current class, designed for the general community college population, which did not. He began with just two classes that fall, to "see how it goes" (Interview, 16 June 2016).

Jaime was initially positive about his experiences at Mountain Ridge. He enjoyed his first remedial English class, which featured an integrated reading/writing curriculum, a range of fiction and non-fiction texts that Jaime said he found interesting, and multiple opportunities to develop his writing through teacher guidance and feedback. Jaime's math course, a two-term, self-paced, online pre-algebra class, was less engaging because it featured material he had learned in high school. He earned passing credit for these classes in his first term, but by that time he had already become far less enthusiastic about his postsecondary experiences. For example, when I asked in an interview four months into the school year if he liked the work he was doing in community college, he explained:

> Well, if I understand it, yeah. If I don't, then I feel, like, frustrated and I don't know what to do, and I just have to wait until the next day to ask questions of someone. Because I mean, you don't really get to communicate with the other students there, since it's just like – as soon as class is over they all leave and stuff. They don't want to talk much…It's different from high school, you know? And I just start thinking, like, "Am I going to be able to do all of this, for like, I don't know how many years?" It's complicated. I just want to get it over with, community college. (Interview, 20 December 2010)

According to Jaime, interactions with classmates were not as common in his community college setting as they were in high school, and he missed those connections not only because of the social environment they created but also for the opportunities they allowed to develop and clarify his learning. Jaime also referenced the long path ahead for completing his studies: The computer science program, for example, required at least ten courses, none of which Jaime was yet taking.

Jaime planned to enroll in the next remedial English class in the sequence and a computer software class in the winter quarter. He was unable to do so, however, because all of the sections were full when he went to register. He also considered taking a Spanish-for-Heritage-Speakers class[6] as an elective but said that in the end he decided he would rather work to earn extra money. Instead, he took on a part-time job and finished the second term of his online math course in the winter, waiting until the spring academic term to take his next English class. Jaime spoke about his second English class in positive terms that were similar to the first one. Although the reading and writing tasks were more demanding, he liked his teacher and enjoyed reading books like *The Autobiography of Malcolm X* (Haley & Malcolm X, 1964) and completing reflective and argumentative writing assignments. Jaime explained that he had to drop out of the English class that term, however, because of personal issues in his family that kept him from attending the class regularly. He returned to Mountain Ridge in the fall term, just a year after he began community college, and completed his second English class, but he did not enroll in any additional classes that term or after.

By the end of his second year after high school graduation, Jaime was working full-time for a local restaurant and was considering returning to school but remained ambivalent about what he wanted to do. When he obtained temporary legal status through the DACA program just a year later, he called it a "life changer," explaining that it—along with his girl-friend's encouragement—was motivating him to pursue further schooling or vocational training. He remained unsure, however, about what he wanted to study:

> First, I wanted to do a doctor assistant for a little bit. That was kind of interesting. Then, I wanted to do like some video production, or maybe get trained for a union job. It all depends, like at what moment I ask myself that question. But I don't know. I just don't want to rush into something, you know? Like in a way it's like, [with DACA] you're a little free to do more things, but then at the same time you have more pressure on you, because now you know you could do something better. (Interview, 19 May 2013)

During the remaining years of the study, Jaime did not return to school, even though he described it as something "I think about every day" (Interview, 24 May 2014). He continued working, however, and in his fourth year after graduation, he left the restaurant where he was employed to take a job at a large technology firm, stocking their breakrooms and dining areas.

Across his various jobs, Jaime consistently worked with colleagues and customers who were Spanish/English bilinguals. As he explained, "I mean, there's always people there that always use both languages, you know?" (Interview, 19 May 2013). In many situations, he described also serving as a bridge (or language broker: Orellana, 2009, Valdés, 2003) between Spanish-dominant co-workers and English-dominant supervisors or customers. For example, at the technology company he received written restocking requests in English and then explained to his Spanish-dominant colleagues what needed to be done. Most reading and writing he undertook at his jobs was in English, including the restocking requests as well as tasks at his previous restaurant job that included labeling food items, reading orders, and taking online tutorials that informed employees about new policies or food items.

The voluntary literacy practices in which Jaime engaged during his community college and working years were quite similar to those during high school. He continued to text and use the latest social media platforms to stay in contact with his bilingual friends and siblings as well as the girlfriend whom he had been dating since high school, peruse Spanish- and English-language websites to keep up with his favorite soccer teams, and read a local English-language newspaper occasionally as well. Jaime described his long-time girlfriend as an avid reader in English who often suggested books to him, although he said, "I only read them once in a while" (Interview, 19 May 2013). As in high school, he reported that his reading in Spanish felt slower than it did in English, and that he did not write in Spanish other than in occasional bilingual social media posts.

Jaime's Longitudinal Interactional Histories

As described earlier in this chapter, Jaime's increasingly tracked high school experiences—and his increasingly limited opportunities to engage in meaningful classroom-based literacy events—built toward the turning point of his enrollment in community college, where he encountered improved literacy instruction and demonstrated development of literacy expertise, but in a context of further academic tracking and a less well-defined institutional pathway that contributed to his decision to leave community college. Literacy events demonstrating these trends both before and after this turning point are presented through LIHA analyses; these events as well as their placement in relation to the turning point are presented in Table 4.1.

Before the Turning Point: Tracking in High School In this section, I use LIHA analyses of two particular literacy events during high school to explore the opportunities and limitations for language and literacy development that Jaime experienced leading up to his turning point, demonstrating how meaningful opportunities to engage in writing were often foreclosed by both instructional choices and discourses of remediation. First, I examine his interest in the topic of a tenth-grade research paper on Pancho Villa in a social studies class but his problematic experiences writing it; second, I analyze an in-class error correction activity from his 12th-grade SDAIE English class, which embodied the limited literacy experiences available to Jaime and other students in that academic track.

"To Get Words to Do the Same Thing": The Research Paper Experience In Jaime's high school experiences, he was required to complete argumentative research papers, particularly in his social studies classes, almost every semester. Topics for these papers ranged from current events to historical topics to exploration of possible careers, all with a focus on learning how to locate sources via library databases and integrate them into students' own writing via standardized citation practices. Although these events did not feature any formal instruction or teacher feedback on writing, they represented the key extended writing opportunities for Jaime in high school and the ones that most closely mirrored the assignments he would be asked to complete in his community college English classes.

This particular literacy event took place in Jaime's tenth-grade social studies class, which was not a SDAIE class but was the lower of two academic tracks offered by the school, one that was open to all students but precluded later enrollment in advanced social studies courses. It did, however, still provide credit toward high school graduation. This class differed from many at West Hills in that it featured periodic collaborative peer learning tasks. In fact, it was the only classroom at the school I saw with desks gathered into tables rather than rows. The teacher, Ms. Evans, often created her own materials, which allowed for a range of tasks like role-plays and other group activities, although she also engaged students in more traditional textbook-driven note-taking, quizzes, and tests. The teacher had a Spanish-speaking assistant, and Jaime described often working with her during class.

The literacy event that I analyze here was the writing of a five-page research paper, in which students were expected to draw from multiple sources and include in-source citations for quotations, summaries, and paraphrases, as well as a works cited page. They were offered a range of over 50 topics or historical figures from which they could choose (aligned with the topics they studied that year), and the purpose of the paper was to present an argument for why their topic or person was important in history. The teacher provided pre-writing activities to help students decide on a topic and organize their notes, a timeline and calendar for each step of the process including an opportunity for peer feedback, and library tutorials on finding resources and citing sources. The teacher also outlined in general terms the kinds of information that should be included in the introduction, body, and conclusion of their paper, along with suggested page lengths.

Interactions Jaime's interactions with both the structure of the assignment and the teacher were influential in the creation of his written text. First, the wide range of possible topics allowed Jaime to choose an individual in whom he was genuinely interested: Pancho Villa. He explained, "I pick him because Mexicans talk about him, so I'm like let's see his history. I didn't really know much about him, just that he was a revolutionary" (Interview, 10 April 2008). Second, several days of class time spent working with his teacher in the school library were key to locating the required English-language sources for his paper. Jaime described his teacher's one-on-one help during this time as extremely useful. Third, the structure of the assignment—in which students gathered sources and completed organizational planning for their papers during class but were expected to draft their paper primarily outside of class—also had an impact on his text and the pace at which he wrote it. Fourth, because

Jaime did not complete a first draft in time to receive peer feedback, a *lack* of interactions with others during the writing process also played an important role in shaping his text.

Impacts Jaime finished the in-class activities on time but did not start writing the paper until two days before it was due. (He acknowledged realizing that he needed to start on the assignment earlier, and being reminded by his teacher to do so, but putting it off because he was busy with other homework and knew he could wait until later to write it.) In the two days during which Jaime drafted his text, he drew upon one of the three sources he had gathered earlier, a 3000-word biography on Pancho Villa from a library database. The assignment guidelines asked students to begin with an introductory paragraph that included a thesis about why their topic or person was important in history before identifying significant events relevant to the topic or person in the body of the paper. Jaime instead followed the organizational pattern in the single biographical source he used: a sequential description of Pancho Villa's life, from birth to death, without a thesis about his importance. In fact, Jaime's reliance on this source involved far more than overall organization, in that he took his writing almost word-for-word from portions of that text, with some paraphrasing but without in-text citations. Table 4.2 shows a representative example of this pattern in his paper.

Jaime relied heavily on his source text—and, indeed, the teacher's written feedback on this paper noted that "this does not sound like you summarized your research in your own words in all places"—but there were several ways in which Jaime attempted to engage in paraphrasing. These included changes to selected vocabulary, like using "begging" instead of "pleading with," "injuring" for "wounding," and "hoop on his horse back and ran away" for "fled on horseback." Such changes were in fact accurate synonyms and demonstrated that Jaime understood what the terms in the original text meant. Other rephrasings like "the owner of the hacianda" for "the hacendado" likewise retained the intended meaning. Jaime also deleted the introductory phrase from his source text but included additional information, like clarifying that Pancho Villa had been working in the field and that the hacienda owner was at his house with his sister, as well as creating a new detail about the hacienda owner being

Table 4.2 Jaime's paraphrasing from sources, tenth grade

Source text	Jaime's text
According to his own recollection, when he returned from the field on September 22, 1894,	When he was working in the field and he return on September 22, 1894,
he saw his mother pleading with	He saw her mother begging
the owner of the hacienda	the owner of the hacienda
to leave his sister Martinita alone.	to leave her sister martita alone.
Sneaking off to the house of his cousin,	He when to his cousin's house
he retrieved a pistol,	and he retrieves a pistol
returned to his home,	and he returns to his house where the owner of the hacianda is with his sister martita
and shot the hacendado three times,	and he shoots the owner of the haciana three time in the back of him,
seriously wounding him;	seriously injuring him;
he then fled on horseback.	then he hoop in his horse back and ran away.

shot in the back.[7] Another notable change was in clause structure, which can be seen in the second sentence. Rather than embedding clauses in each other as the original text had, he used conjunctions (in this case, "and") to join clauses, a feature that is characteristic of developing writers (Schleppegrell, 2004). Other changes included shifting some verbs into present tense, mis-transcribing several words from the source text, and using non-standardized orthography to spell new words he introduced, such as "when" for "went" and "hoop" for "hopped," among others.

Jaime followed this pattern through his entire paper, with a single in-text citation only in the final sentence. During an interview in which we looked over the teacher's feedback about his paraphrasing (earlier in the chapter), he reflected on this aspect of his text. I asked Jaime what the teacher's comment meant to him, and he explained:

Jaime:	To not get it from the thing you're getting it to. Like, try to put it in your own words. Put your ideas. Try to do it the same but not with the same words they're putting. Not just copy it from another paper.
Amanda:	How well do you think you do with that?
Jaime:	About a 6 from a 10.
Amanda:	What keeps you from getting a 10?
Jaime:	Sometimes, it's too confusing to get words to do the same thing.
	(Interview, 9 June 2008)

His efforts, which resulted in some changes at the sentence level but an unfavorable assessment from the teacher, underscored the challenges of "get[ting] words to do the same thing." Notably, the instructional focus for this paper was on the mechanics of citations rather than how to actually *do* the summarizing, paraphrasing, or quoting of sources that would require citing a specific source. In this sense, the complex task of writing from sources was overlooked instructionally as a prerequisite for the formal citation practices required by the assignment.

His teacher's feedback also suggested that he "get some help with proof-reading and fine-tuning of grammar," a comment that was not surprising given the example in Table 4.2, which was representative of his overall text in this regard. However, it remained unclear what Jaime might have even been able to accomplish if there had been time for him to revise and edit his writing. As he explained, "I was just doing, writing fast. I didn't have that much time. I could have done better, you know?" Jaime continued, explaining that regardless of the time he had been able to devote to the paper, "They're going to find mistakes because I'm just, not learning, I've already learned it, but just not as well as [the teachers] have" (Interview, 9 June 2008). He did not earn passing credit for the assignment, but his passing grade for the course allowed him to earn credit toward graduation.

Change Over Time This literacy event made new demands on Jaime. It was the first time that he had been required to locate, integrate, and cite multiple sources, a format that was unfamiliar to him at this point but characterized many of his later writing assignments, particularly in community college. Although he was interested in the topic he chose, found it relevant to his Mexican identity, and spoke with me at length about what he had learned about Pancho Villa's life, his written text did not demonstrate mastery of the literacy-related expectations for the assignment. Such a situation raises several questions about the role that writing instruction (or its absence) played in Jaime's creation of his text. While a lack of effort likely masked Jaime's true ability to engage in this literacy event (echoing a Latinx student profiled in Brooks, 2017), how much might he have been able to accomplish if he had started writing earlier? And might Jaime have begun his drafting sooner if he had more (or different) in-class guidance while writing? If he had completed a first draft on time, would the feedback he received from classmates or his teacher have allowed him to better meet the assignment requirements? Answers to these questions can only be speculative, but the event was significant in highlighting the ways in which Jaime coped with significant literacy demands in the context of limited writing instruction.

"Basic Skills": "Writing" in SDAIE English Class Because of performance on a standardized state assessment in English he took at the end of tenth grade, Jaime was placed in an even lower track designed exclusively for English-learner-classified students—SDAIE—for his last two years of high school English and social studies courses. The English courses featured the same general literary content as those in other tracks but used texts that had been adapted by a publishing company for students at intermediate levels of English proficiency. Ms. Han, Jaime's 12th-grade English teacher, described students in Jaime's class as "very low"—pushing her hand toward the ground to emphasize her meaning—and as not having the "basic skills" for writing (Interview, 19 April 2010). Ms. Han thought that Jaime did not put much effort into his work, and she expected more from him. From Jaime's perspective, however, the class was "for kids who need more help. It's too easy, but oh well" (Interview, 16 June 2010).

In observing this class, I came to see a recurring pattern of literacy events that focused on writing, but not the extended writing tasks I had come to expect from his social studies classes. Rather, most texts students wrote in the SDAIE English class were created by copying directly from the teacher via error-correction activities in ways that enacted her notion of basic skills. Such literacy events embody many of the concerns raised by scholars about EL-classified students' limited access to advanced language and literacy practices or college-preparatory curricula due to placement in remedial or low-track courses (Callahan & Shifrer, 2012; Enright & Gilliland, 2011; Kanno & Kangas, 2014; Umansky, 2016). In the following section I describe one particular lesson, observed in the fall of that year, which was representative of this pattern.

Interactions Jaime's interactions with the curriculum and the teacher's basic skills discourse were highly influential on the texts he created during this literacy event. At the time this particular lesson occurred, students were studying literature from the late medieval period, including Arthurian legends, and this provided an ostensible focus for the lesson. The teacher's understanding of these students as needing remediation, however, led to literacy practices that were disconnected from this literature and positioned students as passive recipients rather than active decision-makers and contributors.

In this activity, which was a daily feature of the class and typically lasted 20–30 minutes, the teacher projected on the front board a written convention "skill" that they would be practicing along with a sentence that included one or more errors that students needed to correct using this skill. On one of the days I observed, for example, it read:

Skill Practiced: Elimination of unnecessary comma in compound conjunction
Practice Sentence: "The Marriage of King Arthur" by Sir Thomas Mallory describes chivalric ideals, and life during the middle ages.

While this sentence ostensibly related this lesson to the literary works students were studying, multiple disconnects from that literature were apparent. For example, in most contexts, "Mallory" is written as Malory, and the work with which he is associated is *Le Morte Darthur* (2004, Shepherd, Ed.). Students had previously read an adapted version of one section of that work, however, entitled "The Marriage of King Arthur," and so this was the only title they had been exposed to.[8] The practice sentence also set up a situation in which there was a very limited challenge for students in understanding the skill they were to practice. There was only one comma in the sentence, and so there could only be one correct answer as to which comma should be removed. And all of this could be accomplished without any attention to the content of the sentence itself.

The teacher led students through this activity in a way that further marginalized the literary context of the sentence and continued to limit their engagement in this literacy event. After asking a student to read aloud the skill they were practicing, as projected on the board, Ms. Han asked students questions about it:

1 Ms. Han:	ok let's see.	
2	do you know what is compound construction?[9]	
3	what should you look for here?	
4	what are the key words?	
5 Student:	unnecessary.	
6 Ms. Han:	unnecessary what?	
7 Student:	comma.	
8 Ms. Han:	comma,	
9	so look for the comma that you don't need.	
10	so even if you don't know what is compound construction,	
11	look for the comma.	
12	where is it Jaime.	
13 Jaime:	what?	
14 Ms. Han:	where is the comma in the sentence that we get rid of.	
15 Jaime:	right there.	
16	where it says ideals.	
17 Ms. Han:	right.	
18	ideals.	
19	Joel why are we getting rid of that comma.	

20	why don't we need it?
21 Joel:	because you have a list of things.
22 Ms. Han:	that's a great idea,
23	thank you.
24	but who thinks you can answer better?
25	OK, what is—
26 Student:	you have a compound construction.
27 Ms. Han:	ah yes.
	(Observation, 24 October 2009)[10]

In this interaction, Ms. Han asked students about the key words in the definition of the skill, building on a student's volunteering of the word "unnecessary" (line 5) to provide a synonym: something you "don't need" (line 9). Rather than moving on to define "compound construction," however, she instead explained that all students really need to do is look for the extra comma in the sentence (lines 10–11). Jaime was called on and quickly identified the location of the comma (lines 12–16). When she called on another student, Joel, to explain why they did so, he offered another rule they had learned recently: that items in a list should be separated by commas (line 21). Ms. Han complimented his idea but asked the group for a better answer, to which a different student simply repeated the phrase in the definition of the skill, "a compound construction" (line 26). Ms. Han accepted this as the correct answer and went on to the next skill to be practiced with this sentence, which was "Capitalization of the name of a historical period." A student immediately supplied that answer ("Middle Ages"), and Ms. Han asked all of the students to copy down the now-corrected sentence. She then turned to a second skill and practice sentence, this time related to correcting a run-on sentence with a semicolon, something students knew how to do immediately. After correcting the sentence, Ms. Han went on to show a 15-minute animated PowerPoint—which she explained she had also shown the previous week—to remind students how to correct run-on sentences. At no time did Ms. Han mention the literary context of the practice sentences or their relevance to the work they were now studying, an adapted version of *The Canterbury Tales*.

Impacts Jaime wrote everything required of him in this literacy event: two correctly punctuated sentences. Despite the existence of these texts, it was unclear exactly what he or his classmates learned about punctuation and capitalization, the meaning of a "compound construction," or the literature they were studying. What was obvious, however, was that youth learned (likely long before this particular lesson) that such literacy events were "games" of finding and articulating a correct answer that had already been presented, rather than opportunities to engage in writing about ideas or thinking critically. And while error-correction lessons did not comprise the entire SDAIE English curriculum, together with the copying of vocabulary words and definitions they made up almost half of each lesson on a daily or weekly basis. During these activities, Jaime did not have opportunities to develop knowledge about literature, or access to authentic literature itself, and writing consisted of copying rather than creating his own texts. In fact, Jaime reported that during the entire year, they were never assigned writing of more than a paragraph at a time.

Change Over Time Both the institutional placement and the curriculum of the SDAIE English course reflected discourses that served to marginalize and racialize Mexican-origin and multilingual students and their language and literacy repertoires. The course represented a dramatic reduction in literacy-related expectations even compared to those Jaime faced in other courses at that time, like his SDAIE social studies class, where he continued to complete research papers with little writing support. Jaime's English class, however, curricularized language (Valdés, 2015) in ways that did not provide him with the literacy expertise to engage in those more demanding tasks. Instead, it relied on teaching isolated features of language (also critiqued in Valdés, 2001), in this case with a focus on written conventions that are in fact commonly misused by *all* student writers, not just English-learning multilingual students (Lunsford & Lunsford, 2008). These practices were divorced from the literary content and students' own writing, used a sentence-correction method that has been critiqued by literacy scholars (Godley, Carpenter, & Werner, 2007), and incorporated very limited opportunities for extended writing. Unsurprisingly, although Jaime's social studies research papers demonstrated a small measure of gradual improvement over time in 11th and 12th grades, none featured consistent use of the written conventions on which Ms. Han spent so much of her instructional time.

After the Turning Point: Challenges and Successes in and After Community College Despite the limited opportunities Jaime's SDAIE English class provided for language and literacy development, it did provide credits toward high school graduation, and he completed all requirements—including passing the state's standardized high school exit exam—in order to graduate on time in the spring of his 12th-grade year. He then decided to attend community college, a choice that served as a turning point in his journey, not because it represented completely new literacy demands—in fact, they were quite familiar (similar to Harklau, 2001)—but because the courses in which he enrolled were no longer placed in a clear trajectory that led to a tangible goal (as his course-taking in high school did). This lack of a pathway became a defining factor in Jaime's eventual departure from community college despite his growth in writing expertise developed in that context.

I use LIHA analyses of two literacy events after Jaime's turning point to explore this journey (See Table 4.1). Specifically, I first explore an argumentative research paper in which his successful negotiation of literacy expectations had little impact in propelling him forward in his community college journey. I then examine a voluntary literacy event in which Jaime participated after leaving school that highlighted the ways in which Jaime was able to fulfill his own definition of a "real" writer, although he did so outside of academic contexts.

"I Put More Heart into It": Writing in Remedial Community College English Class In the first of two remedial English classes Jaime took at Mountain Ridge Community College, he described a final paper he wrote on the DREAM Act[11] as one that he was especially proud of, that he enjoyed writing, and that his teacher rated highly. In this literacy event, Jaime was asked to write about a topic currently being debated in the news, using multiple sources to present arguments in relation to the different sides of the debate and including in-text citations and a works cited page (as he had also been asked to do in his social studies research papers at West Hills High School). Students also wrote a research proposal and annotated bibliographies of their sources, both of which they turned in for teacher feedback. According to Jaime, they spent two or three weeks of class time on this paper, including such activities as analyzing model texts and holding individual teacher-student conferences and peer feedback sessions. This was a high-stakes task, in that it accounted for a large portion of students' final grades.

Interactions Jaime's interactions with his teacher, his own annotated bibliography, other individuals, and discourses of immigration all had notable influences on the text he wrote. First, his one-on-one conference with his teacher played an important role, in that she gave him advice about organizing his paper into multiple sections: an introduction, arguments for and against the DREAM Act, his own opinion about the issue, and the future of the Act. Second, Jaime explained that the annotated bibliography was an important first step in helping him draw ideas from his sources rather than simply paraphrasing them in their entirety. Third, Jaime described spending significant time developing several aspects of his text with his girlfriend and the family friend who helped pay his tuition. Specifically, his girlfriend helped him summarize the articles for his annotated bibliography, select key ideas from them to include in his paper, use in-text citations, and create a works cited page. His family friend, on the other hand, focused on written expression once he had finished his text: "she would be on the phone with me, correcting my grammar and [telling me] what I should take out of a sentence and put in and stuff like that. That helped a lot" (Interview, 20 December 2010). Fourth, Jaime's personal involvement with the discourses of immigration policy surrounding the DREAM Act supported his writing of the text. He explained:

> It influenced me in a lot of ways since I had learned a lot about [the Act]. I know it didn't pass, but I still feel good that I wrote on it, and I spent some time on something that I really wanted to pass. It wasn't something I was like, yeah, I have to do this for a class. I mean, it was, but I was putting

more effort into it, so I could know better about something I was going to get benefit from, so I put more heart into it, like people say. (Interview, 20 December 2010)

In this sense, writing about the Act not only helped him understand the arguments being made about immigration policy but gave him significant motivation to complete his assignment.

Impacts These interactions were notable in their impact on Jaime's text. At the discourse level, the text followed his teacher's advice for overall organization, including each of the sections she suggested. Additionally, his experience creating and using the annotated bibliography—with his girlfriend's help—allowed Jaime to create arguments that integrated ideas from multiple sources, and his interactions with his family friend supported use of the "[correct] grammar" and sentence constructions that Jaime described. For example, in a paragraph that outlined political and ideological arguments opposing the Act, he included three different sources, all with accurate in-text citations and conventional language usage:

> There are many people who do not agree that the DREAM Act should pass. Because the DREAM Act was added onto the Defense Spending Bill, many people think that it was Senator Reid's way to gain many Latin American votes in the state of Nevada. There was also not enough debate on the bill before people could vote on it and many feel that there would be more illegal immigration if the border does not gain more security. Other people think that the DREAM Act would forgive the illegal immigrants for what they did and give them an easy way to gain citizenship (MacPhee). There is an argument stating that giving in-state tuition rates to undocumented individuals amounts to giving them taxpayer-financed education. To some, giving illegal immigrants this "gift" of education will cost taxpayers money, especially when

the rates are rising throughout the nation ("DREAM
Act: Development, Relief, and Education for Alien
Minors Act"). A woman by the name of Leticia
Novoa, who came to the United States from Cuba,
states that it would reward criminals for crossing the border. She claims, "there is always a
way to do everything legal. To allow these people
to have the same rights as I do is rewarding them
for their criminal actions, and that's wrong...if
they want legalization, they have to go through
the legal process." (Cano)

As seen, Jaime's use of paraphrasing developed in tandem with the use
of multiple sources and conventional usage. For example, Table 4.3 presents the third-to-last sentence of this paragraph alongside the source text
from which it was taken.

Jaime employed additions ("A woman by the name of" and "for crossing the border"), deletions (of the year of her immigration), and rephrasings ("it" for "the DREAM Act" and "states that it would reward criminals
for crossing the border" for "opposes the DREAM Act because 'it is
rewarding criminals'"). In many ways, these strategies were similar to
those he used in tenth grade. What differed more dramatically, however,
was his maintenance of complex clausal structures, consistently
standardized spelling and language use, and his use of this paraphrased
text as part of a multi-source argument that employed appropriate citation conventions.

Table 4.3 Jaime's paraphrasing from sources, first year of community college

Source text	Jaime's text
Leticia Novoa,	A woman by the name of Leticia Novoa,
who came to the United States in 1968 from Cuba,	who came to the United States from Cuba,
opposes the DREAM Act because "it is rewarding criminals."	states that it would reward criminals for crossing the border.

Such differences appeared to have had a notable impact in terms of teacher assessment. Jaime's strategies for using source texts were seen as inappropriate by his tenth-grade teacher, but those he employed in this literacy event were met with approval by his community college instructor. Jaime earned an "A" on this paper, although because it was a final assignment he never received additional feedback. With this grade he passed the class and was able to proceed to the next remedial English course at Mountain Ridge.

Change Over Time The structure of the assignment described in this literacy event resembled those Jaime completed in his high school social studies courses, although with further writing-focused pedagogical structures in place. However, Jaime's performance was markedly different on this task than on his tenth-grade research paper, both in terms of the final textual product as well as the process through which he completed it. First, this more sophisticated engagement in writing from sources appeared to be a result of several textual strategies in combination rather than any single element in isolation. Second, the process through which Jaime created his text gave him opportunities to employ and refine those strategies through his own revising and through interactions with others:

> I actually spent the time on it and reviewed it, trying to make it good. But I mean, that's what I enjoyed, I learned if I want to do something good, I have to put more effort into it and ask people, because before, I was like nah because people just criticize. So now, I see it in a different way. And now it's like, yeah, it helps a lot. (Interview, 20 December 2010)

Such a pattern suggests that literacy expertise did not simply develop through participation in solitary reading and writing practices: Integral to change over time in Jaime's case was his engagement with revision and editing with others (consistent with Leki, 2007). In several ways, his participation in this literacy event also helped to answer some of the questions I first posed about Jaime's tenth-grade writing. For example, he did start drafting earlier after receiving in-class writing instruction, and completing his draft on time also allowed him to solicit and receive additional feedback from multiple other people. Given the structure of the assignment and the many layers of interactions Jaime had while writing this text, working with others was fundamental to his ability to meet literacy expectations in this particular context.

"Actual Reading and Writing": Becoming a Writer After Leaving School Jaime passed his first English class—largely because of his success with the DREAM Act assignment—but encountered a range of issues described earlier that slowed and eventually stopped his progress through community college, including a lack of available courses in either the remedial sequence or his area of academic interest (technology), family issues that forced him to drop a course (although he later retook it), and what he described as the attractiveness of work, which provided him a modest income and gave him a sense of independence.

Jaime and I continued to meet and talk regularly after he left community college, and in these encounters, I was struck by his repeated insistence that he no longer "wrote," even though he described engaging in a wide range of literacy practices across languages. As he explained to me, his conceptions of reading and writing were closely tied to formal schooling:

> When I think of writing, I'm thinking like you know, a paper, more like something important, that has to do for school. When it comes to reading I guess I'm thinking of that too, you know, like a topic for your research paper. That's what I consider like, actual reading and writing. Texting, I just consider as, anything like that's just communication, I guess. (Interview, 24 May 2014)

In this sense, Jaime saw his own successful literacy practices outside of school—from texting to other daily practices—as "communication," not "actual" reading and writing. Yet when I asked him how he defined the term "writer," Jaime described a broader notion, unconstrained by school or other institutional contexts:

Really, to me, really, it's like to express something, a point of view that you really have. I mean, it's something I could go back to later on and reflect on, like it's a permanent point of view for myself. (Interview, 24 May 2014)

In this sense, writing for school was not necessarily what made one a writer. Rather, it was expressing an authentic perspective, one that you "really have" and that can serve as a point of reflection in the future. Further, Jaime included himself as someone who could potentially be a writer, although he presented it as a hypothetical act ("I could go back…") rather than a regular practice. Such framing was not unexpected: Jaime arguably engaged in this kind of writing in the DREAM Act text, but it was not a frequent school-based practice overall, and he did not report engaging in such literacy practices outside of school.

And so I was somewhat surprised when, at the very end of his fourth year after high school, more than two years after he left community college, Jaime texted me to tell me he was sending me some writing. I opened his email, which contained only the document itself, entitled "confused." Inside was a nearly 1000-word text in which he contrasted what he described as a happy childhood and adolescence with his current frustrations about not "mak[ing] something of myself." Through this piece of writing and his telling of these experiences, he expressed a point of view that in many ways fulfilled his own definition of a "writer."

Interactions Jaime described creating "confused" on his computer at home and not talking with others about it, but the traces of previous in-school writing tasks and various interactions with policies and discourses related to immigrant students' academic and vocational success were nonetheless visible. In ninth grade, Jaime wrote a Turning Point essay, as all of the youth in this study did, and he wrote "confused" in a similar narrative style, drawing in particular on similar childhood memories. Also apparent in his text were ways in which he was interacting with larger expectations for doing well at school and having a career that would allow him to have a "comfortable life," especially in the context of having legal status through the DACA program.

Impacts In both his ninth-grade Turning Point essay and in "confused," which he wrote almost eight years later, Jaime described similar childhood memories, including enjoying the company of his family in Mexico at a lake they would visit. In the former text, these moments were explored with great attention to sensory detail, in keeping with the design of that assignment (see also Chap. 8) and teacher feedback. In the later text, however, these scenes were used only as a brief starting point to frame a more somber narrative:

> What happen to all the joy and happiness that I always carry with me everywhere I went, that's the question I ask myself. Let's go back and figure this out, ok when I was living in Mexico I remember those were my favorite years of my life, reason why I say that is because I was so happy with what my family had to offer like going to the lake with the whole family...

In this way, the narrative framing was used in "confused" to address what had become a new turning point: his experiences at community college. He went on to explain:

> Things started to catch up to me after I graduated from high school I went to college for a year didn't do much there and from then things started to pilled up on me making me so stress and feeling unhappy all of the time.

Such ideas closely mirror those of other unauthorized/undocumented youth. As Gonzales (2016) found in his work with young adults who shared this status, "a chasm opened up between their stressful, precarious present and a happy, more inclusive past" (p. 215) as they transitioned from adolescence into adulthood. Further, Jaime described his community college experiences in ways that reflected a discourse of academic failure, despite the successes he had there. His framing of these events— "[I] didn't do much there"—also focused on his own action, or lack thereof, rather than the institutional, familial, and economic factors that made his postsecondary academic experiences more challenging.

Finally, after further explanation of the stress he was experiencing, Jaime reflected on the new opportunities provided by his new legal status and identified them as a source of both hope and frustration, particularly in relation to discourses of being "successful":

```
I want to be someone in life I want to have a
comfortable life, I know anyone can be success-
ful if they put their mind to it and I want to
succeed but there's something about that won't
let me do anything it frustrates me that I can't
do anything I know am destined to make something
of myself because I owe it to my family to make
something of myself I don't want to be the guy
working 2 jobs and not having a life.
```

He described these aspirations in fairly general terms, without reference to any particular type of success or career path, but in light of the new work opportunities he had through the DACA program, such possibilities as an immigrant youth seemed to gain immediacy, in that it was at that point more feasible for Jaime to "make something of [him]self" through schooling and access to employment. His frustration at not doing so dominated both this text and several of our interviews.

Change Over Time This literacy event echoed Jaime's ninth-grade Turning Point essay in its narrative structure and initial framing, but his exploration of entry into adulthood through and beyond his community college experiences took his writing in a far different direction. Although lacking the sensory detail of his ninth-grade narrative essay or the careful assistance with editing he received on school assignments like the DREAM Act essay, Jaime's text clearly communicated "a point of view that you really have," which is what he thought was most important to being a writer. This text also represented a new literacy practice related to extended writing that Jaime employed only after his participation in formal schooling had ended. "Confused" did not mark the beginning of frequent writing of this type for Jaime, but it nonetheless demonstrated ways in which he was a "writer" as well as a communicator by his own standards, and the potential for his writing to serve as a point of reflection in the future.

Contradictions Between Expertise and Remediation in the Context of Immigration Policy

Out of all the young people in this study, Jaime perhaps best reflects ongoing scholarly concerns about the impact of academic tracking on minoritized multilingual students (Callahan & Shifrer, 2012; Enright & Gilliland, 2011; Kanno & Kangas, 2014; Umansky, 2016). Although Diego (Chap. 6) encountered extensive remedial coursework at university, Jaime alone had such experiences in both secondary and postsecondary settings. His experiences navigating these contexts make clear that the interactional histories through which literacy events occurred were inextricable from academic tracking but were not shaped only by this issue. Rather, Jaime's experiences suggest that remediation was part of a larger ecological context impacting his language and literacy journey.

Literacy events during Jaime's experiences at West Hills High School highlight the ways in which differing levels of tracking interacted with variations in the rigor of literacy tasks, instructional expertise, teacher beliefs, and student engagement. In the first LIHA analysis profiled earlier, Jaime chose not to complete a challenging tenth-grade research paper until the last minute and did not meet his teachers' expectations for the assignment. This event underscores the complexity of understanding relationships between instruction and engagement for a young person who identified himself as a confident English user but received relatively little writing instruction in the context of a genre in which he had not written before. This experience with extensive literacy demands contrasts with the very limited opportunities to engage in challenging school-based literacy practices as he was moved down into an even lower track— SDAIE—in 12th grade, in which multilingual students' knowledge was further marginalized, literacy expertise was conceptualized as a matter of following written conventions, and course placement evoked minoritized and racialized identities for some immigrant-origin students. Such experiences highlight how both socio-institutional mechanisms and instructional quality can manufacture labels such as "English learner," or as would be applied to Jaime today, "long-term English learner" (Kibler & Valdés, 2016) in ways that reflect institutional arrangements rather than students' actual language and literacy repertoires. In this sense, Jaime's experiences support other scholars' contentions that a seeming lack of "progress" in English language development for minoritized multilingual students like Jaime can be attributed, at least in part, to instructional quality (Brooks, 2015, 2016; Menken, 2013).

Community college, the turning point of Jaime's journey, was an institutional context that afforded new possibilities but also imposed new restrictions. The DREAM Act literacy event provided a venue for Jaime to experience academic success and develop expertise through a task that was similar to those in high school but accompanied by greater instructional guidance and Jaime's own willingness to seek assistance from others to support multiple stages of his writing. Such a milestone, however, was overshadowed by a combination of institutional structures focused on remediation—and the potentially marginalizing messages such placements can send and reinforce (Harklau, 1999; Ruecker, 2015)—as well as familial and economic pressures and issues of authorization/documentation that made Jaime's path through community college a lengthy and uncertain one. Despite Jaime's eventual departure from formal schooling, the final literacy event profiled in this chapter suggests the ways in which Jaime was not only a capable communicator but also a "writer" on his own terms, although outside of institutional structures rather than within them.

Significant to Jaime's journey were the simultaneously facilitative and restricted roles that his Spanish language and literacy expertise played in his academic and vocational success. Jaime had a range of bilingual friends and acquaintances with whom he interacted at South Sierra and West Hills High Schools. Although Jaime and his peers supported each other across both languages during in-class literacy tasks (see Kibler, 2010) and Jaime also benefited from interactions with bilingual teachers or assistants in ninth and tenth grades, Jaime's frequent reluctance to engage in literacy tasks, and his last-minute completion of some of them, somewhat lessened the impact those bilingual resources could have on his eventual written texts. And although many of his interactions with others were bilingual, most of Jaime's institutionally provided opportunities to develop literacy expertise in academic settings were restricted to reading and writing English-only texts. Even classes Jaime took that were designed to promote biliteracy were limited, in that there was relatively little reading and writing other than textbook-related activities in his Spanish-for-Native-Speakers class, and he completed almost all literacy tasks in English for his ninth-grade bilingual humanities class. As a result, even though Jaime explained that he at times read Spanish texts online outside of school and wrote bilingually on social media, it is not surprising that he felt far more confident in his English than his Spanish literacy expertise (which he tended to associated with schooling), a trend that became even more prominent throughout this study. Further, it is notable that the Spanish-for-Heritage-Speakers class in community college that Jaime eventually decided not to take did not fulfill any immediate program requirements for him at a point in time when he had many competing interests, including work. While such a pattern is not surprising, given the limited attention to immigrant-origin students' multilingualism in US postsecondary schooling contexts (García, Pujol-Ferran, & Reddy, 2013), it is clear that language and literacy expertise in Spanish was seen as peripheral rather than central to his progress in this academic institution, even though his use of both languages played important roles as he interacted with colleagues and clients at work.

Another notable trend in Jaime's interactions during literacy events is a focus on remediation: first into increasingly lower tracks at high school, and then into remedial community college courses. These institutional structures can be understood as part of broader discourses that discourage Mexican-origin and other Latinx students by labeling them as unprepared, lacking capital, and educationally unsuccessful (Ruecker, 2015), and it is relatively easy to understand how Jaime's SDAIE courses did not support the development of school-based literacy expertise. However, the case of his postsecondary English courses is more complex. The curricula were well-designed, Jaime was positive and at times even enthusiastic about his experiences in the classes, and it was in these contexts that Jaime demonstrated the most development in school-based literacy practices. They also represented a far shorter remedial sequence than those in many community colleges. However, these courses—like those in his high school—existed within a compensatory institutional structure and focused on general writing development instead of allowing Jaime to pursue literacy tasks directly supportive of his longer-term goal (transfer to a university) and area of study (technology). The remedial community college English classes served a clear purpose that would have likely facilitated his success in future courses, but the fact that he did not make it to those courses is clearly problematic, and is unfortunately a common issue for community college students (Xu, 2016), including many multilingual Latinx youth (Patthey, Thomas-Spiegel, & Dillon, 2009; Razfar & Simon, 2011). Sternglass (1997) argued that the development of postsecondary literacy expertise requires engagement in discipline-specific courses rather than simply remedial or basic-level English courses, and more innovative community college offerings (such as those profiled in Kibler, Bunch, & Endris, 2011; see also Reyes, 2013) could have perhaps provided Jaime with more immediate access to his goals and area of study and helped him foster a positive identity as a successful postsecondary student. It is also possible that stronger writing instruction in high school might have helped Jaime develop the literacy expertise to test out of postsecondary remedial courses. However, such efforts would likely not have been a panacea for the complex issues influencing his transitions into and through community college.

In much the way that both Leki (2007) and Ruecker (2015) found with students they researched, the development of literacy expertise alone was not sufficient to ensure Jaime's successful transition into and through postsecondary schooling. Rather, what played a defining role was the larger context of reception (Portes & Rumbaut, 2001, 2006), in which a combination of institutional, economic, and familial issues all played a role (Harklau & McClanahan, 2012; Kanno & Harklau, 2012). For example, the institutional challenges Jaime faced were inextricable from economic and familial pressures he experienced, which were themselves closely tied to issues of immigration and authorization/documentation. As Gonzales (2011) has noted, unauthorized/undocumented students typically experience increased legal barriers to financial aid and employment as they grow into adulthood (Gonzales, 2011). Jaime's family had limited financial resources to support his postsecondary studies, and financial aid was difficult to obtain for individuals without legal status (Rodriguez & Cruz, 2009: see also Chap. 5). Although he had tuition support from a family friend, such resources were far more limited than those to which authorized/documented youth like Diego and Fabiola had access (see Chaps. 6 and 7). As a result, Jaime's choice to increasingly focus on work was not surprising. Further, many of the familial issues with which Jaime coped were, as he described them, related to strains caused by separation and reunification during the family's immigration to the United States. Finally, Jaime saw no hope of legal employment until proposal of the DREAM Act and passage of DACA, the latter of which took place after he had already left school. Looking back on his experiences, Jaime described the effects of his unauthorized/undocumented status on his ambitions even as a child:

> I knew that no matter what I did in school, I was going to end up at the same place, because I'm not going to be able to do anything with what I had accomplished. So that, I always had that in the back of my head right when I went to school, so I never really put – I guess I could've done better myself, but there was always that, you know, like "Oh I could do this but I won't be able to work or do anything for it." So that was there, I guess if I would have known, that there was going to be [DACA], I would have put more effort into my classes, you know try to do better, better grades. I would've like tried to go to an actual [university] but I mean, it was too late. (Interview, 24 May 2014)

Much like Ana (Chap. 5), Jaime described understanding the limitations of his authorization/documentation status from a relatively early age, and at least in retrospect, considered this as a possible explanation for not performing better in school. Such a pattern resonates with other research suggesting that unauthorized/undocumented youth often experience a lack of motivation to persevere with schooling when confronted with legal barriers to education (Gonzales, 2011, 2016) and have lower educational expectations than similar peers with legal status (Perreira & Spees,

2015). Jaime's case was somewhat unique, in that he maintained support networks that helped him attend community college, but even by his own measure, he felt that he could have accomplished more. Jaime considered himself responsible for his lack of academic success, but it is clear that institutions and policies failed *him* by not providing adequate conditions for him to "do better." The access that DACA provided to academic and career possibilities simply came "too late," in Jaime's words, to change the institutionally provided options for language and literacy development during his initial postsecondary experiences.

Notes

1. The DACA executive order was designed to protect DREAMer youth from deportation and provide them with permission to work. It also facilitated access to financial support of postsecondary schooling in some states and at some educational institutions.
2. Tracking systems in US schools are both complex and diverse. At West Hills High School, the SDAIE track was designed for English-learner-classified students who were deemed to need instruction that was more specialized and more intense than what was provided in classes open to the general school population. For students at earlier levels of English proficiency, ELD classes were provided in addition to SDAIE courses.
3. High schools typically add one or more additional grade point average (GPA) points to individual classes that are considered "advanced." In this way, students may earn more than 4 points for advanced courses. Jaime did not have any such courses on his transcript.
4. Please see the Methodological Appendix for an explanation of the transcription conventions used to present data from interviews and informal conversations.
5. At that time in California, unauthorized/undocumented students paid in-state tuition (rather than the more expensive out-of-state tuition they were forced to pay in some other states), but the state laws and federal programs that would later allow greater access to financial aid for this population were not yet in place at the time Jaime began community college.

6. The Spanish-for-Heritage-Speakers course was generally similar in purpose and focus to the Spanish-for-Native-Speakers course Jaime encountered in high school. In this sense, the classes' names reflected institutional choices rather than substantive differences in the courses themselves.

7. The source text did not mention where he was shot, and my perusal of other writings on Pancho Villa suggest that this detail might have been created by Jaime rather than retrieved from another document.

8. I do intend to imply that reading the entirety of *Le Morte Darthur* would have been desirable. More relevant to this argument is that students did not have a larger literary context for the work they were studying.

9. Ms. Han was an English user who spoke Mandarin growing up and began learning English in adolescence. Her language use in this instance ("what is compound construction") likely reflects this history and is pointed out here to provide context for the utterance, not to imply a lack of linguistic competence.

10. Please see the Methodological Appendix for an explanation of the transcription conventions used to present data from observations.

11. This was a federal bill under consideration in the US Congress at the time that would have provided a path to citizenship for youth and adults brought to the country as children but who arrived without government-required authorization/documentation. Although the bill was defeated shortly after Jaime wrote his essay, in less than two years' time, the DACA executive order was signed.

References

Brooks, M. D. (2015). "It's like a script": Long-term English learners' experiences with and ideas about academic reading. *Research in the Teaching of English, 49*(4), 383–406.

Brooks, M. D. (2016). Notes and talk: An examination of a long-term English learner reading-to-learn in a high school biology classroom. *Language and Education, 30*(3), 235–251. https://doi.org/10.1080/09500782.2015.1102275.

Brooks, M. D. (2017). "She doesn't have the basic understanding of a language": Using spelling research to challenge deficit conceptualizations of adolescent bilinguals. *Journal of Literacy Research, 49*(3), 342-370. https://doi.org/10.1177/1086296X17714016.

Callahan, R. M., & Shifrer, D. R. (2012). High school ESL placement: Practice, policy, and effects on achievement. In Y. Kanno & L. Harklau (Eds.), *Linguistic minority students go to college: Preparation, access, and persistence* (pp. 19–37). New York: Routledge.

Carhill-Poza, A. (2017). "If you don't find a friend in here, it's gonna be hard for you": Structuring bilingual peer support for language learning in urban high schools. *Linguistics and Education, 37*, 63–72. https://doi.org/10.1016/j.linged.2016.09.001.

Duff, P. A. (2002). The discursive co-construction of knowledge, identity, and difference: An ethnography of communication in the high school mainstream. *Applied Linguistics, 23*(3), 289–322. https://doi.org/10.1093/applin/23.3.289.

Enright, K. A., & Gilliland, B. (2011). Multilingual writing in an age of accountability: From policy to practice in U.S. high school classrooms. *Journal of Second Language Writing, 20*(3), 182–195. https://doi.org/10.1016/j.jslw.2011.05.006.

Flores, N., & Rosa, J. (2015). Undoing appropriateness: Raciolinguistic ideologies and language diversity in education. *Harvard Educational Review, 85*(2), 149–171. https://doi.org/10.17763/0017-8055.85.2.149.

García, O., Pujol-Ferran, M., & Reddy, P. (2013). Educating international and immigrant students in U.S. higher education: Opportunities and challenges. In A. Doiz, D. Lasagabaster, & J. M. Serra (Eds.), *English-medium instruction at universities: Global challenges* (pp. 174–195). Bristol, UK: Multilingual Matters.

Godley, A. J., Carpenter, B. D., & Werner, C. A. (2007). "I'll speak in proper slang": Language ideologies in a daily editing activity. *Reading Research Quarterly, 42*(1), 100–131. https://doi.org/10.1598/RRQ.42.1.4.

Gonzales, R. G. (2011). Learning to be illegal: Undocumented youth and shifting legal contexts in the transition to adulthood. *American Sociological Review, 76*(4), 602–619. https://doi.org/10.1177/0003122411411901.

Gonzales, R. G. (2016). *Lives in limbo: Undocumented and coming of age in America*. Berkeley, CA: University of California Press.

Haley, A., & Malcolm, X. (1964). *The autobiography of Malcolm X*. New York: Grove Press.

Harklau, L. (1999). Representations of immigrant language minorities in US higher education. *Race Ethnicity and Education, 2*(2), 257–279. https://doi.org/10.1080/1361332990020206.

Harklau, L. (2001). From high school to college: Student perspectives on literacy practice. *Journal of Literacy Research, 33*(1), 33–70. https://doi.org/10.1080/10862960109548102.

Harklau, L., & McClanahan, S. (2012). How Paola made it to college: A linguistic minority student's unlikely success story. In Y. Kanno & L. Harklau (Eds.), *Linguistic minority students go to college: Preparation, access, and persistence* (pp. 74–90). New York: Routledge.

Kanno, Y., & Harklau, L. (2012). Introduction. In Y. Kanno & L. Harklau (Eds.), *Linguistic minority students go to college: Preparation, access, and persistence* (pp. 1–16). New York: Routledge.

Kanno, Y., & Kangas, S. E. N. (2014). "I'm not going to be, like, for the AP": English language learners' limited access to advanced college-preparatory courses in high school. *American Educational Research Journal, 51*(5), 848–878. https://doi.org/10.3102/0002831214544716.

Kibler, A. K. (2010). Writing through two languages: First language expertise in a language minority classroom. *Journal of Second Language Writing, 19,* 121–142. https://doi.org/10.1016/j.jslw.2010.04.001.

Kibler, A. K. (2014). From high school to the noviciado: An adolescent linguistic minority student's multilingual journey in writing. *The Modern Language Journal, 98*(2), 629–651. https://doi.org/10.1111/modl.12090.

Kibler, A. K. (2016). Promises and limitations of literacy sponsors in resident multilingual youths' transitions to postsecondary schooling. In C. Ortmeier-Hooper & T. Ruecker (Eds.), *Linguistically diverse immigrant and resident writers: Transitions from high school to college* (pp. 99–116). New York: Routledge.

Kibler, A. K., Bunch, G., & Endris, A. K. (2011). Community college practices for U.S.-educated language-minority students: A resource-oriented framework. *Bilingual Research Journal, 34*(2), 201–222. https://doi.org/10.1080/15235882.2011.597822.

Kibler, A. K., & Valdés, G. (2016). Conceptualizing language learners: Socio-institutional mechanisms and their consequences. *Modern Language Journal, 100*(S1), 96–116. https://doi.org/10.1111/modl.12310.

Leki, I. (2007). *Undergraduates in a second language: Challenges and complexities of academic literacy development.* Mahwah, NJ: Lawrence Erlbaum.

Lunsford, A. A., & Lunsford, K. J. (2008). "Mistakes are a fact of life": A national comparative study. *College Composition and Communication, 59*(4), 781–806. https://www.jstor.org/stable/20457033.

Malory, S. T. (2004). *Le morte darthur* (A Norton Critical Edition, S. H. A. Shepherd, Ed.). New York: W. W. Norton & Co.

Marshall, S. (2010). Re-becoming ESL: Multilingual university students and a deficit identity. *Language and Education, 24*(1), 41–56. https://doi.org/10.1080/09500780903194044.

Martínez, R. A., & Morales, P. Z. (2014). ¿*Puras groserías?*: Rethinking the role of profanity and graphic humor in Latin@ students' bilingual wordplay. *Anthropology and Education Quarterly, 45*(4), 337–354. https://doi.org/10.1111/aeq.12074.

Menken, K. (2013). Emergent bilingual students in secondary school: Along the academic language and literacy continuum. *Language Teaching, 46*(4), 438–476. https://doi.org/10.1017/S0261444813000281.

Meyer, S. (2005). *Twilight*. New York: Little, Brown and Company.

Orellana, M. F. (2009). *Translating childhoods: Immigrant youth, language, and culture*. New Brunswick, NJ: Rutgers University Press.

Ortmeier-Hooper, C. (2008). English may be my second language, but I'm not "ESL." *College Composition and Communication, 59*(3), 389–419. http://www.jstor.org/stable/20457011.

Patthey, G., Thomas–Spiegel, J., & Dillon, P. (2009). Educational pathways of generation 1.5 students in community college writing courses. In M. Roberge, M. Siegal, & L. Harklau (Eds.), *Generation 1.5 in college composition: Teaching academic writing to U.S.-educated learners of ESL* (pp. 135–150). New York: Routledge.

Perreira, K. M., & Spees, L. (2015). Foiled aspirations: The influence of unauthorized status on the educational expectations of Latino immigrant youth. *Population Research and Policy Review, 34*(5), 641–664. https://doi.org/10.1007/s11113-015-9356-y.

Portes, A., & Rumbaut, R. G. (2001). *Legacies: The story of the immigrant second generation*. Berkeley, CA: University of California Press.

Portes, A., & Rumbaut, R. G. (2006). *Immigrant America: A portrait* (3rd ed.). Berkeley, CA: University of California Press.

Razfar, A., & Simon, J. (2011). Course-taking patterns of Latino ESL students: Mobility and mainstreaming in urban community colleges in the United States. *TESOL Quarterly, 45*(4), 595–627. https://doi.org/10.5054/tq.2011.268060.

Reyes, R. (2013). *Learning the possible: Mexican American students moving from the margins of life to new ways of being*. Tucson, AZ: University of Arizona Press.

Rodriguez, G. M., & Cruz, L. (2009). The transition to college of English learner and undocumented immigrant students: Resource and policy implications. *Teachers College Record, 111*(10), 2385–2418.

Rosa, J., & Flores, N. (2017). Unsettling race and language: Toward a raciolinguistic perspective. *Language in Society, 46*(3), 621–647. https://doi.org/10.1017/S0047404517000562.

Ruecker, T. (2015). *Transiciones: Pathways of Latinas and Latinos writing in high school and college*. Logan, UT: Utah State University Press.

Schleppegrell, M. J. (2004). *The language of schooling: A functional linguistics perspective*. Mahwah, NJ: Lawrence Erlbaum.

Sternglass, M. S. (1997). *Time to know them: A longitudinal study of writing and learning at the college level*. Mahwah, NJ: Lawrence Erlbaum.

Umansky, I. M. (2016). Leveled and exclusionary tracking: English learners' access to academic content in middle school. *American Educational Research Journal, 53*(6), 1792–1833. https://doi.org/10.3102/0002831216675404.

Valdés, G. (2003). *Expanding definitions of giftedness: The case of young interpreters from immigrant communities*. Mahwah, NH: Lawrence Erlbaum.

Valdés, G. (2001). *Learning and not learning English: Latino students in American schools*. New York: Teachers College Press.

Valdés, G. (2015). Latin@s and the intergenerational continuity of Spanish: The challenges of curricularizing language. *International Multilingual Research Journal, 9*(4), 253–273. https://doi.org/10.1080/19313152.2015.1086625.

Xu, D. (2016). Assistance or obstacle? The impact of different levels of English developmental education on underprepared students in community colleges. *Educational Researcher, 45*(9), 496–507. https://doi.org/10.3102/00131 89X16683401.

5

"It's Going to Take a While for This Country to Get Used to Us": School and Vocational Interactional Histories in the Context of Immigration Policies

Born in a small town a few hours west of Mexico City, Ana was just two years old when her father left to seek job opportunities in the United States. He worked as a landscaper for several years before sending for Ana, her siblings, and her mother. When they arrived in the South Sierra community, ten-year-old Ana was introduced both to a new country and to a father she had only known through pictures and telephone calls. She began school in South Sierra in fifth grade, which she remembered as a difficult time:

> The teachers would make me like write things in English, or look in the dictionary, and then talk in front of the class. I found that really humiliating, because why you going to put a little girl, like she don't know how to speak English, in front of the class where others are going to make fun of her? I really didn't like that. (Interview, 20 May 2013)

Although her classmates were often bilingual, she explained, they rarely helped her with classwork. She was so frustrated by these experiences that

---

Portions of this chapter draw from data first published in Kibler (2011b) and Kibler (2016).

© The Author(s) 2019
A. K. Kibler, *Longitudinal Interactional Histories*,
https://doi.org/10.1007/978-3-319-98815-3_5

one day she went home and begged her mother to take her back to Mexico. Describing this experience in her 12th-grade exhibition presentation (explained further later in the chapter), Ana recalled:

> I said, mommy, let's go back to *México*. People here are making me feel like trash. And then she's like, *mija*[1] it's OK, it's going to take a while for this country to get used to us. And then ever since she told me that I just kept on trying, kept on trying, kept on trying until I became who I am, a better person. (Observation, 5 May 2010)

As Ana progressed through school and became more confident in her ability to communicate with others at school in both English and Spanish, she developed loyal friendships with classmates and participated with them in extra-curricular activities like a soccer club. She remained ambivalent about school, however, and her early high school experiences were often dominated by disciplinary referrals for defying teachers or peer conflicts, as well as frustrations about the limitations of her unauthorized/undocumented status. In tenth grade, for example, she explained:

> I do want to go to college, but I want to study for nurse or probably police, but you have to have papers to do those. [To] do it would just be a waste, they're not going to accept me because I don't have papers. So why I am going to study if I'm not going to do it? (Interview, 28 February 2008)

These concerns, which resonate with Jaime's (Chap. 4) and those found in other research on the educational aspirations and academic motivation of unauthorized/undocumented youth (Gonzales, 2011, 2016; Perreira & Spees, 2015), continued throughout her high school career. As graduation approached, Ana also realized how few scholarship opportunities for postsecondary funding were available to unauthorized/undocumented youth at the time, or as she described it, those who don't have a "social [security number]" (Interview, 4 June 2010).

Key to understanding the ways in which Ana's uses of languages and literacies—as well as her engagement in academic and vocational settings—developed over time, was the turning point of her story (see

Table 5.1): her relationship with Ms. Torres, a bilingual and biliterate Mexican-origin Latina[2] student-teacher. Ms. Torres taught Ana's 12th-grade humanities class and made a notable impression on her language and literacy journey. In addition to sparking Ana's interest in the class Ms. Torres taught (humanities) and helping her develop a newfound pride in her bilingual and biliterate identities, this teacher also encouraged Ana to turn away from the "drama" of peer conflicts and toward academics and her postgraduation plans. Ana decided to enroll in a cosmetology program at a local community college that a friend had recommended to her, and in her final year of high school, she eagerly completed class assignments as well as cosmetology program paperwork. Ana enlisted her homeroom advisor, counselor, and me in helping her wade through the labyrinth of documents needed to enroll in the cosmetology program and even persuaded a former teacher to loan her part of the money she needed to pay for tuition, fees, and supplies.

This motivation continued throughout her cosmetology program, where she completed a 13-month course that included literacy events such as lectures, quizzes, and hands-on practice and assessments of skills ranging from hairstyling to makeovers to manicures. Even before finishing coursework, she started cutting friends' hair, and then upon graduation accepted clients privately at her parents' home. Ana employed her bilingual and biliterate communicative repertoire extensively in these vocational situations, interacting with and texting English and Spanish-speaking clients, reading up on the specifics of different products she used, and investigating the latest hair styles online. Her aspirations as a hairstylist, however, were often overshadowed by the legal restrictions she experienced due to her unauthorized/undocumented status.

Here I first provide an overview of Ana's language and literacy experiences during the eight years of the study. I then use a longitudinal interactional histories approach (LIHA) to analyze two literacy events before and two after her turning point of meeting Ms. Torres (see Table 5.1). Each LIHA analysis explores the interactions influencing her production of texts, how they did so, and patterns of change over time in relation to her turning point.

Table 5.1 Ana's turning point and literacy events presented through LIHA analysis

Literacy Event	Before the turning point		Turning Point: Bilingual and Biliterate Latina Teacher	After the turning point		
	"Good words"	"I did not choose the artist"		"You can see how much I've grown"	"I'm more into hands-on"
Year	Grade 10	Grade 10		Grade 12	Grade 13
Task	Essay based on class novel (argumentation[a])	Artist research paper (report)		Exhibition (explanation/reflection)	Makeover project (account)
Institutional context (if applicable)	Untracked high school humanities class	Untracked high school art class		Untracked high school (humanities class and school-wide)	Cosmetology program

Notes: [a] Genre labels in parentheses are aligned with those originally presented in Kibler (2014), as adapted from Schleppegrell (2004)

Overview of Ana's Language and Literacy Experiences

During High School In her first year at South Sierra High School, Ana was enrolled in the school's ELD course but in English-medium classes in all other subjects and years. These latter courses were all untracked, unlike Jaime's courses at West Hills. She took all the required courses necessary to graduate, including English-medium classes in math, science, humanities, and art. She also took computer technology, a community college course in reading, and two Spanish-for-Native-Speakers courses. Her weighted GPA was a 2.16 out of 4, reflecting a pattern in which she typically earned Cs or Ds (on an A-F scale) in her first three years but As and Bs in her final year.

As early as ninth grade, Ana positioned herself as a skilled English user. For example, in describing the speech of some of her classmates who had come to the United States more recently, she explained:

> Once you know English and you see Latino people talking, you're like, hmm, he don't know English so much, so yeah. Like you know, Fabiola, when she's talking, I know that's her second language, that she can't speak English that well, like me. (Interview, 28 February 2008)

Ana added that her favorite class at South Sierra High School in ninth grade was ELD, which she enjoyed because "I knew English and I could help other people, like Diego and Carlos, liked to help them, liked to encour—, how do you say, encourage them? That their work, they could do it." I regularly saw Ana spontaneously engaging in this kind of support and sometimes also taking on academic "helping" roles with fellow students in other informal contexts, like the after-school tutoring sessions that she occasionally attended. In other classroom settings, however, Ana engaged with peers and teachers very differently. In observations of Ana's tenth-grade humanities and mathematics classes, for example, some days she would raise her hand and energetically call out "I don't get it!" until the teacher stopped and addressed her question, but most days she remained silent throughout classes. Several factors, both including and extending beyond linguistic and academic ones, might have contributed to such a pattern. An obvious issue was her frequent absences from class, the causes of which ranged from illness to tardiness to being sent out by her teachers for behavior issues, which led to her frequently missing information the first time it was presented.

Ana employed English and Spanish to skillfully communicate with a variety of bilingual and monolingual peers and teachers at South Sierra High School, but I often observed that she was reluctant to read or write in either language for school tasks. In relation to reading assignments for school, Ana voiced frustration as a tenth grader about not being able to remember what she read in any language, and even as a 12th grader, she explained that "I hate it. I get sleepy when I read" (Interview, 4 June 2010). My observations showed a similar trend. During in-class reading time in her tenth-grade humanities class, for example, Ana interspersed moments of apparent intense concentration on the class novel with doodling, texting, or putting her head down. Although her attitudes about reading remained unequivocal throughout high school, her perspectives on writing changed over time. Early in high school, she described being frustrated about not explaining herself well when writing in English for her classes ("Sometimes I see, like I'm writing it, and then two days later, what is this paper about?") or being overwhelmed by the amount of writing she had to do ("Like when they tell you to do five paragraphs, I'm like oh my god, it's too much, I quit." Interview, 28 February 2008). I observed the latter situation many times: Ana would often submit partially completed school essays, or make progress on first drafts of texts but never finish them. (Such patterns primarily applied to her writing in English. She wrote in Spanish only in the context of her Spanish-for-Native-Speakers classes, and those typically required limited writing.) In her 12th-grade year, however, Ana reported that although she still felt that she was slower than some of her classmates in getting her ideas onto paper, her confidence in school-based writing had grown. When asked how she had changed since ninth grade, she responded:

Ana: I kind of like writing. Not very well.
Amanda: Do you think you've gotten better at it?

Ana: Yeah.
Amanda: What makes you think that?
Ana: Because I don't know, I just can write, without having some-
           one be there, [saying] write this, write that, write this.
           (Interview, 4 June 2010)

Although Ana predicted that writing would be a challenge in her cosmetology program, primarily in terms of taking notes from her textbook,
this change in motivation—which coincided with her experiences with
Ms. Torres (explored below)—was notable.

Outside of academic contexts, Ana wrote profusely. In addition to her
self-reported journal writing, her written notes to friends, text messaging,
and social media postings were a constant feature of my fieldnotes during
observations. In her first three years of high school, Ana typically engaged
in these activities alongside, or more often instead of, her classwork. A
texted conversation with a bilingual friend during one class in tenth
grade, for example, spanned more than 15 minutes and 20 messages,
during which they joked and made plans for what they were going to do
after school. These were typically texts that employed communicative
resources spanning multiple languages and language varieties—embody-
ing some scholars' descriptions of translanguaging (García, 2009)—such
as Ana's message about what she would do that afternoon: "Am goNNA
TAKE ET To THE METRO STORE *PARA VER K TIENE* / to see
what they have." Such texts used a range of features typical of that
medium and the language varieties she and other youth at the school
used at the time, including using unconventional capitalization and "*k*"
for "*que*/what", shown here, as well as other features such as "3" for "e,"
"foo" for "fool," "lol" for "laugh out loud," and "dnd" for "didn't."

In other respects, Ana had relatively fewer opportunities to engage in
institutionally supported literacy practices outside of school than did
some of the other youth in this study. For example, the extracurricular
activities Ana enjoyed and chose to participate in tended to be related to
sports (e.g., soccer), unlike others' more academically focused activities
(e.g., the academic enrichment program Upward Bound for Maria, or the
weekend writing program that Diego, Fabiola, and Maria attended). Ana
did, however, explain that she was often tasked with helping her parents

translate documents from English into Spanish, even though she claimed her older sister was better at doing so than she was. Such biliterate activities are well-documented in the literature in terms of both their prominence in immigrant families and the linguistic and literate dexterity they require (Orellana, 2009; Valdés, 2003).

During and After Cosmetology School Ana enrolled in the cosmetology program a few months after her graduation from high school, and by the end of the first semester, she described her full-day program as, "intense. It was like, a lot of work, a lot of like quizzes and then a lot of doing things…[practicing] up-dos, dyeing hair, cutting hair, makeup, nail" (Interview, 5 January 2011). The program—in contrast to community college academic pathways that include coursework in traditional academic disciplines—was comprised solely of cosmetology content and included both classroom based and practical courses. In her two classroom-based courses, both of which she attended every day, Ana explained that the primary activity was note-taking during lectures, which she reported being challenging: "It's hard to pay attention and write at the same. They talk fast, and I'm like, 'WAIT!'" She described working to improve her notes by staying in the classroom during break times to reread and rewrite them, and during one of our interviews she proudly showed me her binder full of handwritten pages. Most of her written course assessments were multiple-choice tests, based on the lectures, which Ana described as a new and somewhat difficult task. Another key assessment was a multimodal final project documenting a makeover she had done (described later). In her practical courses, Ana had opportunities to learn skills like haircutting, which were assessed through "practical tests" in which she was observed by instructors and assessed on a checklist. Many of her classmates, she said, were not serious about the program, coming to class unprepared or chatting with friends while the teacher was talking. She described her own attitude, however, as more committed.

When Ana finished her program, she started accepting clients at her home, where she lived with her parents and had set up a small salon station in their garage with a chair and mirror. She described engaging in reading online to learn about the hair-care products she was using, an English-medium literacy practice that she said distinguished her from other stylists in her community. She gave me an example:

Ana: Instead of using bleach to take out the black, I try to search something else, that's not bleach, but would take out the color. I find like three different ones and I just read, and then I figure out which one is the best. I did. It works. The other stylists are [asking me], why you reading it? [I say,] because you never know how you use this. [They say,] you just mix. I'm like, one of these days you will make a mistake with that.
Amanda: Are these other stylists you know, that sometimes say that?
Ana: Yeah. But they don't know English.
          (Interview, 20 May 2013)

In this sense, Ana's confidence in navigating English-language websites to learn more about products she used provided her with additional knowledge not available to colleagues who did not, in Ana's view, have the literacy expertise in English to do so.

By her third year after high school graduation, Ana had received her "social" through the DACA program (see details in Chap. 4). With this new authorization, Ana worked for a short time at a local retail chain, which she said paid better than salon-related work she had been doing. There she described interacting frequently with non-bilingual and non-Latinx customers but "switching" into Spanish when Latinx customers asked her if she spoke the language. Ana said she grew impatient with her bosses' insistence that she work only as a cashier rather than take on other roles, and decided to return to her home-based salon, where she continued to have a primarily Latinx and bilingual clientele and arrange appointments via text. Outside of work, she kept up with family and friends primarily through texting, and these messages tended to employ features of both English and Spanish, as they did in high school.

Ana's Longitudinal Interactional Histories

As described earlier, Ana's early years of high school were characterized by a reluctance to engage in school-related literacy events, but the turning point of her relationship with Ms. Torres led to consistent investment in these same types of events in her last year of high school. These were followed by further use and development of her literacy expertise through vocational practices that drew upon her bilingual and biliterate resources in varied ways. Literacy events demonstrating these trends both before and after this turning point are presented through LIHA analyses; these events as well as their placement in relation to the turning point are presented in Table 5.1.

Before the Turning Point: "Do Whatever They Say" Ana's first three years of high school—before she met the young Latina teacher who made such an impression on her and marked a turning point in her language and literacy journey—were characterized by difficult experiences with school-based literacy events. Ana summed up her frustrations well one morning in tenth grade as she and I walked to her homeroom advisor's classroom from her art class, where she had been kicked out of class for not bringing a draft of her paper-in-progress. She told me:

Ana:	Oh, and I HATE writing.
Amanda:	Why do you hate writing?
Ana:	Because I don't know it's just I don't know…it's dumb I don't like writing.
Amanda:	But you write sometimes like outside of school, right? for yourself?
Ana:	Yeah, but I don't like writing stuff for school.
Amanda:	Mmhm, how are they different you think?
Ana:	Because you have to do whatever they say, and when you're writing by yourself you can write whatever comes in your mind. It's not important if you wrong or right.
	(Observation, 7 March 2008)

Writing in school, then, was not a process of discovery for Ana. Instead, the answers were already known, and she was simply doing "whatever they say" while trying to avoid the "wrong" way of doing so. In this sense, school-based writing for Ana was a matter of complying with instructors' expectations rather than communicating ideas to which she was actually committed.

The two literacy events analyzed below through LIHA analyses demonstrate the complex ways in which Ana navigated her teachers' expectations for school-based writing early in her high school career. The first of these explores how she complied with a teacher's suggestions for certain registers of language while writing a humanities essay in efforts to use the "good" words she (and her teacher) felt were required for the text. The second event documents how a highly structured writing assignment provided limited opportunities for Ana to develop her own opinions and led her to resist these efforts through both her engagement with the process and the writing itself.

"Good Words": Coping with Teachers' Expectations for School-Based Registers In an interview during tenth grade, I asked Ana to describe the writing she was doing in her humanities class with her teacher, Mr. Smith. She told me, "All the classes are different because you have to write the same words but you have to like, in this class, you have to use more like, good words? I don't know, difficult words" (Interview, 12 June 2008). She was not alone in describing writing in this class, or in school more generally, in such ways, but the dilemmas she and her teachers faced in navigating the use of particular educational registers[3] of language in her writing were nonetheless a consistent feature of her early high school experiences across subject areas.

The literacy event described here involved the writing of an essay, the culminating assignment for a humanities unit featuring the reading of *Nectar in a Sieve* (Markandaya, 1954), a novel about industrialization in mid-twentieth-century India. Students were to write the essay in the form of a letter from the point of view of one character in the novel to another, using examples from the novel to argue that industrialization was either "progress," a "problem," or "promise" for the future. Ana wrote her letter from the perspective of Ira, the daughter of the family featured in the novel, and focused on industrialization as a problem. As is typical in many US high school classrooms, students had time during class periods to draft their essays, and as part of this process they completed a series of pre-writing tasks and two drafts of their essays. The humanities teacher, Mr. Smith—who was licensed as a social studies teacher rather than an English teacher and who at the time did not have any formal preparation in writing pedagogy or teaching multilingual youth—often walked around during class time to answer questions and check in with students about their writing. (I call these activities "informal conferences" to distinguish them from the more structured writing conferences described in pedagogical literature: see Atwell, 5. For more details on this assignment, see Kibler, 2011a, 2013.)

Interactions Two key sets of interactions were most influential on Ana's engagement in this literacy event. First were her interactions with the texts and classmates while reading *Nectar in a Sieve* and discussing it in small groups. As described earlier, Ana read this book during in-class silent reading times, albeit with sporadic attention. In her discussion group, although she rarely completed the written work designed to go along with the daily discussion tasks they were assigned, her oral contributions to their conversations demonstrated an understanding of the key characters and plot of the book. In this way, Ana was able to build knowledge through reading and discussing the narrative and the larger issues raised in the novel, all of which she later drew upon to write her essay. (Such interactions differed in key ways from Diego's experiences with this same novel and literacy event: see Chap. 6.)

Also highly influential, and more contentious, were her interactions with her teacher as he helped her refine her essay draft. He was quite explicit that he intended to shape her writing in particular ways, explaining the following after reading a draft of her writing:

1 Mr. Smith: so I understand what you're trying to say?
2   like what you're trying to express,
3   I understand the MEANING of that,

4		um,
5		but some things are just,
6		the word choice is a little unclear,
7		or some things need to be REVISED,
8		so that it makes it makes more sense to someone who might be a little more strict?
9		about the writing?
10		I guess?
11		you know what I mean?
12	Ana:	mmhm.
13	Mr. Smith:	so if it's the grammar or if it's word choice or where you PUT words,
14		where you PUT THE WORDS is kind of out of order,
15		maybe um,
16		but I understand it,
17		but we want to try to work on that so that it's more clear and coherent,
18		and that it makes sense to anybody who reads it in English,
19		does that makes sense?
20	Ana:	mmhm.
		(Observation, 14 March 2008)

Mr. Smith mentioned several issues in this interaction, including word choice, grammar, and syntax (lines 6, 14–15). He distanced himself from a negative assessment of Ana's writing, however, explaining that these concerns were important not for him, because he understood what she was saying (lines 1–3), but for "someone who might be a little more strict about the writing" (line 8–9) or for "anybody who reads it in English" (line 18). These comments, along with his use of hedges ("I guess?" line 10; "maybe," line 15) and appeals with upward intonation (e.g., "you know what I mean?" line 11; "does that make sense?" line 19), indicated that Mr. Smith may have sensed the potential for correcting Ana's work to be a face-threatening act (Goffman, 1967). Nevertheless, he viewed it as his responsibility to help Ana write in educational registers that differed from those she was using.

One such example of these efforts that was representative of Ana and her teacher's interactions throughout this literacy event was an informal conference that took place after Ana had written several sentences about the economic effects of industrialization that characters in the novel experienced. It said:

```
When your factory moved in to our village, the
things became more expensive for every one. In
the bigining wen my brothers Arjun & Thambi whent
to work in the factory. Everything was okay for
us because they were bringing money into our
home. Then they lost their job and we didnt have
money for or nothing and then everything for us
and other people was becoming more and more
expensive. Even though my brothers___
```

Earlier that day in class, Mr. Smith had asked students to read models of ways they could assert and reject a counterargument in their essays. After reading these examples, Ana wrote down the phrase "Even though my brothers___" on her paper, following the model phrasing her teacher used: "Even though ___, ____." Ana then called over Mr. Smith to her table to ask him what she should do next. After quickly reading her draft and re-explaining the idea of rejecting a counterargument, Mr. Smith offered a suggestion for her next sentence:

1 Mr. Smith:	so you're Ira, right?
2	are you talking about family here?
3	or,
4 Ana:	is the,
5	the economy.
6 Mr. Smith:	so you could say,
7	(.)
8	"even though my brothers were employed,"

9	or "even though my brothers worked for your factory they were forced,
10	they were fired and forced to move to a different country to work,"
11	does that make sense?
12 Ana:	yeah.
	(Observation, 7 February 2008)

Once he and Ana confirmed the topic of her paragraph (lines 1–5), Mr. Smith began by offering Ana an explicit suggestion (lines 8–10), ending his speaking turn by appealing to Ana to see if what he has said "make[s] sense" (line 11), as he did in the previous transcript. The content of his sentence used the structure Ana had written down ("even though") and drew from material she had already written in the paragraph, along with a bit of new information: that the two brothers were forced to leave the country to find work. Mr. Smith also used the phrases "were employed" rather than Ana's "worked" and "were fired" rather than her phrasing "lost their job." Such constructions differed from Ana's written text in both the choice of words and in the use of passive rather than active voice.

After confirming with Mr. Smith a few facts about the character, Ana then paraphrased Mr. Smith's suggestion:

47 Ana:	so put,
48	"even though these names they work at your factory but,
49	then,
50	(1)
51	they they had to leave.
52	(.)
53	and then you told them to leave the factory and some other country (xxx)."
54 Mr. Smith:	"even though my brothers were employed or WORKED at your factory,
55	eventually they were forced,
56	they were FIRED,

57	…
58	and (xx) um,
59	forced to work far away."
	(Observation, 7 February 2008)

Ana's paraphrasing continued to draw upon the "even though" counterargument structure but not some of Mr. Smith's other wording (lines 48–53). In turn, Mr. Smith's rephrasing took out some of the conjunctions Ana had added (but, and), emphasized one of his earlier suggestions ("FIRED"), and repeated another suggestion along with its synonym ("were employed or WORKED") (lines 54–59). In this sense, Mr. Smith used a form of recasting that served to "[edit] discourse" rather than to simply correct errors (Mohan & Beckett, 2001, p. 138).After this repetition, Ana noticed one of Mr. Smith's wording suggestions and asked him for its spelling:

60 Ana:	how do you spell that?
61	ployE:D?
62 Mr. Smith:	employed?
63 Ana:	yeah.
64 Mr. Smith:	um,
65	"even though my brothers were employed,"
66	e- m- e- m- plo- yed,
67	employed,
68	you know what that MEANS,
69	right?
70 Ana:	yeah.
71 Mr. Smith:	OK.
	(Observation, 7 February 2008)

As Ana sought assistance in writing down her teacher's suggestion, she pronounced the word ("employed") with a dropped initial syllable and an extended, emphasized "-ed" ending (line 61). Mr. Smith repeated the word, offered a spelling, and then asked Ana directly about her knowledge of the word, perhaps in response to her unconventional pronunciation. This last move was followed by the tag "right?", implying a preferred response (Schegloff, 1988) of "yes" that Ana supplied, although without providing further information to suggest that she did indeed understand the word. This pattern, in which Mr. Smith provided spelling without asking Ana to demonstrate her comprehension of the words he was using, continued for the remainder of the interaction about this sentence, as Ana copied down each phrase that Mr. Smith dictated and spelled for her.

Impacts At the end of Mr. Smith and Ana's conference described above, her assertion and rejection of a counterargument placed at the end of her paragraph read:

```
Even though my brothers were employed at your
factory, eventually they suffered from low pay
and hard work. In the end you forced my brothers
to move to another country to work.
```

This new text followed the rhetorical pattern suggested in Mr. Smith's lesson and also closely mirrored the language and structures Mr. Smith modeled during the conference. In this way, Mr. Smith maintained Ana's ideas but exposed her to a different register of written language through his explicit suggestions. Mr. Smith's phrasing in some ways shared features of educational registers described by functional linguists (Schleppegrell, 2004), like particular ways of presenting logical relationships and using an initiating phrase to make connections across sentences. However, it can also be argued that other aspects of his language were not more typical of school registers according to any structural criteria: They were simply *different*. In this sense, Mr. Smith's position as the teacher made his suggested language the de facto preferred educational register in the classroom, regardless of its particular features.

Mr. Smith's insistence upon the use of certain phrasing thus shaped Ana's text and helped her create an essay that eventually earned a passing grade. Such interactions also potentially provided a meaningful bridge for Ana as she learned new written registers. The structure of the informal conference, however, in which Ana acted primarily as a repeater and a scribe, made it difficult to assess whether or not this was the case.

Change Over Time When viewed from the perspective of Ana's initial days in the United States as a fifth grader, the English literacy practices in which she engaged during this event were impressive. She comprehended a class novel well enough to participate in discussions and later write about its characters and plot. She was also successful in soliciting her teacher's repetition of wording and his support with transcription in ways that resulted in a text that closely adhered to the teacher's expectations for school-based written registers of English. However, such interactions had particular limitations, in that Ana did not revise other sentences in her draft without Mr. Smith's assistance, and the final essay she submitted was missing at least two of the paragraphs she originally planned to write, including her conclusion. Perhaps more importantly, Mr. Smith's guidance likely also reinforced for Ana the ways in which writing in school was largely a process of "doing whatever they say," a process that may have been pedagogically useful but distanced Ana from an identity as a writer in school contexts.

"I Did Not Choose the Artist": Negotiating Autonomy in School-Based Writing Ana also took an art class in her tenth-grade year, and her experiences writing a research paper for that course served as both the immediate impetus for her declaration of "I HATE writing" (earlier) and for a rare instance of overt resistance to the restrictions she felt were placed upon her school-based writing. In this assignment, students were asked to choose artists who painted or drew self-portraits, to write a report about their lives, and to draw a copy of one of their works. Ms. Crichton, Ana's teacher, created packets that provided a highly structured means of completing the paper. First, students were provided with a series of websites where they could find information about their artists and several guiding questions to answer in writing as they did so. Next, they were given a checklist to use while writing their drafts that dictated what information should be included in each sentence of each paragraph of the text. Finally, they were required to incorporate drawing into their assignments by copying one example of the artist's work.

Interactions Ana's interactions with the implementation of the assignment structure and with her teacher were key to the development of her text. Ms. Crichton adhered strictly to the step-by-step processes outlined in the packet, for example, requiring all guiding questions to be fully answered before drafting could begin. Students were also required to bring their packet in order to stay in class and work on their paper, and later to have brought their paper-in-progress in order to continue drafting it in class. Otherwise, they were sent out of class as punishment and had to sit in their homeroom advisor's room for the remainder of the period and work on their own. This happened to Ana on multiple occasions when I observed her class.

A one-on-one interaction with her teacher was also significant in this literacy event. When Ana did not show interest in any particular artist for this assignment, Ms. Crichton suggested one: Frida Kahlo. When Ana remained noncommittal while other students had already begun their research, Mrs. Crichton told her that she was now assigned this artist.

Impacts The design of the task and its implementation had a range of impacts on Ana's engagement in the writing process and her written text. Although Ana had a clear understanding of biographical details about her artist as a result of reading the teacher-provided, English-medium websites, Ms. Crichton's insistence that students have their packet or have already completed a certain portion of the task to stay in class led to Ana being sent to her homeroom advisor's room multiple times. There, she did not work on the paper (as other art students were doing during class time), and as a result fell further behind the teacher's schedule for the assignment. I observed Ana on her third day of removal from the class, and I suggested that we work together on the task. During this time, Ana started writing her introduction without complaint, if not with enthusiasm, but the response to one checklist item (to include in her introduction paragraph) made clear her frustrations with the writing assignment:

Amanda: What is the next thing that you need to put in?
Ana: ((Reading from assignment page)) "Why did you choose this artist?" Because Ms. Crichton TOLD ME TO. She didn't let me choose my own, she was all, you're going to choose her,

you're going to DO IT. Fine then, I'm going to put, "I did not choose the artist." How do you spell Crichton?

Amanda: I'm not sure, let me look it up.

Ana: Sarah [Ms. Crichton's first name], I'm going to put SARAH choose it, ((talking aloud while writing)) "Sarah choose it." (Observation, 7 March 2008)

For this question, Ms. Crichton undoubtedly intended for students to explain why they were interested in the artist, rather than to recount the logistical or practical reasons that may have determined their choice of artist. Ana's resistance, shown through writing about the latter rather than the former, was underscored by her choice to also mention her teacher by first name only, not an acceptable convention in this school where teachers were always referred to as Mr. or Ms. and by last name. Shortly after she wrote this sentence, I asked Ana what she thought about it. She laughed, acknowledging the transgressive nature of what she had written, and said, "I like it. But still it IS true, the teacher didn't let me choose my own one." In this sense, Ana recognized the expectations she was defying but claimed her right to do so because of the truth it represented.

Ana's sentence stayed in her draft unchanged, and during the remaining two days of in-class writing time she continued to work on her first draft, responding to her teacher's checklist and putting in the required information. Given the initial days of class she missed, however, she did not complete her paper by the due date. She eventually submitted a completed typewritten version and her drawing to Ms. Crichton, but because she did so after the deadline, the teacher did not read or assess it.

Change Over Time Similar to her participation in the humanities essay, Ana's engagement in her report on Frida Kahlo demonstrated an ability to gather information from written resources (this time from the Internet) and to write a text that responded to her teacher's instructions and guidance. Because this literacy event occurred at close to the same time as the previous one, its importance lies not in showing distinct signs of development but in highlighting a different way in which school writing represented doing "whatever they say" for Ana. The drafting process itself was highly regimented, such that missing required steps meant losing out on instructional time in her art class. Further, the structure that Ms. Crichton provided via the guiding questions and checklist allowed Ana to learn about Frida Kahlo and produce writing on that subject, but it gave her few opportunities to develop her own ideas in writing. In fact, saying "whatever comes in your mind"—in this case, explaining who really chose Ana's artist—amounted to a direct challenge to the task itself and to the teacher. Ana was in this sense likely responding to marginalizing institutional discourses (Compton-Lilly, 2017) that restricted the ways in which she was able to employ her literacy repertoire.

After the Turning Point: Bilingual, Biliterate, and Multimodal Practices as Assets Although the literacy events in which Ana participated throughout her first three years of school varied over time, tensions regarding her ownership of the texts she wrote remained a constant feature, a trend that co-existed with her ambivalent feelings about school more generally. Twelfth grade, however, marked a turning point. Specifically, her interactions with Ms. Torres in her humanities class that year appeared to support a dramatic change in academic motivation and pride in her own bilingual and biliterate identities. I began to realize this teacher's importance to Ana when we met to talk about her experiences and discuss writing samples she had shared with me in the spring of her 12th-grade year. We were in the midst of talking about a presentation she had recently done for her math class when Ana abruptly changed the subject:

Ana: You know what I've been thinking? I feel like there's this teacher. Ms. Torres. She's a Latina, right, and when I start thinking of her, I'm like, man, I wish I could speak like her. Like smart words …I want to talk like that. I just want every single smart word to come out. Every time I see her, I want to keep on trying, keep on trying.

Amanda: Yeah, it's great to have examples like that.

Ana: And when she gets nervous, she does the same thing as me, she talks Spanish.

Amanda: Really?

Ana: She's like, *y*, like, and, *y*. I'm like, OH MY GOD. They [other
            students] have been telling me, since she was our teacher, is
            that your sister? She kinda looks like me. [They ask] are you
            guys related? ((laughing))
            (Interview, 3 March 2010)

These comments, as well as their spontaneity, suggested how strong
Ana's connections to Ms. Torres had become. Ana's admiration of Ms.
Torres, as well as the ways that this teacher motivated her, was a topic to
which she returned in nearly every interview for the rest of the study. For
example, when I asked her four years after graduation what she had
learned from high school that still impacted her, she explained:

> The only – the one that like, opened up my eyes like alot was Ms. Torres. I
> don't know why, but she like inspired me to do good. Because, even the
> junior [eleventh-grade] year I was bad. I didn't get good grades. And then
> when I started meeting her, she was good. My grades went up. (Interview,
> 24 May 2014)

As Ana's journey progressed, and as I continued to reflect upon the various influences on her experiences over time, the positive experiences Ana
had with this teacher echoed through her subsequent language and literacy practices in ways that were strikingly different than those that took
place, particularly with school-based writing, before meeting Ms. Torres.

I use LIHA analyses to explore the significance of this turning point as
reflected in two literacy events that took place after it (see Table 5.1).
These include Ana's 12th-grade exhibition, which she used as a venue to
highlight her bilingual and biliterate growth, and a makeover project in
her cosmetology program that demonstrated the ways in which her communicative repertoire encompassed not only multiple languages and literacies but also multiple modalities, all of which were key to her vocational
goals.

"You Can See How Much I've Grown": The 12th-Grade Exhibition The
major annual assessment at South Sierra High School for Ana and her
peers was an exhibition, in which students submitted a written text,

which varied by topic and genre each year, and gave an oral presentation. A committee of judges, including teachers, community members, and peers, served as the audience for these presentations and assessed them according to school-wide rubrics. Exhibitions figured into graduation requirements and honors, and students took them seriously. They were often able to recall their own and others' performance in and achievement on the exhibitions even when other memories of schooling had faded. (For more details about this assignment, see Kibler, Salerno, & Palacios, 2014.)

Exhibition topics connected to each grade's curriculum, and in grade 12 the focus was a self-reflection on academic and personal achievements during high school. Specifically, students in that year were asked to create and present a website with several elements, most prominent among them a personal statement and an explanation of how well they met each of the five "habits" upon which they were graded in high school (Personal Responsibility, Social Responsibility, Critical and Creative Thinking, Application of Knowledge, and Communication). For each habit, students had to summarize what it was, list evidence that showed their fulfillment of it, and include images of that evidence, which were often school assignments or photos of youth engaging in activities. Students prepared written work and presentations in their humanities class, which for Ana was taught by Ms. Torres.

Interactions Perhaps unsurprisingly, given Ana's turning point, her interactions with Ms. Torres were the most decisive in their influence on her 12th-grade exhibition. In addition to the general sense of motivation Ana felt in her class, the written comments Ms. Torres provided on Ana's drafts played key roles in the creation of her text. Ms. Torres's feedback was frequent and varied, often including several questions asking Ana to provide further explanation and information. For example, when Ana wrote that during high school she had grown "not only in the English but also in Spanish," Ms. Torres responded by saying, "Good. Be specific…what can you do both in English and Spanish? Why is this important?" Other types of feedback were those in which Ms. Torres pointed out sections of the text that Ana had not yet included, often adding place-holders to visually indicate where this information should be placed. She also made a handful of corrections related to grammar and conventions, but these were far less frequent than her more content-focused comments. The final aspect of Ms. Torres's feedback was her encouragement for Ana to continue writing. Such comments included: "Very strong introduction. Keep going!" "Great start...keep going ☺" and later, "Beautiful...finish up the conclusion then you are ready to move on!"

These were not the only interactions that influenced Ana's exhibition. The structure of the 12th-grade exhibition as a reflective portfolio, for example, emphasized a discourse of growth and development, which Ana took up in her written texts, with a particular focus on her bilingual and biliterate practices as assets. She also drew upon the multimodality of the exhibition to use the venue of the oral presentation to extend these narratives of growth into a recognition of the role her Latina teacher played in that development.

Impacts In contrast to writing assignments she undertook earlier in her high school career, Ana completed the written and multimodal components of her exhibition relatively quickly, finishing before other classmates and well before it was due. She explained enjoying this process, saying "I didn't got frustrated – I had fun with it. You know? I think I was the calmest one [out of all the students]" (Interview, 4 June 2010). The design of the assignment clearly played a role: In contrast to writing in which there were "wrong or right" answers, the reflective portfolio allowed Ana more autonomy with her text. As she explained in that same interview, one reason she liked the process was "because it was about you, you know?"

Another aspect of this process that likely contributed to her timely and full completion of the task was Ms. Torres's feedback. Unlike earlier experiences in which teachers often focused on shaping Ana's written language into particular educational registers, Ms. Torres's comments encouraged her to continue drafting and adding ideas, with explicit validation of the work she had produced so far. Ana revised in response to each and every one of Ms. Torres's questions and suggestions, often conferring with her in class to further clarify the feedback and develop new ideas. This process was clearly successful: Ana's exhibition judges were complimentary of her final written texts, with one noting that "your writing is way better than it has been in the past," although he acknowledged that "college papers will ask for a step more" than what was required by this reflective assignment (Observation, 19 May 2010).

Because the exhibition was designed to showcase students' growth in the school habits over time, Ana's newfound academic focus in 12th grade provided clear evidence for such a pattern. One area in which Ana highlighted her growth in these ways was the habit of Communication. To do so, she drew upon two different assignments: an economics essay she wrote in Ms. Torres's class and a written exam for her Spanish-for-Native-Speakers class.

For Ana's economics essay, both her website and oral presentation mentioned the ways in which the quality of her text and her determination while writing it showed growth from earlier years. In the oral presentation, she also made a more personal connection, saying:

> When I [saw the grade I received] like, tears came out because when I was a freshman like, I didn't know how to, communicate or, just like, communicate through paper, it was really hard for me. And when I saw this I'm like, oh my gosh I can like communicate and I was so happy…And that made me really proud because, ever since I met Ms. Torres, like I'm like, oh my gosh I want to be like her, you know, because she's a Latina girl and she overcome, like, obstacles that are, different from me but, they're like, definitely, what made her stronger. (Observation, 19 May 2010)

This excerpt in particular demonstrated the ways in which Ana connected with her teacher as a "Latina girl" and hinted at how this strengthened sense of cultural and ethnic/racial identity may have supported Ana's sense of self-esteem (in line with other research on Mexican-origin adolescents in the United States: see Umaña-Taylor, Yazedjian, & Bámaca-Gomez, 2004).

Such descriptions of her development in English writing and the important role her teacher played were complemented by her use of Spanish-language texts as further evidence of improved communication. For example, in describing a Spanish-for-Native-Speakers exam for which she received the highest mark possible, Ana wrote the following on her website (and read it aloud in her oral presentation):

```
This demonstrated how I have grown not only in
the English language but also in Spanish. I can
communicate in Spanish and English through my
essays and through language. This is important
because when you're older your going to have more
open doors in your life, if you know more than
one language... This shows that I have grown in
Spanish writing because when I was taking Spanish
in my sophomore year I would get low grades, but
now in my senior year I am doing great and get-
ting higher ones in communication.
```

This text reflected not only Ana's revision in response to her teacher's feedback (earlier in the chapter) about what she could accomplish in both languages and why that was important; it also publicly highlighted her bilingual and biliterate growth. Notably, Ana was the only student in the study at South Sierra High School to use Spanish-language texts as evidence for growth in the exhibition, or to reference Spanish language and literacy practices as assets, or evidence of growth, rather than to characterize uses of Spanish as evidence of *not knowing* English, as Diego did (see Chap. 6). Such moves, through which Ana positioned herself as an accomplished bilingual/biliterate Latina by the end of high school, were seen positively by her exhibition judges. They awarded her a distinction, the highest rating possible, and most also complimented her growth over time, with one noting "one of the strong points of your presentation was your ability to reflect but also to show us in the evidence how you grew, like your evidence demonstrated that, and I think that really it was clear to us" (Observation, 19 May 2010).

Change Over Time Ana's composing process, written texts, and oral presentation for the 12-grade exhibition embodied notable changes that occurred in her uses of languages and literacies, as well as her own perceptions of them, after meeting Ms. Torres. She successfully presented herself through the growth discourse that this literacy event was designed to elicit, doing so with an emphasis on her bilingual and biliterate development and the influence of her teacher. Further, Ana's engagement throughout the writing, revision, and presentation process suggests that this literacy event provided her with a unique opportunity to reflect upon and have validated the bilingual and biliterate identities she developed through academic engagement and motivation in both English- and Spanish-medium classes in her last year of high school.

"I'm More Into Hands-on": Engaging Across Modalities and Languages As described earlier, after high school, Ana attended a cosmetology program at a local community college, where she undertook coursework and written examinations along with practical tasks and assessments in a program designed to prepare students to work in a range of cosmetology-related positions and to pass the state licensure exam for the profession. Despite Ana's contention that she was "more into hands-on" than reading and writing (Interview, 19 June 2012), a range of literacy practices across languages was inherent to both her English-medium cosmetology program tasks and her later work as a hairstylist. In this final section, I present a literacy event that occurred during Ana's vocational training in order to address the different ways that she employed varied multimodal and bilingual/biliterate practices through her engagement in cosmetology.

The final project for Ana's first cosmetology course was a multimodal task in which she had to complete a makeover and create a step-by-step manual, including photographs to document what she had done, so that another stylist could re-create the same look. Using her mother as a "client," Ana completed a haircut and style with makeup, using multiple photos and a written description to explain each step of the process.

Interactions A range of interactions influenced Ana's creation of this project. First, the assignment guidelines presented a concrete set of activities about which she must write; models of completed projects were also available in the classroom for students to read, and Ana said she reviewed them briefly. The assignment also required a particular register, or "good words" as she called them in high school. She explained, "I had to use the specific vocabulary, not just like, 'cut it this way then cut it the left way and then this,' you have to [write] like, 'high graduation to low graduation'" (Interview, 5 January 2011). She described interactions with her textbook, the teachers' lectures, and in-class practice with hairstyling as all helping her recall and use this language accurately in writing her manual. For the hair coloring, she described reading labels and instructions to ensure she was using the products correctly. Also, Ana explained that although one of her bilingual friends in class gave her advice about how to *do* the makeover, she wrote this project on her own at home. Finally, Ana interacted with her Spanish-speaking mother, the client, to consult with her about the style she wanted.

Impacts Ana's multimodal text followed the guidelines of the assignment, in that it was framed as a manual for other stylists and employed a range of terms specific to cosmetology as presented in course texts and lectures. For example, she wrote:

```
It is important to analyze you clients hair
before you start any haircuts or coloring. This
will help you decide the style that will fit them
better. Always make sure for the texture of each
hair strand, flexibility, diameter (fine, coarse,
medium). For this style any hair type would be
fine. The client I choose has long, medium-low
density, curly and fine hair.
```

She followed this text with two photos of her client's hair before the makeover, showcasing its texture. Similarly, in describing the steps she took during the haircut itself, she explained the process as follows:

```
Solid cut: Section the hair in four grab sections
of 1". Let the hair fall in the natural hair
growth and cut straight across in horizontal
line. Start with a small section to have control
of the hair, also to have your guideline, and
follow all the way around.
```

This text was accompanied by five pictures, showing the sectioning, the natural fall, the use of a small section, the straight horizontal cut, and its completion across all the hair in that section. Each subsequent step of the makeover followed a similar pattern, with reminders to the reader about the needs of the client, the technical steps taken, and photos documenting what occurred.

My conversation about this text with Ana also reminded me of the interrelationships between these steps and the writing she undertook. In explaining how her friend helped her with this assignment, she told me:

Ana: Well, she just said, just make sure how you're holding the fingers, how you're cutting the hair, how to start like, the hair color, and the makeup, what product to use. Stuff like that.

Amanda: Yeah. So she was giving you advice more about how to do it rather than how to write about it?

Ana: No no no, because it's the same thing, like you have to like, however you did it, you have to write it like on the paper how you did it.

(Interview, 15 May 2011)

Ana's final comment, explaining that the doing and the writing were "the same thing," not only demonstrated how her friend made an impact on the actions Ana took, which in turn shaped the text she produced; it also positioned haircutting itself as an inherently literate practice that necessarily projected a text to be written about it. At the same time, Ana's text was also inherently a bilingual one, although all of the writing she submitted was in English. Ana's conversations with her mother about the kind of makeover she wanted took place in Spanish, and subsequent conversations with her bilingual classmate about technical advice utilized both languages.

The transformation of these activities into English writing was met with not only a passing grade for her assignment but also a satisfied client. As Ana explained to me in an interview and included in the last sentence of her project, "My model is happy with the style that I did on her." Such a comment underscored the extent to which Ana's profession depends on language and communication to engage in the sorts of social interactions that help stylists understand clients' desires and adapt their technical repertoires to clients' needs (Rose, 2004).

Change Over Time Literacy events such as this one represented both continuity and change from the writing Ana completed in high school. It required particular registers of language, especially in the use of profession-specific terminology, but this type of language was closely tied to the doing of her makeover, rather than being imposed by teachers as a "right" way of using language. Although Ana still described the writing process for this project as "hard" (Interview, 15 May 2011) and her text showed signs of developing (and also, as she explained, unedited) English writing, her completion of the project demonstrated her motivation to persevere with a lengthy literacy-focused task, a pattern she began in 12th grade and continued into her vocational studies. Finally, although her makeover project did not provide a venue for her to explicitly mention her bilingual or biliterate expertise as her 12th-grade exhibition did, it nonetheless played important roles in the creation of her text. Such communicative practices were vital to her work as a stylist, in which she engaged in English reading to determine appropriate hair products and interacted face-to-face and via texting with Spanish- and English-speaking clients.

Contradictions Between School-based Writing, Bilingual/Biliterate Meaning-Making, and Immigration Policy

Ana's ambivalence about schooling, as well the disciplinary referrals she often received in her first three years of high school, complicated her teachers' efforts to understand her full linguistic and academic capacity, a pattern also found with Jaime (Chap. 4) and in other research (Brooks, 2017; Compton-Lilly, 2017). Those experiences were inextricable from a larger context of reception (Portes & Rumbaut, 2001, 2006) in which Ana felt unwelcome, through both her early experiences with teachers and peers and an immigration policy that precluded her from pursuing many postsecondary pathways upon graduation. In both of these ways, her mother seemed to be correct in noting that, "it's going to take a while for this country to get used to us."

Within these larger contexts, the first two literacy events profiled earlier offer micro-level insights into Ana's frustrations with in-school writing as simply a matter of having the "right" answers. In these cases, teachers' efforts to assist Ana included emphasizing a particular register of language (in the humanities essay), as well as both deciding the content that should be included in each sentence of a text and providing a series of guidelines and due dates aimed at ensuring students brought materials to class and completed the task step-by-step (in the art research paper). While my observations of these teachers indicate that they were clearly people of good will who were dedicated to supporting youth's academic success, and Ana did not actively resist the assistance her tenth-grade humanities teacher provided, the design and enactment of these literacy events served to further confirm to Ana that writing in school was simply doing "whatever they say."

Such a pattern was not inevitable, however. The turning point Ana experienced highlights the ways in which a linguistically minoritized student's perspective on schooling and literacy events can change in the context of a linguistic and cultural role model as well as curricula that explicitly include opportunities to support those identities. The notion that well-prepared bilingual Mexican-origin teachers can have positive academic impacts on their Mexican-origin students is commonly found in research (see Gándara, 2015), and one might ask why all youth in the study who had Ms. Torres as their humanities teacher (Diego, Fabiola, and Maria) did not have a similarly notable experience. There are several possible factors, including the ways in which gender may have helped Ana relate better to a "Latina girl" than Diego would have, for example, or the fact that the other young people (but not Ana) had a memorable bilingual/biliterate Latina teacher in their ninth-grade bilingual humanities class. The timing of Ana's experience with Ms. Torres—as she neared the end of high school—may have also made her particularly ready to make changes in her life and seek mentors as she looked into her future. Regardless of exactly *why* this occurred, it suggests the important roles teachers can play in replacing linguistically minoritized labels and identities with explicit support for bilingual and biliterate identities and repertoires, even for youth who see themselves as already "know[ing] English."

During literacy events that Ana found more relevant to her bilingual/biliterate identities and vocational interests, she engaged with those tasks and consistently completed them. The 12th-grade exhibition provided Ana an opportunity to enact a bilingual/biliterate growth discourse that was seen favorably by her judges and that was supported in its creation by ongoing feedback from her teacher. Ana's cosmetology final project represented a literacy event in which both her self-ascribed bilingual/biliterate and her hands-on identities were inherent to the creation of her text, resulting in a multimodal project that employed a range of technical language and depended on focused reading of the course texts and products she used. Although the project did not feature opportunities for writing feedback, as the exhibition did, and I was not able to access her teacher's assessment of the project, the satisfaction of Ana's client offered a different kind of evaluation, one—along with her bilingual and biliterate expertise—that was key to her later professional success.

Such a performance suggests why educators and scholars should consider vocational students as deeply engaged in literate and intellectual pursuits. Many individuals underestimate the sophisticated cognitive, numerical, and literate practices involved in working-class occupations, Rose (2004) argued, and the ways that, for Ana's profession in particular, "language and communication are central to the work itself" (p. 203). Further, also relevant to Ana's experience was the fact that although she was enrolled in a community college—a common option for many Latinx students (Krogstad, 2016)—she had immediate access to the cosmetology coursework she desired and a clear path toward her vocational goal. In this sense, her experience was far different from those of Jaime (Chap. 4), Diego (Chap. 6), and the many other community college and university students enrolled in gatekeeping remedial coursework (Patthey, Thomas–Spiegel, & Dillon, 2009; Razfar & Simon, 2011) that may have little connection to their interests and aspirations.

Despite the expertise Ana developed and employed, her story, like Jaime's, is nonetheless overshadowed by the impact of immigration policy and the timing of immigration reform. Around the same time that DACA was announced, several state laws in California went into effect that made it easier for unauthorized/undocumented youth like Ana to obtain scholarships and financial aid for postsecondary education. Such developments were significant but occurred after Ana completed her cosmetology training. And although Ana finished her high school and cosmetology programs, she described a certain lack of motivation much as Jaime did (Chap. 4), resonating with other research on unauthorized/undocumented youth who are faced with legal barriers to education and careers (Gonzales, 2011, 2016). For example, when I asked Ana if her high school and later experiences would have been different if she had known she would eventually receive permission to work and eligibility for licensure by the state as a cosmetologist, she said:

> I would've pay attention more…like focus more on what I want. And I would've focused more in school for cosmetology if I knew I would have a social, I can get my [cosmetology] license. But since I didn't know I was just like, whatever. I'm not even going to study for that. (Interview, 24 May 2014)

Ana's DACA permission eventually did come through, but by that time she realized that she would need to return to school to prepare for the cosmetology licensure exam, and doing so would have required time and financial resources that she did not have. Ana aspired—and still aspires—to own a salon as a business, and her bilingual and biliterate communicative repertoire would be integral to its success. However, the window for obtaining a license, which would be a first step in achieving that goal, came belatedly, and her potential to realize those dreams remained tied to the economic circumstances in which she was placed by current immigration contexts, regardless of her bilingual or biliterate assets.

Notes

1. *Mija* (a shortened form of *mi hija*, or "my daughter") is an affectionate term used by parents or other adults to refer to daughters or young women.
2. As noted in Chap. 1, I use "Latinx" as a generic term but Latino/Latina when individuals used those terms or described themselves or others in those ways.
3. Halliday (1986/2007) described the ways that language is used in school settings as multiple and dynamic "registers of education" through which students are socialized into schooling contexts (p. 304). Wells (1999) argued that this socialization process occurs as students simultaneously learn language and learn *through* language.

References

Atwell, N. (2015). *In the middle: A lifetime of learning about writing, reading, and adolescents*. Portsmouth, NH: Heinemann.

Brooks, M. D. (2017). "She doesn't have the basic understanding of a language": Using spelling research to challenge deficit conceptualizations of adolescent bilinguals. *Journal of Literacy Research, 49(3), 342–370*. https://doi.org/10.1177/1086296X17714016.

Compton-Lilly, C. (2017). *Reading students' lives: Literacy learning across time*. New York: Routledge.

Gándara, P. (2015). Foreword. In R. E. Zambrana & S. Hurtado (Eds.), *The magic key: The educational journey of Mexican Americans from K-12 to college and beyond* (pp. ix–xiv). Austin, TX: The University of Texas Press.

García, O. (2009). *Bilingual education in the 21st century: A global perspective*. Malden, MA: Wiley-Blackwell.

Goffman, E. (1967). *Interaction ritual: Essays in face-to-face behavior*. Abingdon, OX: Routledge.

Gonzales, R. G. (2011). Learning to be illegal: Undocumented youth and shifting legal contexts in the transition to adulthood. *American Sociological Review, 76(4), 602–619*. https://doi.org/10.1177/0003122411411901.

Gonzales, R. G. (2016). *Lives in limbo: Undocumented and coming of age in America*. Berkeley, CA: University of California Press.

Halliday, M. A. K. (1986/2007). Language across the culture. In J. J. Webster (Ed.), *Language and Education* (pp. 291–205). London: Continuum.

Kibler, A. K. (2011a). "*Casi nomás me dicen qué escribir/*they almost just tell me what to write": A longitudinal analysis of teacher-student interactions in a linguistically diverse mainstream secondary classroom. *Journal of Education, 191*(1), 45–58.

Kibler, A. K. (2011b). Understanding the "mmhm": Dilemmas in talk between teachers and adolescent emergent bilingual students. *Linguistics and Education, 22*(3), 213–232. https://doi.org/10.1016/j.linged.2010.11.002.

Kibler, A. K. (2013). "Doing like almost everything wrong": An adolescent multilingual writer's transition from high school to college. In L. C. de Oliveira & T. Silva (Eds.), *L2 writing in secondary classrooms: Student experiences, academic issues, and teacher education* (pp. 44–64). New York: Routledge.

Kibler, A. K. (2014). From high school to the *noviciado*: An adolescent linguistic minority student's multilingual journey in writing. *The Modern Language Journal, 98*(2), 629–651. https://doi.org/10.1111/modl.12090.

Kibler, A. K. (2016). Promises and limitations of literacy sponsors in resident multilingual youths' transitions to postsecondary schooling. In C. Ortmeier-Hooper & T. Ruecker (Eds.), *Linguistically diverse immigrant and resident writers: Transitions from high school to college* (pp. 99–116). New York: Routledge.

Kibler, A. K., Salerno, A., & Palacios, N. (2014). "But before I go to my next step": A longitudinal study of adolescent English language learners' transitions in oral presentations. *TESOL Quarterly, 48*(2), 222–251. https://doi.org/10.1002/tesq.96.

Krogstad, J. M. (2016). *5 facts about Latinos and education*. Washington, DC: Pew Research Center. Retrieved from: http://www.pewresearch.org/fact-tank/2016/07/28/5-facts-about-latinos-and-education/

Markandaya, K. (1954). *Nectar in a sieve*. New York: Penguin Putnam Books.

Mohan, B., & Beckett, G. H. (2001). A functional approach to research on content-based language learning: Recasts in causal explanations. *The Canadian Modern Language Review, 58*(1), 133–155. https://doi.org/10.3138/cmlr.58.1.133.

Orellana, M. F. (2009). *Translating childhoods: Immigrant youth, language, and culture*. New Brunswick, NJ: Rutgers University Press.

Patthey, G., Thomas–Spiegel, J., & Dillon, P. (2009). Educational pathways of generation 1.5 students in community college writing courses. In M. Roberge, M. Siegal, & L. Harklau (Eds.), *Generation 1.5 in college composition: Teaching academic writing to U.S.-educated learners of ESL* (pp. 135–150). New York: Routledge.

Perreira, K. M., & Spees, L. (2015). Foiled aspirations: The influence of unauthorized status on the educational expectations of Latino immigrant youth. *Population Research and Policy Review, 34(5)*, 641–664. https://doi.org/10.1007/s11113-015-9356-y.

Portes, A., & Rumbaut, R. G. (2001). *Legacies: The story of the immigrant second generation*. Berkeley, CA: University of California Press.

Portes, A., & Rumbaut, R. G. (2006). *Immigrant America: A portrait* (3rd ed.). Berkeley, CA: University of California Press.

Razfar, A., & Simon, J. (2011). Course-taking patterns of Latino ESL students: Mobility and mainstreaming in urban community colleges in the United States. *TESOL Quarterly, 45(4)*, 595–627. https://doi.org/10.5054/tq.2011.268060.

Rose, M. (2004). *The mind at work: Valuing the intelligence of the American worker*. New York: Penguin Group.

Schegloff, E. A. (1988). On an actual virtual servo-mechanism for guessing bad news: A single case conjecture. *Social Problems, 35(4)*, 442–457. https://doi.org/10.2307/800596.

Schleppegrell, M. (2004). *The language of schooling: A functional linguistics perspective*. Mahwah, NJ: Erlbaum.

Umaña-Taylor, A. J., Yazedjian, A., & Bámaca-Gómez, M. (2004). Developing the ethnic identity scale using Eriksonian and social identity perspectives. *Identity: An International Journal of Theory and Research, 4(1)*, 9–38. https://doi.org/10.1207/S1532706XID0401_2.

Valdés, G. (2003). *Expanding definitions of giftedness: The case of young interpreters from immigrant communities*. Mahwah, NH: Lawrence Erlbaum.

Wells, G. (1999). *Dialogic inquiry: Towards a sociocultural practice and theory of education*. Cambridge, UK: Cambridge University Press.

6

From "An Inspiration" to Not Knowing "The Basics": Tensions Between Classroom Interactional Histories and Institutional Expectations

Diego was born in the South Sierra community, where his family had arrived from Mexico several years before. He lived and attended school there until first grade, when he moved with his family to a rural *rancho* in Mexico because of a job opportunity for his father. Diego described not being able to continue formal education during his years at the *rancho*, and only at age 12 did Diego return to the United States and to school. Tall, athletic, and adept at the latest technology, he could often be found during lunchtime at South Sierra High School playing pick-up games of basketball on the asphalt schoolyard or showing friends the newest photos he had taken on his digital camera.

Even though living conditions at home sometimes made it difficult for him to do schoolwork there, Diego earned high grades in high school, graduating with a 3.78 (out of 4) weighted GPA, and had a reputation among teachers and peers as a hardworking student who was particularly skilled at math. With teachers' help, and the benefit of US citizenship that made him eligible for postsecondary funding, he won a competitive

Portions of this chapter draw from data first published in Kibler (2011a), Kibler (2013), and Kibler (2016).

A. K. Kibler, *Longitudinal Interactional Histories*,
https://doi.org/10.1007/978-3-319-98815-3_6

scholarship that paid his full tuition and living costs for any university to which he was accepted. He elected to attend four-year Ocean College, a small private university a few hundred miles away that scholarship advisors told him would provide personalized guidance and assistance. Just before graduation, he spoke excitedly to me about his upcoming experience at Ocean College, his future roommates, his interest in playing on the school's sports teams, and his plans for earning a degree in business finance.

The turning point in Diego's language and literacy journey during this study was his transition from secondary to postsecondary schooling (see Table 6.1). More specifically, although he left high school recognized by teachers and others as a confident English user,[1] once at university, he quickly came to believe he "didn't know the basics," especially in writing. At Ocean College, he was placed in a sequence of remedial and introductory classes—rather than the business courses he was looking forward to—and, despite the help of teachers and a mentor provided through his scholarship, struggled to pass several of them.

In an interview with Diego after his second year at Ocean College, he surprised me by explaining that he would not be returning there the following fall. According to Diego, his scholarship organization had advised him that, because of rising tuition rates, they could not afford to continue covering all of his expenses there. Diego explained that he would instead be staying at home and attending a local community college, which the scholarship program committed to funding. While I knew that he could earn a two-year associate's degree at that particular community college in business administration or accounting, somewhat similar to his initial career aspiration of business finance, I was still puzzled. In his 12th-grade exhibition (explored in more detail later in the chapter), he had said of his future plans, "I will get a college degree, extra activities, and more time, with friends, and good career ... but if, that didn't–NONE of that happen, which I want–I don't want a bad thing happen, I will go to community college, work, maybe live with my parents and help them" (20 May 2010). Returning home and attending a community college was clearly not what Diego or his scholarship program—which boasted a 90% bachelor's degree graduation rate for their recipients—had in mind when he began university studies. His explanation that the scholarship could not cover rising tuition rates, something I attempted to confirm but was never able to, could account for his departure from Ocean College, but I also wondered if his lack of academic progress also played a role. At that point in time, Diego also stopped responding to my texts and requests to meet, meaning that such questions remain unanswered (although he did text me once after the study ended with a brief greeting and update: see Chap. 9).[2]

Yet, the data I collected until that point provide insights into why Diego's language and literacy journey may have unfolded as it did, and how his university experiences both resonated with and marked a turning point away from those in high school. In the next two sections, I provide a broad overview of Diego's language and literacy experiences to contextualize his journey during high school and university. I then use a longitudinal interactional histories approach (LIHA) to analyze two literacy events before and two after his turning point of beginning university studies (see Table 6.1) in order to explore the interactions influencing his production of texts, how they did so, and patterns of change over time in relation to this turning point.

Overview of Diego's Language and Literacy Experiences

During High School I first met Diego when he was enrolled in Ms. Gutiérrez's bilingual humanities course at South Sierra High School in ninth grade. He also took ELD courses in ninth and tenth grades, but apart from those, which were designated exclusively for English-learner-classified students, his other English-medium classes in high school were untracked. During high school, he took humanities, math, science, statistics, Spanish-for-Native-Speakers, and community college courses. Diego met all graduation requirements, including the standardized state high school exit exam, although he had to retake it multiple times to earn a passing score, while the other students in the study passed it on their first or second attempts.

Table 6.1 Diego's turning point and literacy events presented through LIHA analysis

Literacy Event	Before the turning point		Turning Point:	After the turning point	
	"Me 'tan dando todas las respuestas"	*"I have been increasing my English"*	**Turning Point: Attending University**	*"She was giving me more pages"*	*"I was caring… but he made it really hard"*
Year	Grade 10	Grade 12		Grade 13	Grade 14
Task	Essay based on class novel (argumentation[a])	Exhibition (explanation/ reflection)		Essay based on class novel (argumentation)	In-class mid-term exam
Institutional context (if applicable)	Untracked high school humanities class	Untracked high school (humanities class and school-wide)		Remedial university English class	Introductory university philosophy class

Notes: [a]Genre labels in parentheses are aligned with those originally presented in Kibler (2014), as adapted from Schleppegrell (2004)

In his first year of high school, Diego showed an eagerness to have teachers check the accuracy of his work and often stayed after school for help, interactions in which he was often able to engage using Spanish because many of his teachers in ninth grade were bilingual to varying degrees. In subsequent years, more and more of his teachers were monolingual English speakers, and he took great pride in conversing with them in English to seek similar forms of assistance both in class and after school. Such patterns of interaction quickly earned him a reputation among teachers as a diligent and hardworking student, particularly once they learned about his interrupted schooling experiences. This situation resonated in some ways with a case Harklau (2000) documented, in which teachers tended to assign immigrant ESL high school students a shared social identity of "kids with determination" (p. 45) that in many ways essentialized or stereotyped youth but nonetheless brought them supportive relationships and positive teacher assessments. Diego and his teachers' interactions, detailed later in the chapter, clearly aligned with this depiction, but it should be noted that many other immigrant and English-learner-classified students at South Sierra High School did not invoke this representation or have teachers who did so in describing them.

At the beginning of high school, both my own observations and Diego's standardized English language proficiency assessment scores suggested he was at early stages of English language development, but he was confident that his English expertise would develop over time. For example, and when I asked him in tenth grade what he thought his English would be like ten years from then, he explained:

Mi inglés, pues sería, estuviera,[3] pues, no exactamente perfecto, pero ya, ya la mayoría ya me sé el inglés … Ya tuviera,[4] ya, yo ya ha aprendido todo el inglés, y, este, como, pero no perfectamente así, como profesional. (Interview, 7 February 2007)

(My English, well, would be, well, not exactly perfect, but already, for the most part, I already know English … I would have, I have already learned all of English, and, well, like, but not perfectly, like a professional.)

He felt similarly about maintaining his uses of Spanish (at least in spoken form), saying that "*pues mi español, pues ese nunca se me va a dejar de olvidar*[5] *porque siempre con mi, entre mi familia, siempre hablamos puro español.* / Well, my Spanish, well, I will never forget that because always with my, in my family, we always speak only Spanish" (Interview, 7 February 2007). Diego also communicated with others online, most notably on MySpace, the social media venue of the time, where he posted messages to friends, statements of love to his girlfriend (e.g., "I love u ___ with all my *corazón* / heart"), and *dichos*, or sayings ("*Es mejor tarde que nunca* / Better late than never"). He also attended a Saturday writing program for several months in tenth grade that provided opportunities to write a range of traditional and multimodal texts in any language, and where he chose to write multiple texts in English. These language and literacy experiences and positive perspectives continued throughout high school, but he felt particular pride in his growing proficiency in English. By 12th grade, for example, he explained that in school "now I could understand everything: how to do my work and without problems with the English" (Interview, 19 April 2010).

Diego described himself as a beginning English reader when he returned to the United States in seventh grade after missing several years of schooling, saying that "they were teaching me, like, little books, baby books. Like, 'the cat is running.' That's because I actually needed it, and it helped me a lot because I couldn't read, like, big words or a sentence" (Interview, 19 April 2010). In ninth grade, however, he moved on to high school and almost without exception was given the same texts as his fellow classmates rather than texts for early readers, without any individualized reading instruction. This seeming "leap" over a short period of time did not appear to align with the pace of his reading development. For example, in many classroom observations of in-class silent reading during tenth grade, I often saw Diego turning no more than one or two pages of the assigned class novel during the session even though typical reading assignments were 8–15 pages (which some, but not all, other students completed). Such patterns of participation led me to believe that his reading might have been much less fluent—and/or involved less comprehension—than his teacher assumed. Diego's participation in subsequent small-group discussions bore this out, in that he often asked classmates to explain what had occurred in the day's reading assignment. In terms of the texts he read in high school, all were in English with the exception of the first novel read in his bilingual humanities class (which he was given in Spanish translation) and the Spanish-language texts that formed the curriculum for the single Spanish-for-Native-Speakers class he took. Although Diego described those as somewhat easier to understand, I was not able to observe him often enough in the latter course to know if he was indeed better able to comprehend those texts.

In terms of writing, Diego initially wrote in Spanish for his ninth-grade bilingual humanities course, but he was encouraged by his teacher—who felt pressure to prepare her students for an English-medium humanities course the next year—to increase the amount of English writing with each assignment. As a result, he shifted to writing almost all-English texts by the end of his ninth-grade year. Drafts of writing during that transition indicated ongoing and increasing communication with his teacher and classmates about how to translate phrases from Spanish into English (see also Kibler, 2010 for a similar pattern with fellow students in tenth grade). These bilingual interactions included both in-class conversations and written communication via teacher feedback. Diego progressed steadily in his uses of written English at school, and an excerpt from an assessment given at the end of his ninth-grade year represented what he was able to accomplish in English when writing a descriptive passage independently:

> My *importante* porsend is my mom she is very nice to me she help me with the materials for the school. My mom is strict, is a good *cocinera* [cook], and a good clin up the house.[6]

Although by tenth grade Diego still felt that he was not yet writing with the "*palabras grandes* / big words" expected in his humanities class, or writing like a scientist as his biology teacher expected (see Kibler, 2011b), his comments about school-based writing in English became more positive over time. In an interview just before his high school graduation, I asked him about how his writing for school had changed over time, and Diego explained this growth in terms of his English writing alone. He said:

> Now I know how to write in English. In my sophomore [tenth grade] year, I was still not that good on writing, but I was writing in English. Then, like, from junior [eleventh grade] and senior [twelfth grade] now, I can write bigger paragraphs and more, like, vocabulary, with different details and ideas and knowledge. I couldn't do it before. (Interview, 14 June 2010)

He acknowledged that university might be more challenging, explaining that there would be "more writing, more reading, more books to read almost every week, every day. On my writing skills, I know that I'm going to need to, like, to write more than high school and speak more and read more every day" (Interview, 14 June 2010). However, he felt that his teachers had prepared him well for these tasks. Further, he explained that he had already looked at one of the Ocean College business finance textbooks, and "it doesn't have big words that I don't understand, so it seems like I'm not going to struggle when reading that book" (Interview, 14 June 2010).

During University Academic life at Ocean College, the private four-year university Diego then attended, was quite different than what he expected. In fact, Diego took no business classes at all during his time there. Instead, he was enrolled in a range of remedial English and math courses, alongside other introductory requirements. As a result of standardized placement tests given upon his arrival at university, in his first semester Diego was enrolled in the two lowest remedial English courses (multiple levels below the English courses required for graduation), an Intermediate Algebra course two levels below the Math course required for graduation (Calculus), and an elective Interpersonal Communication course.

The English placement in particular was an unwelcome surprise to Diego. As he explained, "Well, I was expecting that this was going to happen to me … okay, I'm going to be like lower English classes because I already know that. But THAT low?" (Interview, 29 June 2011). To him, the message of his English placement and early remedial experiences was clear: "I went there, now [they're] telling me that I actually didn't learn the basics things on high school about how to write a paragraph or an essay." Once courses began, Diego quickly became overwhelmed with the language and literacy expectations of his English classes, and because of failing grades had to retake both the next semester. In fact, during his two years at Ocean College, Diego took seven remedial English classes in all, three of which he did not pass, and still had not reached any of the English courses required for graduation. He progressed more steadily in math, however, and began courses in calculus by his second year. He also began electives like art and music, along with other liberal arts prerequisites like introductory science and philosophy, but he reported withdrawing from or not earning passing credit in the latter two courses.

The English-medium texts Diego read for his various university classes were diverse, ranging from memoirs and essays to textbooks and workbooks targeting issues such as basic sentence grammar, vocabulary development, and locating main ideas and summarizing. In relation to book-length texts he read for English classes, he consistently described these as difficult to comprehend. For example, in explaining his first semester's experience reading the memoir *I Will Plant you a Lilac Tree* (Hillman, 2005), he said, "I wasn't understanding anything because that one, because of the reading ... I couldn't like understand it that much, all the words" (Interview, 29 June 2011). He had a similar experience with *Burro Genius* (Villaseñor, 2004), the memoir he read when he retook that class the next semester, which is explored later in the chapter. Diego also described textbook reading as difficult, particularly in relation to the philosophy course he took (also profiled later in the chapter).

Diego told me that time management was a constant challenge in keeping up with the readings and assignments for his classes (a common experience for first-year community college and university students: Conley, 2008), but issues with writing were particularly frustrating to him. He explained that during his first vacation home from university, he returned to his high school to tell his former teachers what had happened:

> I explained to [the counselor] and another teacher that, no this is what I'm learning and I think I'm supposed to learn already this on high school ... I print out one, a paper that I'd got in high school, and it supposedly was like really good. And I showed it to my English teacher over there [at Ocean College], and ... she just told me, oh, this is like a D paper. And

then I showed them over there at high school, [and said,] "this is an A paper that I got here, and this is a D paper. This is supposed to be a D paper over there, so that means that we're doing like almost everything wrong." (Interview, 29 June 2011)

However, as Diego continued his university coursework, his perceptions of university-based writing events gradually became more positive. In fact, when I asked what skill had advanced most during his first two years at Ocean College, he explained it was writing:

> My writing skills increased a little bit more. I don't make, not perfect essays, but like better essays and paragraphs. To improve my writing is, I just followed what they actually told me to do so, which is really helpful. (Interview, 20 July 2012)

He spoke with great detail and enthusiasm about what he was learning across his various English courses in terms of how to develop main ideas and supporting details in paragraphs, how to vary sentence length, and how to use sentence structure and punctuation more effectively. He also enjoyed those classes requiring reflective essays (e.g., "What did you learn this semester, and how did you learn it?") that allowed him to practice developing main ideas and supporting details, but he continued to find essays based on book-length texts more difficult because he rarely completed the reading. For assessments that included relatively less writing, like short answer and multiple-choice tests—the latter of which Diego described having little experience with in high school—he explained that their level difficulty varied depending on the particular class.

Diego was never advised to enroll in any Spanish language or literature classes at Ocean College, and in fact, the university's course catalog explicitly stated that "Speakers of Spanish with native-like fluency will not receive credit for [Spanish] courses except with advance approval from the instructor and department." No Spanish courses for heritage speakers were offered, and neither did he report receiving any encouragement to use Spanish language resources, oral or written, to support his learning in other classes. His teachers and fellow students were almost exclusively non-Spanish speakers as well, Diego explained, and although his friends and roommates were from both the United States and abroad—such as a young man from China from whom Diego learned to play ping-pong, a main hobby of his at university—they were not Spanish speakers. However, he still used Spanish almost exclusively with his family and friends in the South Sierra community, either in person, on the phone, texting, or online.

In many ways, Diego's language and literacy experiences at Ocean College were not unique: They were similar in various ways to those of many Latinx and multilingual postsecondary students in the United States, in that coursework focused heavily on remediation (Razfar & Simon, 2011), took place in English without support for bilingual or biliterate development (García, Pujol-Ferran, & Reddy, 2013), and led to challenges in managing the demands of reading and writing tasks and writing essays (Kanno & Grosik, 2012; Kanno & Varghese, 2010). And although Diego noted growth in his English literacy development both in high school and university, and was often enthusiastic about his learning, this progress appeared to be insufficient to consistently meet institutional or instructor expectations for success after the turning point of beginning university studies.

Diego's Longitudinal Interactional Histories

As explained earlier, Diego's high school experiences with language and literacy built toward a turning point in which he left high school with a GPA and other academic accomplishments and identities that marked him as a confident English user, but the transition into university studies—the turning point in his journey (Table 6.1)—led to very different trajectory, including remediation, frustration, and difficulties meeting his instructors' expectations. Literacy events demonstrating how these trends developed both before and after this turning point are presented here through LIHA analyses; these events as well as their placement in relation to the turning point are presented in Table 6.1.

Before the Turning Point: Becoming an English User in High School To describe the ways in which Diego built a growing identity as an eager student and eventually an accomplished user of English in high school, I use LIHA analyses to explore two distinct literacy events. The first is an essay from tenth grade, in which he and his teacher, Mr. Smith, both agreed that Diego put in substantial effort but relied too heavily on his teacher's help to write it. The second is from 12th grade, when Diego completed a multimodal writing task in ways that allowed him to successfully present himself (and be recognized by others) as a hardworking, competent English user who met his school's academic expectations.

"Me 'Tan Dando Todas las Respuestas/They Are Giving Me All the Answers": Novel-Based Essay Writing in Humanities Class As Diego began his tenth-grade year, he shifted from Ms. Gutiérrez's bilingual humanities course, described earlier, to an English-medium humanities class taught by Mr. Smith, who did not speak Spanish and did not have formal training to work with multilingual students at the time this event took place (see also Chap. 5). Writing assignments for this tenth-grade class were all completed in English—including multiple-draft essays on assigned class novels—and Diego's interactions while creating such texts highlighted the ways that he and his teacher managed these challenging literacy events early in his high school career. As described in Chap. 5 and elsewhere (Kibler, 2011a, 2013), a tenth-grade assignment all students at South Sierra completed was an essay, in which they had to write about whether industrialization in the novel *Nectar in a Sieve* (Markandaya, 1954), set in mid-twentieth-century India, was an example of "progress," a "problem," or a "promise" for the future. Students read the book in small groups over a period of several weeks, and afterward began working on their essays through a series of in-class pre-writing and drafting tasks.

Interactions Several interactions were prominent as Diego wrote this essay, first among them those with the text itself. As mentioned in Chap. 1, school discourses emphasized that students should read "thick, important books." These discourses were influential, in that a book-length novel from an internationally recognized author served as the text upon which this assignment was based. The book was a challenge for Diego, however. Consistent with patterns mentioned earlier, I observed him struggling to read and understand the novel, despite conversations with classmates during small-group activities as they discussed the text in class.

During a pre-writing activity in which students were to brainstorm ideas for their essays, an interaction among Diego, his teacher, and two other students in Diego's small group made this apparent:

1 Mr. Smith:	ok so what do you think you remember MOST from the book.	
2	(3)	
3 Mr. Smith:	maybe if you just had to pick a character and talk about that character?	
4	just talk to me about anybody.	
5	(1)	
6	let's just have a conversation,	
7	about what you read and what you think about that person.	
8 Daniel:	that she kills the the her daughter?	
9 Mr. Smith:	Diego [your voice] changed,	
10 Jaime:	[DIEGO DI]EGO,	
11	(6)	
12 Jaime:	*de cuáles de cuál te acuerdas más güey.* ('which ones which one do you remember the most about dude.')	
13 Diego:	*de NINGUNO.* ('about NONE.')	
14 Jaime:	NONE,	
15	he said none. (Observation, 4 February 2008)	

In this informal conference, Mr. Smith attempted to begin a "conversation" about the novel's characters (line 1), and after silences when he likely expected a response from Diego (lines 2 and 5), he rephrased his question multiple times. However, even another student's more succinct translated version of the teacher's question (line 12) did not elicit a response from Diego. In some senses, this silence was surprising to me, because Diego often enthusiastically participated in other English-medium classroom conversations, especially with teachers. Although certain social or linguistic factors unrelated to this assignment or nonverbal cues not captured in the data might have influenced his behavior in this informal conference, it was likely that Diego's interactions with the novel to this point were simply not sufficient to discuss its characters or begin the writing assignment.

After this conversation, Diego received a two-page summary of the book from Mr. Smith, and this became the new text upon which he based his essay writing. From that point onward, Mr. Smith and Diego's interactions were quite frequent and far more interactive. They had 26 informal conferences about Diego's text, both during and outside of class. Early on, Mr. Smith often engaged with Diego during these conferences to check his comprehension of the summary text and brainstorm ideas for writing, using questions and upward intonation to cue Diego to particular answers. As Diego began writing, Mr. Smith used this same pattern of intonation as well as explicit suggestions for rephrasing to provide Diego with sentence-level wording, much as he did with Ana (see Chap. 5). Mr. Smith would often provide phrasing for a sentence orally, and then recast Diego's wording as they discussed the idea and as Diego transcribed it, until Diego's written version approximated the original teacher suggestion. (See Kibler, 2011a for further discussion of this process). A key difference between Ana and Diego, however, was the intensity of support, in that Mr. Smith assisted Diego in this manner with almost all of the sentences in his essay.

Diego became increasingly active in these interactions over time, first by responding to Mr. Smith's questions and later by appealing for his teacher's help in transcription, using repetition, rephrasing, and upward intonation to elicit his teacher's approval of what he had written. Mr. Smith also gave written feedback on the draft twice, and in almost all instances Diego implemented his teacher's suggested changes either on his own, with the teacher, or with the help of fellow Spanish-speaking students, who sometimes also served as language brokers in conversations with Diego and Mr. Smith.

Impacts The lack of interaction between Diego and the novel—but his frequent interactions with Mr. Smith, the written summary, and his classmates—played key roles in shaping his essay (see full text in Kibler,

2013). All of his main topics were suggested by Mr. Smith, and details provided in the essay could all be found in the summary or were suggested by his teacher or other students. Further, his written expression of those ideas was closely tied to his interactions with Mr. Smith: Several of Diego's written sentences were nearly identical to his teacher's oral suggestions. Written feedback from the teacher was also very influential on Diego's final text, in that he changed his essay to comply with all of Mr. Smith's suggestions, which included comments on both content and written expression. This attention to detail helped Diego produce a very "clean" text. His 250-word essay, in fact, contained only two language patterns that readers might readily identify as "typical" for multilingual writers at early stages of English language proficiency ("our village *need* this land to *reproduce* rice"), both of which occurred in the last sentence of his essay. A final impact of Diego's interactions was, as one might expect given the many informal conferences in which he engaged, that he ran out of time to write the essay. As a result, his teacher suggested he include just two topics in his essay instead of the three topics expected of the other students.

Reflective interviews that I conducted with Mr. Smith and Diego after the essay was completed and assessed suggested that they both understood how fundamentally teacher-student interactions influenced Diego's writing, but their perspectives on this phenomenon differed. For example, Mr. Smith explained:

> So with Diego I felt that I was almost writing his essay at one point, which was really hard. When we worked together, he would write a few words, then I would have to finish it or it just felt that I was writing the essay for him, so he's not learning how to write. I mean he's learning something I think, but I felt he was too dependent on me to complete the task. (Interview, 18 April 2008)

Diego's perspective, as he expressed it to me in an interview, was somewhat different, in that he described relying upon others only to help him begin his paragraphs and doing the rest himself. In this way, instead of requiring other people's help to *finish* his writing, as Mr. Smith explained and I observed, Diego understood the assistance he received as focused on helping him *begin* to write. When considering an audio-recorded in-class interaction between Diego and a friend, yet another possible explanation emerged: In it, he confided to his friend that the essay writing was difficult but "*ahorita todo esto lo 'toy sacando de los maestros, me 'tan dando todas las respuestas.* / now all this I'm getting it from the teachers, they're giving me all the answers" (14 February 2008). There were several possible reasons why Diego might have characterized his experiences this way to his friend, but his comments nonetheless highlighted the ways in which he negotiated school expectations for English literacy expertise in ways that allowed him to complete the assignment.

Change Over Time In the context of Diego's long-term English language and literacy experiences, this event marked an important change over time from those early in ninth grade, in that his essay was written entirely in English, and although conversations with classmates occurred in Spanish, interactions with texts and his teacher took place primarily in English (when not language-brokered by fellow students). Although the essay itself did not meet the teacher's expectations in terms of process or quality (it received the equivalent of a "D"), this event nonetheless demonstrated Diego's success in eliciting support to negotiate challenging English literacy events. He did so both through bilingual peer support and through extensive assistance from his English-only teacher, although his interactions with the teacher were done in ways that transgressed certain norms (McDermott & Roth, 1978) held by Mr. Smith and many other teachers in US classrooms about students writing with a level of independence.

"I Have Been Increasing My English": The 12th-Grade Exhibition As described in Chaps. 5 (Ana) and 8 (Maria), students at South Sierra High School participated in annual exhibitions that included individual oral presentations to a committee of teachers, community members, and other youth at the school. In 12th grade the focus was a self-reflection on students' academic and personal achievements during high school: Diego and his peers were each asked to create and present a website with several components that allowed them to discuss their accomplishments during high school (see Chap. 5 for further details).

Interactions In ways that were somewhat similar to his tenth-grade composing process, Diego had a range of interactions with teachers and other students while writing that helped him both develop and express his ideas. Although I was not present to observe and audio-record these interactions, Diego described receiving oral and written feedback on both his "ideas" and "spelling" (likely encompassing several issues of written expression) from a range of adults, including his teacher, homeroom advisor, and scholarship mentor. He also described having two friends, both of whom were Spanish-English bilinguals, work with him on the project: "they helped me put in more – more evidence, more – more writing in the paragraphs, and put it in here what each [habit] means" (Interview, 14 June 2010). Extensive interactions around revision did not seem to be as prominent as they were during the tenth-grade event, however. As Diego explained, due to an illness, he missed most of the in-class opportunities for feedback and did not revise on his own.

Unique elements of this assignment created additional contexts for interactions not present in more traditional essay-based literacy events. As explored in Chap. 5 (Ana), reflective assignments like this one explicitly encouraged students to engage in a discourse of growth, which influenced Diego's writing and his oral presentation. His use of multimodal resources, including his use of pictures on the webpage and additional oral explanations during the exhibition presentation itself, together allowed him to create a more complete reflection in line with this larger discourse.

Impacts To better explain the influence of these various interactions, I take one habit, Application of Knowledge, which Diego judged as his strongest, and examine how the webpage (Table 6.2) and Diego's oral presentation combined to create a multimodal text demonstrating Diego's successful self-presentation as a developing user of English through a discourse of growth over time.

Table 6.2 Diego's website page on application of knowledge, 12th grade

	Application of Knowledge *Understand Class Content *Demonstrate Content Skills	
[Superhero Graphic]		
	This habit is when you are practicing your skills in the class when you know most of the activities that we need to do in class. Is when you demonstrate content skills in a test and when the teacher ask you a question you need to know if you are understanding the class contents. Also show your knowledge on each class and you will know in what you are good at and what you need help with. I have demonstrated growth in this habit through my Gardner's test, Maslow test, math exhibition, and in my research paper.	
[Image: Test on Howard Gardner's Multiple Intelligences, grade 9]	[Image: Test on Abraham Maslow's Hierarchy of Needs, grade 9]	[Image: Math poster for a presentation, grade 9]
	[Image: Research presentation on Irish immigration to the US, grade 11]	
	[Image: "Where I Am From" poem, grade 9]	[Image: "I Am a Dream" poem, grade 12]

On his Application of Knowledge webpage, Diego presented a three-part explanation of this habit: as practicing skills you know in class, as demonstrating knowledge for the teacher, and as using these demonstrations to self-reflect. He also listed four examples of tasks through which he demonstrated this habit (two tests, a math exhibition, and a research paper) and posted images of this work as evidence. An additional image on the page—that of a superhero pointing to a chalkboard proclaiming "Knowledge is Power"—is one Diego explained he chose "because every time that we are growing our knowledge, we are growing more powerful. [It is] showing that we're actually learning more stuff: Now I can do it" (Interview, 14 June 2010). He was well aware that he could rely on these images as part of his overall communicative repertoire to carry part of the meaning of his text. In the same interview he explained that he preferred multimodal texts like his website because "on the regular essays you have to write everything."

The orality of his presentation was another key element of the final text he created for his judges at the exhibition. In presenting his webpage to the judges, he first read aloud the text that he had written but then launched into a further explanation that included new information beyond what was written on the page, much as Ana did to show her alignment with a Latina role model (Chap. 5). In Diego's case, his oral explanation allowed him to present himself as an increasingly accomplished English user according to the growth discourse implicit in the assignment, as noted in the following in bold:

This is one of my first evidence, the m- gar- Maslow's test. **When I was in ninth grade, I was trying my best because even though that I didn't know English still, I was practicing hard, and, I said I needed to stay for office hours, and, and stay with the teachers to help me.** And another one is … the multiple intelligence. So this is another test and I know I knew that I practiced a lot, because I showed the knowledge to my teacher and to the class because of, th- I even, I almost got, twenty two points. I just got twenty one but I showed that I actually paying attention to the class and I'm, **I'm learning more English and, showing what I know.** My next evidence is my, my math exhibition. So, this is my poster. (2) I was staying with my algebra one teacher, and I **I show her that I always stay after school and sometimes I was the only one.** And, and I actually I show her by presenting this exhibition passing it with, with distinction so and she was proud because I actually demonstrating what I know and, presenting all the the judges that, I I know this concepts and answered their questions. And, this is, the Irish moving to America so this is my, my research paper that I do for junior year [eleventh grade] last year. So, the there were different kind of groups that we, that we can chose. I choose Irish people, and how they were moving to to the United States. And, and **I showed to the teacher too that I, that I, even though that I don't, I'm not good at English I show him that I can, I can do better and I can learn more new stuff.** And, my knowledge, the section on the bottom, and, this part, this poem, **I write it when I was in, a fr- freshman year, but I write it in English and Spanish because I didn't know the, a lot of English and, and for now, I write this for humanities twelve, I write**

another poem. And this time I write it all in English and more, with more knowledge and, so, I compared these two **because in the freshman year, I didn't know that much English and then from, from NOW I have been increasing my English, and knowing more stuff.** (Observation, 20 May 2010)[7]

In this oral explanation, Diego referenced his growth as a learner of English multiple times, suggesting growth from "I didn't know English" (fall, ninth grade) to "I'm learning more English" (spring, ninth grade) to "even though … I'm not good at English I show him that I can, I can do better" (eleventh grade) to "NOW I have been increasing my English" (12th grade). Such a growth discourse was presented in the opposite way for Spanish literacy, however: He described writing in Spanish in ninth grade only "because I didn't know the, a lot of English" rather than as evidence of opportunities to use or develop his biliteracy expertise. In fact, he showcased an all-English poem in 12th grade as evidence of his development away from Spanish in school contexts. Alongside these growth discourses were also explanations of practicing hard and staying after school for office hours to receive help from the teachers for the first two assignments, even when "sometimes [he] was the only one" among his peers who did so.

Judges' assessments provided affirmation that Diego fulfilled the criteria for demonstrating academic and personal development during high school. He passed 9 of 10 categories with a ranking of meeting or exceeding the standard (4 or 5 out of 5 points, respectively). Beyond these numerical ratings, however, judges' comments to him at the end of the exhibition suggest that Diego was seen by the judges as a student who had grown to meet the school's expectations. For example, one judge explained, "I think you represent what this school is all about … it's really amazing how far you've come and how much you've accomplished," while another told him, "I admire you for your strength and determination … you're definitely an inspiration to me." Yet another complimented his communication with the audience, saying, "You're really good at interacting with people." However, the panel's one suggestion for improvement highlighted his English literacy development in particular: The lead judge explained, "We all noticed some issues in your writing with spelling and grammar, and I think with time it's something that will get ironed out, but it's something you do need to focus on … [at university] they will have a lot of resources to help you with that." In this sense, Diego's challenges in writing were framed as "some issues" with surface-level expression rather than rhetorical and conceptual concerns, and the judges appeared confident that they would "get ironed out" through effort and assistance he could seek in university.

Change Over Time Diego's performance in this culminating event allowed him to navigate an identity as an increasingly competent English user, moving from someone whose teacher "wrote [an essay] for him" to someone whose "issues" with writing were noted but not seen as detracting from his broader academic accomplishments and readiness for university, a next step that was decisive in his language and literacy journey. Several issues and interactions remained relatively hidden through this event, however, including his bilingual and biliterate practices, which were referenced only through his use of Spanish in writing earlier in high school and framed as evidence of limited proficiencies in English rather than an ongoing resource, and his challenges earlier in high school when interacting with lengthy texts, a trend that was unaddressed in the exhibition but played an important role in his university experiences.

After the Turning Point: Coping with Challenges of University Literacy Events Diego's entrance into university served as the turning point in this analysis (see Table 6.1). It was at this moment that the hardworking and increasingly competent English user identity he developed through literacy events in high school was confronted by the institutional realities of tertiary course placement and remediation, leading him to believe that he didn't know "the basics" in writing when he arrived. The two literacy events after this turning point examined below through LIHA analyses demonstrate the ways in which university contexts presented Diego with challenges both familiar and new. The first analysis uncovers the ways in which the teacher-reliant interactional processes through which Diego wrote essays about book-length texts in university remedial English classes mirrored the same strategies he drew upon in high school. The second literacy event explores new literacy practices unique to Diego's university experience, ones in which his previously successful interactional strategies proved ineffective.

"She Was Giving Me More Pages": Teacher Support in University Writing Classes The primary assignment in a remedial English course Diego retook during his second semester at Ocean College was writing an essay about an important theme from *Burro Genius* (Villaseñor, 2004), a memoir about the Mexican-origin author's childhood experiences in 1940s' Southern California. Students had to complete both the reading and essay drafting outside of class, a common pattern in universities but a notable change from the in-class writing (Harklau, 2001) and reading prominent in the experiences of many high school students, including Diego. His English teacher, Ms. Harwood, was the same instructor as when he first took (and did not pass) the course in the fall. Although I was not able to gather specific information about her professional background and preparation, Diego described her in positive terms as a helpful teacher. He did not share with me the written handouts or guidelines that she provided, but Diego reported that the in-class activities for this particular essay focused on basic organizational structures: introduction, conclusion, and supporting paragraphs that are linked together. In terms of paragraphs in particular, he explained being retaught (and then using) the same pattern of "main idea-supporting information-quotation-analysis" that he had originally learned in ninth grade.

Although this assignment was similar in many ways to the *Nectar in a Sieve* essay Diego completed three years earlier, the institutional setting was clearly different. Rather than being in an untracked, majority-Latinx and Spanish-speaking class, Diego was now in a beginning-level remedial university English course, with few or no other Spanish-speaking or Latin-American-origin students. The curriculum focused primarily on grammar, sentence structure, punctuation, paragraphs, and short essays, according to assigned textbooks and the course description.

Interactions Diego's interactions with both textual resources and his teacher were particularly influential in this literacy event. Perhaps most critical was that, like in his tenth-grade assignment, Diego explained that he did not read the book upon which the essay assignment was based:

> Well, first because when I read the first chapter, I can't understand it at all. And so from there, I just like kind of like stopped reading it, and then like the teacher wasn't telling us anything about the book, like "how are you coming on your reading" or something ... And so I just read the first chapter, and then it was kind of confusing, and then at the end like, like it was boring. (Interview, 29 June 2011)

His teacher did not provide a summary of the text, as Mr. Smith did in tenth grade, but Diego developed ideas to write about through another means: an in-class activity part-way through the essay drafting process, when classmates shared with each other the theme from the book about which they were planning to write. Diego reported, however, that rather than drawing from other students' ideas, he decided to use the initial example his *teacher* provided at the beginning of the activity:

> She was like giving us an example, "oh, so I here, I have like the theme about making mistakes. He did a lot of mistakes on the, on the story and when he was little and when he was older." And so she just, she just like give us like simple quotes. And then so that came to my mind, and so I write about making mistakes. But I didn't use her quotes. I used different ones. (Interview, 29 June 2011)

Diego went on to explain that once he decided upon this theme, Ms. Harwood helped him locate quotations in the book to use in his essay: "she was giving me more like pages, like 'oh, so you can use like this example of some mistake, or you can use this one or this one, but you only need like three.' So I'm like oh, okay." Diego described completing drafting outside of class and not receiving written feedback from the teacher before submitting his final version of the essay.

Impacts As Diego recounted these experiences to me, I was struck by their similarity to the assistance Mr. Smith provided in tenth grade through their one-on-one interactions. Because I learned of Diego's university writing experiences through his interviews and written texts but not through direct observation, it was impossible to know exactly how similar Ms. Harwood's assistance was to that of Mr. Smith, but Diego's interactions with her appeared to provide key content for his final essay (see full text in Kibler, 2013). For example, in addition to closely following the paragraph pattern he was taught, Diego used a theme—"Victor succeeds because he learned from his mistakes"—that was almost identical to the one Ms. Harwood provided in class. In addition, the three main paragraphs of his essay each contained quotations, which Diego explained were provided by his teacher, and almost all of the information Diego included about the characters or plot of the memoir could be gleaned directly from those quotations. In fact, he described going back to the book after being given the quotations in order to "read like a little bit from the page from for where was the quote so I can get an idea how to start the paragraph to make it clear when I'm going to get to the quote" (Interview, 29 June 2011). Also visible from the final text's lack of a conclusion paragraph—and confirmed in interviews—was that Diego did not have time to complete the essay, which is perhaps unsurprising given that he decided upon a theme only after other students had done so. Finally, language patterns readers might expect from multilingual writers (e.g., "it makes you successful of not repeat the mistakes") were actually more frequent in this essay than in his tenth-grade text, likely because he did not have as many opportunities for in-class drafting or written feedback as he did in high school. And although Diego explained that he was anticipating a low grade on the essay, he reported earning a B plus, which allowed him to pass this class on his second try and advance to the next remedial English course the next fall.

Change Over Time This literacy event underscores how Diego's university experiences resonated with the past but also showed evidence of development over time. Because the *Burro Genius* essay assignment was in many ways similar to the tenth-grade *Nectar in a Sieve* writing task, certain measures of progress in his writing were visible. For example, he was increasingly able to use consistent paragraphing structures and had a clearer overall focus for his essay, and his completion of drafting out-of-class, without constant support from his teacher or classmates for written expression, also suggested a measure of progress. In terms of the process through which the essay was created, consistent with his high school experiences, Diego seemed to "form as well as perform" (Bartlett & Holland, 2002, p. 14) similar identities as a hardworking student who was motivated to complete classroom assignments and eager to enlist his teacher's help to do so. These enactments of identity, and the support from Ms. Harwood they appeared to elicit, helped Diego navigate this event and (eventually) pass the class, even without reading the assigned text. However, when put in the context of the long string of remedial English courses Diego had yet to take, and the dismal rates of success for students in such classes (Razfar & Simon, 2011; Xu, 2016), this success appeared somewhat muted.

"I Was Caring ... But He Made It Really Hard": Leaving the University Although Diego's interactions while writing his *Burro Genius* essay clearly demonstrated some of the ways in which literacy events presented him with challenges in his English classes, he reported not earning passing credit in a range of other courses, including those that featured textbook reading and multiple-choice and short-answer questions on quizzes and tests. One such class was philosophy, an introductory course that fulfilled a liberal arts requirement for Ocean College. (Diego had not yet completed the English course prerequisite for the class, but he was nonetheless permitted to enroll.) In this final literacy event I profile Diego's account of preparing for a mid-term test in this philosophy class, which included both multiple-choice and short-answer questions. His extensive description of this event, which occurred during an interview just after he explained that he would be leaving Ocean College, appeared to sum up Diego's frustrations and literacy-related difficulties with his coursework there. Although extended writing was not a key feature of this literacy event, I have included it in this chapter because of its importance in understanding Diego's language and literacy journey through university settings.

Interactions Infused throughout Diego's descriptions of the mid-term philosophy test and his preparation for it was a discourse of shared struggle with his fellow students. Specifically, he consistently described having a group of several close friends in the class with whom he interacted and who had the same experience as Diego: "Everybody said like they hated that class and it was really hard" (Interview, 20 July 2012). He also described many of his assessment preparations and experiences as shared. For example, he explained that "everybody reads the book," and "everybody makes a lot of note cards," and in relation to the test itself, "we see the test" or "we don't know the answers" (Interview, 20 June 2012). I was not able to observe these events, and so it was impossible to know exactly how similar Diego's experiences were to those of other students, but the consistency of these descriptions suggested a disconnection from his teacher—unlike his experience with Ms. Harwood or teachers in high school—and a possible sense of connection with peers.

Interactions with the teacher, textbook, and fellow classmates were significant in Diego's preparation for his mid-term test, which he described preparing for in the same ways as he had for other tests and quizzes in the class. He reported following the teacher's instructions for reading: "We needed to read the book so I read the book. [The instructor] said, 'You'd better start to pay attention to every single thing the book says,' [and so I] did" (Interview, 20 June 2012). He also described making note cards with important vocabulary words and facts from the reading, even though this was not a strategy explicitly suggested by the teacher. Diego reported studying with other students outside of class, quizzing each other on words from the textbook using their note cards.

Impacts Such interactions, however, appeared to have been insufficient to prepare for the mid-term test. Diego explained that, "We see the test and then we start reading. We don't know the answers. There's nothing the same as what we studied." He then described particular challenges with questions that required students to apply their learning:

> We'll read something an important person did – he did this and that. And the test wants, "What makes him do that and his reasoning to do that?" We actually [didn't] pay attention to that. And then he writes, "What is the opposite or meaning of this word?" So we don't know the opposite of the meaning of that word. And then he writes, "What is the difference between this person and this person?" We don't know that. (Interview, 20 June 2012)

In this sense, Diego's (and possibly his classmates') preparations, which seemed to focus on memorization rather than application, were a mismatch for the kinds of questions that the instructor posed on the mid-term. Diego related ongoing struggles with these types of questions, suggesting that even after first encountering them on the mid-term, he was not able to better prepare for similar ones on subsequent quizzes and tests.

Diego's difficulties with these test questions had a clear impact on his instructor's perception of him, which I gained insight into through his written feedback on a take-home essay Diego completed later in the semester. For this assignment, students had to answer guiding questions about an imaginary scenario and their opinions of the ethics of what the people involved did, or should have done. The scenario drew upon ideas in the course readings, but the assignment itself did not require explicit references to the textbook. At the end of Diego's paper, the instructor wrote a single final comment: "OK. B, 85%. Imagine what you could get if you cared about your work." Surprised by this, I asked Diego in an interview what his reaction was when he received that feedback from his teacher. He said,

> We already took like two quizzes and the mid-term before we wrote that, so probably that's why he meant that, like "why you don't get like better grades on the quizzes and tests too if you got like a really good grade on the essay?" Well that's how I took it. Because I mean like I would [like to] tell him, "Oh well your quizzes and tests are really hard. It's kind of like I cannot understand that much about what you talk about in class and what we read." … Like I was caring about to pass that class, but he made it really hard. (Interview, 20 July 2012)

Whether or not the teacher was contrasting quiz and essay performance, as Diego understood, or simply communicating an overall assessment of Diego's achievement in the class, the comment's highly critical nature made it clear that Diego was unable to sustain a hardworking student identity in this class. Also notable was that the teacher tied Diego's performance, or as he saw it, underperformance, to a lack of effort and commitment rather than difficulties understanding the material or preparing for the assessments. In the abovementioned interview, however, Diego argued that he cared about the class and tried to do well but struggled with both comprehension of lectures and test preparation. Perhaps because the university English course required for graduation was a prerequisite for this class, the philosophy instructor may have assumed students already had sufficient preparation in the language/literacy and critical thinking practices his course required.

Change Over Time According to Diego's description of the mid-term literacy event, the ways in which he read did not appear to be the "real" literacy practice in which his teacher was expecting him engage: that of reading critically in order to apply rather than simply recall ideas and information. Unfortunately, Diego's recounting of this event did not provide any evidence that his interactions with other people or resources helped him develop expertise in those literacy practices through the semester, in that he prepared for each quiz and test in the same way. Further, the institutional setting—a non-remedial class in which particular language and literacy practices were supposedly prerequisites rather than the subject of learning—as well as the outlook of this particular teacher led to a situation in which Diego's hardworking identity was not sustained, his needs as a developing English user were not considered, and his bilingual and biliterate expertise appeared to be ignored completely. He was instead seen as academically (and perhaps by extension linguistically) competent but not putting forth effort, an identity with which Diego did not agree.

Contradictions Between Identity, Classroom Performance, and Institutional Expectations

As a student in an untracked high school, Diego supposedly had access to curricula that would prepare him for postsecondary schooling (a concern raised by many researchers of EL-classified students: see Chap. 4). Further, his high school grades appeared to be a testament to mastering these curricula. However, his experiences suggest a far more complicated picture of language- and literacy-related university readiness, one in which there were deep contradictions between Diego's identity as an eager student and an increasingly competent English user, the success that his interactions with some of his teachers allowed as he participated in literacy events, and the limitations of those efforts in supporting his academic success.

Like Jaime (Chap. 4), Diego navigated a postsecondary education system that positioned him as needing remediation and offered a long and uncertain pathway before he could engage in courses that were directly tied to his interests, unlike Ana (Chap. 5), Fabiola (Chap. 7), and Maria (Chap. 8). Diego was unique, however, in reporting ongoing and consistent difficulties with reading comprehension over the years of the study, even in the context of remedial courses. In this sense, it appeared that secondary and postsecondary teachers and institutions did not adequately address his unique literacy background and instructional needs, which were shaped at least in part by his history of interrupted education. (Such issues resonate with a larger concern about services for multilingual immigrant students in US schools not being adequately differentiated for students with limited or interrupted schooling: see DeCapua, 2016).

Diego made important strides in English language and literacy development during his time in high school and university, developing from a 14-year-old who rarely spoke or wrote in the language, to a teenager who captivated his 12th-grade exhibition audience through a 45-minute multimodal presentation in English, to a 20-year-old who was successful in university Calculus classes. These accomplishments—especially in light of his interrupted education, his family's extremely limited financial resources, and his status as a first-generation high school graduate and university student—are remarkable. Further, Diego's identity as a dedicated and hardworking student was far from only a performance. In my observations, he really *was* the person who often stayed after school for office hours, and who was deeply committed to learning and succeeding in school.

In light of these clear strengths, a pressing question is: Why did a student like Diego, who graduated from high school recognized as an increasingly competent English user who met and even exceeded academic expectations, then struggle so dramatically once in university? Postsecondary (or "college") readiness is a multifaceted concept, encompassing interacting factors such as cognitive strategies, content knowledge, academic behaviors, and contextual skills and awareness about how to navigate institutions (Conley, 2008). In Diego's case, these factors played varied roles in his transition to university. In terms of his initial placement in university classes, classroom performance—in which he could appeal for teacher assistance, seek help from other students in Spanish, or draw upon multiple modalities to communicate his message—suddenly mattered less than individual performance on a standardized placement measure, which labeled Diego as needing remediation and thus deviating from a "normal" postsecondary student (Harklau, 1999). Once in remedial English classes, early teacher assessments of his writing reinforced a sense of not knowing the basics, but by the end of the second semester, he appeared to again be able to successfully navigate literacy events through interactions with teachers. Diego's identity as a hardworking student and an increasingly competent English user were key to his classroom-based approach to writing, which provided him a level of success in completing assignments and eventually passing classes in ways similar to a university L2 writer profiled in Leki (1999), who developed survival skills that helped him complete courses but that did not fully support his learning or development of critical thinking skills.

Such classroom- and teacher-based strategies were not as applicable or successful in all classes. In Diego's philosophy course, for example, he was not able to develop or sustain either academic success or a hardworking identity in a course whose main assessments (quizzes and tests) relied on critical reading and out-of-class preparation rather than in-class writing activities through which he could interact with fellow students and teachers. He also clearly faced challenges with reading and then writing about book-length fiction and memoir across both high school and university. There are many possible explanations why these genres and texts might have posed particular difficulties for Diego: their length, the necessary background knowledge needed to understand the historical and sociocultural contexts in which they were set, the use of metaphorical and figurative language and nonlinear or elliptical structures, their limited visual representations to support the written text, and other textual complexities. What is key, however, is that Diego's high school teachers did not engage in individualized reading instruction that recognized his unique needs and potentially could have supported his later engagement in writing about texts, given the mutually reinforcing roles that reading and writing have been shown to play, particularly in postsecondary settings (Leki, 2007; Spack, 1997; Sternglass, 1997). Further, neither high school nor university teachers "saw" Diego's difficulties with reading comprehension until essay writing was already underway. This is an unfortunately common oversight in many secondary and postsecondary classrooms, and teachers' subsequent actions were sympathetic and understandable choices given institutional demands and expectations related to curricula and assessments. Yet their efforts to support his completion of the assigned essays unfortunately did not provide Diego with new tools to cope more successfully with such literacy events in the future. Further, Diego's experiences with his philosophy mid-term highlighted ways in which his approach to reading textbooks—as a memorization activity—was similarly mismatched with instructor expectations, and his teacher's response exemplifies the ways that literacy-related difficulties can be misinterpreted as problems of motivation and effort.

Missing so far from this discussion is the extent to which Diego's journey was also a bilingual and biliterate one, and this absence was a key part of his story. In many ways, Diego's uses of multiple languages and literacies were a prominent feature of his academic and social experiences, particularly in high school. For example, Diego first developed his identity as a hardworking student in ninth grade through interactions in Spanish with his bilingual teachers. Further, many of Diego's school-based texts in high school were created through interactions with not only his teachers but also his classmates, almost all of whom were fellow Spanish/English bilinguals with whom he fluidly used resources across both languages to develop his writing. Likewise, bilingual resources were key to many other oral literacy practices, such as informal and small-group conversations during high school with bilingual peers about (English-medium) texts students were reading and other academic content they were learning. To these more school-based experiences with bilingualism and biliteracies can be added the many ways in which Diego's social relationships with family and friends were built and sustained through both languages via social media, texting, and face-to-face conversations throughout his teenage and young adult years. However, Diego engaged in discourses of academic growth in ways that highlighted a linguistically minoritized identity, for example, presenting his written uses of Spanish in ninth grade simply as evidence of weaknesses in English. In many ways, this pattern was unsurprising, given broader discourses minoritizing non-English languages as well as the transitional nature of his bilingual humanities course, in which shifting into English-medium writing was a major focus of instruction. Diego's investment in a hard-working English user identity appeared to come at the cost of recognizing his bilingual and biliterate expertise, a pattern that unfortunately did not bring him the institutional academic success to which he aspired.

Notes

1. I employ the term "user" (Cook, 2002) to emphasize the ways in which Diego was seen by others as not simply learning English for later use but actively using his existing linguistic resources for the real-life task of learning academic content through English. All the students in this study were English users, but my emphasis on the term in this chapter highlights the ways in which Diego was increasingly recognized as such by his high school teachers, rather than as a "learner" deemed unable to use English to accomplish his goals at school.

2. See also Chap. 3 for a discussion of the methodological implications of this development.

3. Diego uses the conditional form of "*ser*" (*sería*), followed by the imperfect subjunctive form of "*estar*" (*estuviera*). Given the question he is responding to, in this transcript it is assumed that the meaning he intends is conditional ("My English would be...").

4. Diego uses a similar construction to that described in the previous footnote, this time using the imperfect subjunctive form of "*tener*" (*tuviera*). Given the question he is responding to, in this transcript, it is assumed that the meaning he intends is conditional ("I would have...").

5. Diego's expression "*nunca se me va a dejar de olvidar* / I will never forget" (or literally, I will never stop forgetting) can be interpreted as a combination of the two phrases "*nunca se me va a olvidar* / I'm never going to forget" and "*nunca lo voy a dejar de recordar* / I'm never going to stop remembering," given the information that follows this utterance ("*entre mi familia, siempre hablamos puro español*" / in my family we always speak only Spanish).

6. It should be noted that Diego's ninth-grade bilingual humanities teacher used what some might today consider to be a translanguaging approach (García, Ibarra Johnson, & Seltzer, 2016) in her writing pedagogy, in that she encouraged students to use their Spanish resources when writing in English (and vice versa), for example, using words in Spanish when they did not know them in English. His writing here likely reflects that guidance.

7. Because of its length, this data is presented somewhat differently from other instances of audio-recorded, observed classroom interactions: I did not divide intonation units into separate lines, and to improve readability I capitalized the beginning of intonational units at the beginning of the data and after stopping fall or rising tone. See the Methodological Appendix for a full listing of transcription conventions.

References

Bartlett, L., & Holland, D. (2002). Theorizing the space of literacy practices. *Ways of Knowing Journal, 2*(1), 10–22.

Conley, D. T. (2008). Rethinking college readiness. *New Directions for Higher Education, 2008*(144), 3–13. https://doi.org/10.1002/he.321.

Cook, V. J. (2002). Background to the L2 user. In V. J. Cook (Ed.), *Portraits of the L2 user* (pp. 1–28). Clevedon, UK: Multilingual Matters.

DeCapua, A. (2016). Reaching students with limited or interrupted formal education through culturally responsive teaching. *Language and Linguistics Compass, 10*(5), 225–237. https://doi.org/10.1111/lnc3.12183.

García, O., Ibarra Johnson, S., & Seltzer, K. (2016). *The translanguaging classroom: Leveraging student bilingualism for learning*. Philadelphia: Caslon.

García, O., Pujol-Ferran, M., & Reddy, P. (2013). Educating international and immigrant students in U.S. higher education: Opportunities and challenges. In A. Doiz, D. Lasagabaster, & J. M. Serra (Eds.), *English-medium instruction at universities: Global challenges* (pp. 174–195). Bristol, UK: Multilingual Matters.

Harklau, L. (1999). Representations of immigrant language minorities in US higher education. *Race Ethnicity and Education, 2*(2), 257–279. https://doi.org/10.1080/1361332990020206.

Harklau, L. (2000). From the "good kids" to the "worst": Representations of English language learners across educational settings. *TESOL Quarterly, 34*(1), 35–67. https://doi.org/10.2307/3588096.

Harklau, L. (2001). From high school to college: Student perspectives on literacy practice. *Journal of Literacy Research, 33*(1), 33–70. https://doi.org/10.1080/10862960109548102

Hillman, L. (2005). *I will plant you a lilac tree*. New York: Simon & Schuster.

Kanno, Y., & Grosik, S. A. (2012). Immigrant English learners' transitions to university: Student challenges and institutional policies. In Y. Kanno & L. Harklau (Eds.), *Linguistic minority students go to college: Preparation, access, and persistence* (pp. 130–147). New York: Routledge.

Kanno, Y., & Varghese, M. M. (2010). Immigrant and refugee ESL college students' challenges to accessing four-year college education: From language policy to educational policy. *Journal of Language, Identity and Education, 9*(5), 310–328. https://doi.org/10.1080/15348458.2010.517693.

Kibler, A. K. (2010). Writing through two languages: First language expertise in a language minority classroom. *Journal of Second Language Writing, 19*(3), 121–142. https://doi.org/10.1016/j.jslw.2010.04.001.

Kibler, A. K. (2011a). "*Casi nomás me dicen qué escribir*/They almost just tell me what to write": A longitudinal analysis of teacher-student interactions in a linguistically diverse mainstream secondary classroom. *Journal of Education, 191*(1), 45–58.

Kibler, A. K. (2011b). "I write it in a way that people can read it": How teachers and adolescent L2 writers describe content area writing. *Journal of Second Language Writing, 20*(3), 211–226. https://doi.org/10.1016/j.jslw.2011.05.005.

Kibler, A. K. (2013). "Doing like almost everything wrong": An adolescent multilingual writer's transition from high school to college. In L. C. de Oliveira & T. Silva (Eds.), *L2 writing in secondary classrooms: Student experiences, academic issues, and teacher education* (pp. 44–64). New York: Routledge.

Kibler, A. K. (2014). From high school to the noviciado: An adolescent linguistic minority student's multilingual journey in writing. *The Modern Language Journal, 98*(2), 629–651. https://doi.org/10.1111/modl.12090.

Kibler, A. K. (2016). Promises and limitations of literacy sponsors in resident multilingual youths' transitions to postsecondary schooling. In C. Ortmeier-Hooper & T. Ruecker (Eds.), *Linguistically diverse immigrant and resident writers: Transitions from high school to college* (pp. 99–116). New York: Routledge.

Leki, I. (1999). 'Pretty much I screwed up': Ill-served needs of a permanent resident. In L. Harklau, K. M. Losey, & M. Siegal (Eds.), *Generation 1.5 meets college composition: Issues in the teaching of writing to U.S.-educated learners of English as a second language* (pp. 17–43). Mahwah, NJ: Lawrence Erlbaum.

Leki, I. (2007). *Undergraduates in a second language: Challenges and complexities of academic literacy development.* Mahwah, NJ: Lawrence Erlbaum.

Markandaya, K. (1954). *Nectar in a sieve.* New York: Penguin Putnam Books.

McDermott, R. P., & Roth, D. (1978). Social organization of behavior: Interactional approaches. *Annual Review of Anthropology, 7*(1), 321–345. https://doi.org/10.1146/annurev.an.07.100178.001541

Razfar, A., & Simon, J. (2011). Course-taking patterns of Latino ESL students: Mobility and mainstreaming in urban community colleges in the United States. *TESOL Quarterly, 45*(4), 595–627. https://doi.org/10.5054/tq.2011.268060.

Schleppegrell, M. (2004). *The language of schooling: A functional linguistics perspective.* Mahwah, NJ: Erlbaum.

Spack, R. (1997). The acquisition of academic literacy in a second language. *Written Communication, 14*(1), 3–62. https://doi.org/10.1177/0741088397014001001.

Sternglass, M. S. (1997). *Time to know them: A longitudinal study of writing and learning at the college level.* Mahwah, NJ: Lawrence Erlbaum.

Villaseñor, V. (2004). *Burro genius: A memoir.* New York: Harper Collins.

Xu, D. (2016). Assistance or obstacle? The impact of different levels of English developmental education on underprepared students in community colleges. *Educational Researcher, 45*(9), 496–507. https://doi.org/10.3102/0013189X16683401.

7

Becoming a "Mexican Feminist": Disciplinary Becoming Through Interactional Histories Across Communities and Contexts

Fabiola was born in the California community of South Sierra but moved with her family to Mexico, where her parents had been born and raised, before beginning formal schooling. She recalled her family living paycheck to paycheck in her childhood but supporting her academically: Fabiola explained that because her mother completed high school (which many other parents in the community had not), she was more aware of her children's educational needs than most and was also able to support Fabiola with schoolwork. Fabiola completed nine years of Spanish-medium schooling in Mexico, through the end of *secundaria* (grades 7–9). She recalled performing well academically at her local public school even though her teachers often seemed to have had limited expertise in education and pedagogy. When she was 15, Fabiola and her mother decided that Fabiola should move back to South Sierra to live with her aunt and attend school there, with hopes of her earning a university degree and having a career in the United States.

Portions of this chapter draw from data first published in Kibler (2016), Kibler (2017), and Kibler and Hardigree (2017).

At South Sierra High School, Fabiola finished her homework regularly and earned higher grades in her classes than did many of her peers. At times, she maintained a distance from classmates in order to complete schoolwork. For example, youth typically used study times in advisory (or homeroom) classes for socializing, but Fabiola claimed a corner of her 12th-grade advisor's room with a sign saying "Fabiola's Office – Quiet!" This focus paid off. Although standardized state assessments labeled her English as *beginning* (the lowest of five proficiency levels) when she began high school, she went on to easily pass the state's standardized high school exit exam, earn a 4.12 weighted GPA, and receive the school's Founders Award at graduation, which was designated for "a student who shows determination and overcomes significant challenges to graduate." Fabiola also had a strong network of friends at school, composed primarily, but not exclusively, of youth whom she first met in Ms. Gutiérrez's bilingual humanities class in ninth grade. Apart from academics, Fabiola participated in Student Council and worked 20 hours a week throughout high school at a local convenience store, where her multilingual supervisors and co-workers came from a range of different countries but none spoke Spanish.

Through teacher recommendation, Fabiola was accepted and awarded a scholarship to a top-tier state university, West Coast University (WCU), where she entered with interests in international business but later chose to complete a Gender and Women's Studies (GWS) major instead. Through writing-intensive courses such as "Introduction to Feminist Theory," "Transnational Feminism," "Cultural Representations of Sexuality," and "Chicana Feminist Writers," among others, Fabiola came to self-identify as a "Mexican feminist," suggesting a strong sense of disciplinary becoming (Stevens, O'Connor, Garrison, Jocuns, & Amos, 2008) developed through her literacy practices in the major. At the same time, however, her identity as a linguistically minoritized writer constrained some of the potential that this disciplinary becoming provided.

As a result of the significant ways in which this disciplinary engagement shaped her language and literacy development during the eight years of the study, I examine her choice of the GWS major as the turning point in her journey (see Table 7.1). In the sections that follow, I first provide an overview of Fabiola's language and literacy experiences to describe larger contexts of development during the study. Then, I use a

Table 7.1 Fabiola's turning point and literacy events presented through LIHA analysis

	Before the turning point		Turning point	After the turning point	
Literacy event	"She helped many people"	"Dishwashers and aprons"	Declaring GWS major	"I sent it to my aunt"	"I'm a Mexican feminist"
Year	Grade 12	Grade 13		Grade 14	Grade 16
Task	Presentation on democracy in Jordan (argumentation/ report[a])	Advertisement analysis (argumentation)		Research paper (argumentation)	Blogs (argumentation/ narration/ recount)
Institutional context (if applicable)	Untracked high school humanities class	First-semester university writing class		University Chicano studies/GWS class	University GWS class

Notes: [a]Genre labels in parentheses are aligned with those originally presented in Kibler (2014), as adapted from Schleppegrell (2004)

longitudinal interactional histories approach (LIHA) to analyze two literacy events before and two literacy events after this turning point in order to understand the interactions influencing her production of texts, how they did so, and patterns of change over time as she developed a Mexican feminist identity both inside and outside of disciplinary contexts.

Overview of Fabiola's Language and Literacy Experiences

During High School At South Sierra High School, Fabiola was enrolled as a ninth grader and placed in a bilingual humanities course, an ELD course, and untracked English-medium classes in all other subjects. Other than a single additional ELD course in tenth grade, Fabiola was enrolled in untracked courses for the remainder of her high school career: These included humanities, math, science, community college classes, and two Spanish-for-Native-Speakers courses.

Fabiola engaged bilingually with classmates and Spanish-speaking teachers throughout her high school career using resources across languages, but even in courses taught by instructors who did not speak Spanish, she participated in lessons by asking questions and contributing to discussions when asked to. She did so only reluctantly in her first years of high school, however, and often expressed to me her insecurities about speaking English in those settings. As she told me, *"No me gusta mi pronunciación en inglés,* so *por eso prefiero no hablar.* / I don't like my pronunciation in English, so that's why I prefer not to talk" (Interview, 12 February 2008). This concern seemed to gradually diminish during her time in high school, in that Fabiola became a far more active participant and was even at times reprimanded by her teachers for dominating (English-medium) classroom conversations.

Fabiola aspired to be both bilingual and biliterate. As a tenth grader envisioning herself at age 25, she said, *"Ya los voy a tener los dos [inglés y español] bien metidos. Para hablar, va a ser difícil, pero para escribir y leer, yo pienso que van a estar igual, van a ser bien.* / I will already have both [English and Spanish] well in place. To speak, it will be hard, but to write and read, I think they will be the same, they will be good" (Interview, 12 February 2008). She also felt confident in her reading expertise, explaining that even as a tenth grader, "*Lectura [en inglés], puedo entender casi todo. Oh, y leer en español, me encanta leer en español.* / Reading [in English], I can understand almost everything. Oh, and reading in Spanish, I love reading in Spanish" (Interview, 12 February 2008). Although I did not have many opportunities to observe Fabiola reading or discussing Spanish texts,[1] I found that her reading self-assessment proved largely accurate in relation to the English texts she read in her classes. For example, in reading assigned books in her tenth-grade humanities class, although she at times asked bilingual classmates or adults for help understanding individual words or phrases she encountered in those texts, her written work and participation in group discussions demonstrated that her reading comprehension was generally on par with many students in her class, including those who were US-born and educated. (This stands in contrast to Diego's experiences: See Chap. 6.)

During high school, Fabiola drew upon her bilingual and biliterate expertise to write a range of texts outside of classroom requirements, including messages composed for her MySpace account and texting, and, less often, in a personal journal she shared with me. In her MySpace page, Fabiola typically used English-language templates and posted graphics with inspirational quotations in English, but also created texts of her own that employed diverse language resources (García, 2009) as well as bilingual wordplay (e.g., Martínez & Morales, 2014). Examples of her online texts included tag lines about herself during high school such as, "I misS My PaPi Y mAmi VeRi MucHo" (I miss my dad and mom very much) and "HeCha X LoS mEjOrEs FaBrIcAnTeS (MAMI Y PAPI)" (Made by the best manufacturers, Mom and Dad). Comments with friends used similar language patterns, including a range of conventions typical of texting and social media at the time. Such online communications with family and friends in South Sierra, elsewhere in California, and in her hometown in Mexico helped her maintain ongoing connections locally, translocally, and transnationally, much as Lam (2009) found in the adolescent immigrant she studied.

Fabiola also participated in a Saturday poetry-writing program over the course of several months during tenth grade in which youth had opportunities to write both traditional and multimodal texts in any language. Although she completed many of those in English, the final poem she wrote, which was included in the glossy magazine published by the program, employed resources spanning multiple languages:

```
The eye
  The eye is small but with a center
  Eye is like humans
  humans can show feelings;
  When you are sad you can make an ocean
  in your own world.
  When you are happy you show it
  with a naked teeth
  Eye is like humans
  Eye can feel the nothing
  see nothing or
  hear nothing.
  Eye reflect feelings of the heart
  but just eyes know the value of love
  The center of an eye can show the
  value of a true love.
  El iris del ojo parpadea
  cuando siente amor.
  A veces esa pequeña pupila
  se queda sin parpadear
  como el corazón se queda sin su amor.²
  Eye can betray feelings
  just with a gaze.
```

In looking at her poem, which was placed on the first page of the magazine anthology, she described feeling proud because her writing had never been in a venue where so many people could read it. Notably, among the youth in this study who attended the program, she was the only one who chose to write a translingual (Canagarajah, 2013) text of this type for the magazine. When asked what she enjoyed about the program, Fabiola described the freedom they were given to write about their own ideas and feelings in whatever form and language they chose.

In school contexts, Fabiola's ninth-grade bilingual humanities course offered opportunities to write in either English or Spanish (or a combination of the two[3]), and while her first essays were in Spanish, her essays and in-class assignments later in the year increasingly used English, drawing admiration from her ELD teacher, who responded to a short text she wrote at the end of ninth grade by saying, "I am so proud of you for writing the whole thing in English! Good job!!" (I problematize the implications of this rapid push toward a transition into English later in this chapter and elsewhere in the book.) Fabiola's own confidence in her English writing grew substantially through her high school career. In tenth grade, she was already noting the presence of "more formal" words in her writing (Interview, 13 March 2008) and even boasted to her humanities teacher about a journal entry she wrote ("What about if my journal, it's like excellent?" Observation, 8 January 2008). In other moments, though, she felt that her writing had improved relatively little during the early years of high school. Yet, when I asked her to describe a persuasive essay she wrote in 12th grade, she explained, "It was much better than other years. *Pienso que este año estoy escribiendo como lenguaje más profesional, no como antes que usaba palabras más cortitas.* / I think that this year I'm writing language that's more professional than before, when I used shorter words" (Interview, 3 June 2010).

Despite these positive assessments of her English writing by the end of high school, Fabiola was somewhat critical of the writing instruction she received there. In an interview at the end of her 12th-grade year, she spoke positively about the ways in which the school helped her grow as a person, but faulted it for not preparing her and other students well for writing at the postsecondary level, explaining that "*Muchos dicen que van a la universidad y la escritura que nosotros tenemos es de lo peor, que no sirve, sino que tenemos que empezar de cero.* / Many [former South Sierra High School students] say that they go to university and our writing is the worst, that it doesn't work for them, and that we have to start from nothing" (Interview, 3 June 2010). As a result, Fabiola readily predicted writing to be the most significant challenge she would face in university.

During University In her first semester at WCU, Fabiola was enrolled in three (non-remedial) courses: a compulsory writing class, an English course that focused on literature and ethnic studies, and pre-calculus. In reflecting on her experiences during an interview just a month into her first semester at the university, she told me:

> *Estás rodeada de mucha gente tan inteligente que te quedas así como,* "Wow I don't fit here." *Es como que no hay [mi] lugar. Yeah, es raro. Pero gracias a Dios no soy la única así.* / You are surrounded by a lot of very smart people so that you sit there thinking, "Wow I don't fit here." It's like this place isn't for me. Yeah, it's strange. But thank God I'm not the only one like that. (Interview, 28 September 2010)

She went on to mention that many of her classmates and fellow scholarship recipients had similar experiences, and that simply knowing they shared this experience was reassuring.

Fabiola identified writing as a key struggle at that time, as Kanno and Grosik's (2012) participants did. Her writing courses (two in total, one per semester of her first year) required Fabiola to produce English writing more frequently and with higher teacher expectations than she had experienced before. During her first semester Fabiola asked me to give her feedback on drafts of her writing, something that I had previously offered to do if she thought it would be it helpful (see Methodological Appendix). I did so at her request for each of the major writing assignments she completed during her university studies, although I was rarely the only person from whom she solicited feedback.

Fabiola described her first-semester writing instructor as being critical of her writing in many respects, including her arguments, evidence, and organization, as well as language use more generally. On one essay, for example, he wrote, "Overall, it seems to me that you are struggling with the very basics of essay writing and also of reading: I suspect that you have some language issues that keep you from expressing yourself as clearly as you might otherwise." Despite his warning to her that she might not pass the class, which was assessed according to a final portfolio graded by other instructors, Fabiola earned a C+ (on a scale of A-F, with A-C as passing). Her instructor advised her not to take the next required writing class in the sequence the following semester but to wait a year or two for her English to develop, but because of a lack of courses available, she decided to enroll in the second writing class despite his warning. Her second writing course was a far better experience, she explained, because her teacher gave more "concrete" suggestions for revision and allowed students to select the topics about which they would write. By the end of that class, Fabiola noted improvement in both her writing and her instructor's assessment of it:

> *Al final me dijo la maestra que mi escritura no era muy aun,* "professional level" *dice, "pero está bien a comparación de tu primer* essay." / In the end the teacher told me that my writing was not really at the "professional level," she says, "but it's good compared to your first essay." (Interview, 22 June 2011)

As might be expected, Fabiola continued to experience challenges related to university writing assignments after her initial writing courses. Her GWS classes required a range of essays and reading responses, and multiple-draft essays were typically the primary and sometimes only forms of assessment. Fabiola at times received critical comments noting that her writing was, in her words, "all over the place" (Interview, 21 June 2012), or needed to be "more formal" (Interview, 9 November 2012). Based on my reading of written feedback she shared with me throughout her university studies, it was often constructive and supportive, but in other instances it also critiqued Fabiola's argumentation, interpretations of readings, and grammar. Representative comments of this sort were: "You seem to be misinterpreting the reading here"; "Your argument isn't clear"; "The essay, however, really falls apart in the second half"; and "There're quite a few grammatical mistakes in your paper." Over the years, however, her teachers' evaluations gradually became more positive, and Fabiola herself noted progress not only in her writing quality but also in her ability to write increasingly longer texts while keeping up with lengthy, dense readings and demanding deadlines. My own analysis of her writing showed development as well, particularly in terms of the argumentative essays she was frequently asked to produce (Kibler & Hardigree, 2017). Fabiola's overall strong performance in her major was clear: Although I was not always able to obtain teacher feedback and grades for each individual assignment, she earned a 3.41 (out of 4.0) GPA in her GWS courses, compared to a 2.9 overall for all university coursework.

Fabiola's bilingual practices while in university represented both stability and change. For example, she continued using primarily Spanish with family and close friends in a range of face-to-face and social media venues. In academic and work spaces (the latter of which included university work-study employment in dining services), English remained the official medium of communication with teachers and supervisors, and both English and bilingual communication continued to be more common with fellow students and employees. A notable change from high school to university, however, was visible in her uses of Spanish in school-based writing. She explained to me—a trend that I confirmed by looking at her drafts of writing—that although she worked quickly to transition into English-only writing in high school and actively avoided using Spanish while writing early in her career as an undergraduate, in her later years of university studies, she felt more comfortable doing so and recognized its importance:

> Now when I'm trying to write a sentence and it's not coming, that I don't feel that it's clear, I stop and think in Spanish and say, "How would I phrase this in Spanish?" then I think about it, then I try to write it in English. And then there are words that I just I don't know, I'll just write them in Spanish and then go back later. (Interview, 21 May 2014)[4]

This strategic use of Spanish is typical of advanced writers' continuing uses of resources across languages (de Courcy, 2002; Seloni, 2014) and was clearly helpful in Fabiola's English composing processes. However, these self-sponsored uses of Spanish were in no way the kinds of sustained experiences with writing that would have been necessary for her to create extended Spanish texts in disciplinary registers. While advanced university courses in Spanish could arguably have played such a role, Fabiola never took any Spanish-medium classes. Her scholarship advisors and mentors never actively discouraged her from doing so, but they primarily focused on ensuring she was completing her required courses, of which there were many, especially because she began university with a lighter course load at her scholarship advisors' suggestion. Her schedule was further restricted because she added a minor in legal studies for greater "employability," also upon the advice of advisors and mentors for her scholarship.

Fabiola's lack of school-based Spanish writing experiences in high school and university led to a situation that was predictable, if not foreseen, by Fabiola herself. Just before university graduation, I asked her, "Do you consider yourself a bilingual writer? An English writer? A Spanish writer? Something else entirely?" She responded, "This is embarrassing, but I feel like I'm just an English writer. I feel like my Spanish is so bad right now, you have no idea" (Interview, 21 May 2014). It is important to note that Fabiola's sentiments here equate school-based writing with writing in general, and as a result overlooked her many skillful everyday uses of written Spanish. However, they struck me as particularly poignant given her hopes just six years earlier about her biliterate future (*"Para escribir y leer, yo pienso que van a estar igual, van a ser bien. /* To write and read, I think they will be the same, they will be good." Interview, 12 February 2008).

Writing in GWS By the time she had taken several GWS classes, Fabiola spoke about the writing she completed for her major in unique terms. For example, during an interview in which we discussed her sense of audience when she wrote, I asked:

Amanda: When you think about who your community is, does it change depending on the class or the writing assignment? Does the "we" sort of shift in terms of who you're talking about and the community you're representing?

Fabiola: I think that when I use "we" and "us," it's because I want to include myself in that group. And I've definitely used it more often in my Gender and Women's Studies classes because I feel more a part of the community. Whereas in the Legal Studies classes, I might have been more specific about who "we" are or maybe saying "some people."
(Interview, 15 November 2013)

Her GWS community was also the only context in which university classmates played a prominent role in her descriptions of courses. For example, she talked about having both individual friendships and knowing "lots of people" (Interview, 9 November 2012) in her classes as well as seeking and providing peer writing feedback on assignments. At graduation time, Fabiola decided to attend only the GWS and not the university-wide ceremony, explaining that "I just decided that, you know, GWS, that's where I felt more like I fit in, more comfortable being myself" (Interview, 21 May 2014).

I attended Fabiola's GWS graduation, an experience that helped me understand both the community itself and its relationship to Fabiola's language and literacy development. As the ceremony began, the 22 graduates who proudly filed past represented demographics different from those at West Coast University overall: Many GWS students were Latinx[5] and Black, even though the overall university population was predominantly White and Asian. Once graduates took their seats, a Cuban-born professor in her 50s who served as the GWS department chair began the opening speech. She reflected on students' experiences in the major, emphasizing that the degree was "not just about content … We teach students to write, and edit, and write, and edit some more" (Observation, 22 May 2014). The professor then continued, describing other goals important in the major, like research, critical engagement, and creative expression. Her emphasis on writing was not necessarily surprising, given the many conversations and rounds of feedback in which Fabiola and I had engaged during her time at WCU, but these public declarations clearly highlighted the importance of writing as a means of participating in the GWS major.

As I came to learn through reading Fabiola's university writing, expectations for writing in her major also reflected larger disciplinary trends. Feminist writing is characterized by a range of topics and conventions, but certain commonalities are notable. For example, feminist scholars since the 1980s have often used "the personal as evidentiary" in their writing, according to Spigelman (2001, p. 66). Such a practice involves an emphasis in feminist writing on lived experiences as "relevant and admissible data" (Foss & Foss, 1994, p. 42), in response to the silencing that women and other minoritized populations often experience through traditional Western forms of argumentative writing. In this way, feminist texts both acknowledge issues of power and "put the personal, the particular, the emotional, the subjective and the 'private' on the agenda" (Davies, 2012, p. 748).

These disciplinary distinctions are important because the process of Fabiola's disciplinary "becoming" was deeply intertwined with writing. What makes such uses of writing so complex, however, is that disciplinary writing is far from a monolithic or stable construct in any academic field. Prior (1998) argued that the inherent instability of disciplines; the openness of disciplinary enculturation; and the situated, mediated, and dispersed nature of writing itself all make disciplinary writing a less tangible entity than what many assume.

Such writing, in all its variability, plays important roles in disciplinary becoming, which Stevens et al. (2008) described as developing through three key processes: (1) gaining disciplinary knowledge, (2) identifying oneself (and being recognized by others) as a member of the discipline, and (3) navigating institutional pathways to become officially recognized as having that identity. This development is particularly complex because what counts as disciplinary knowledge (and disciplinary writing) varies depending on the context (Prior, 1998), and identities are often fluid constructions that develop in the context of individual relationships as well as broader power structures (Ivanič, 2006). Further, the navigation of institutional pathways is particularly important when understanding students' experiences, in that they are still learning the conventions of disciplinary writing and as a result may not yet know how to "bend the rules" (Hyland, 2009, p. 29) as more experienced writers do. Students are also in the process of developing a sensitivity to the disciplinary expectations of (sometimes multiple) audiences, which can at times lead them to subvert their own goals and ideas in order to create performances in hopes of meeting instructors' expectations, and in doing so may animate (in Goffman's words, 1981) ideas or ways of writing to which they may have little personal commitment (Hyland, 2012).

Also important to GWS writing were the ways that gender and identity were defined and understood. Two key concepts that arose in Fabiola's studies were that of performativity (Butler, 1990) and intersectionality (Shields, 2008). Performativity relates to the idea that gender is in fact a performance—not simply a biological trait—and one that is socially and historically constructed but also fluid and agentive (see also Kubota & Chiang, 2012, who discuss this in relation to applied linguistics scholarship). Intersectionality—as explained in Chap. 2—relates to the idea that individuals are always multidimensional, in that an individual's race/ethnicity, age, class, sexuality, and (dis)ability, among other factors, all intersect in unique ways to influence processes of privilege and marginalization (see Pavlenko & Piller, 2008, for a description of this process in language learning and education).

As Fabiola's graduation ceremony continued, I came to understand what this intersectionality looked like for students in her GWS major. For example, the aforementioned opening remarks were followed by a lip-synced drag performance by *La Reina* (The Queen), one of the graduating seniors. She performed in Spanish, and many of the graduates and ceremony attendees knew the songs—like "*Como Me Duele*" (How It Hurts Me)—by heart and sang along. The ceremony also included a rap performed by a current GWS student and a commencement speech given by a Puerto-Rican born Hollywood celebrity before the traditional awarding of diplomas. In this way, Fabiola's graduation represented several elements of the GWS disciplinary context at WCU in which she formed her own disciplinary identities through writing.

Fabiola's Longitudinal Interactional Histories

To understand the roles writing played in Fabiola's disciplinary becoming, I explore her literacy experiences through the turning point of selecting GWS as her undergraduate major. I first examine two literacy events preceding this choice that demonstrate ways she used writing to initially explore her interest in feminism in ways that led to the turning point of formally studying GWS as a discipline. I then turn to two key literacy events that occurred after her selection of this major to illustrate how she forged intersectional but circumscribed disciplinary identities through writing. These literacy events are presented below through LIHA analyses; their placement in relation to the turning point is presented in Table 7.1.

Before the Turning Point: Developing Interests in a Discipline Fabiola told me that her mother loves to tell a story about how Fabiola was a feminist even as a child. Frustrated that her younger brother was not responsible for any household chores while she had many, she forced him to help her do the dishes every night. Although this family tale is told in jest, Fabiola more seriously reported having been exposed to the idea of feminism informally as a pre-teen, but not formally or systematically, and not in the context of her academic studies or the writing she undertook. The literacy events in which Fabiola participated were diverse in high school and before she declared her university major, but the two analyzed here demonstrate the beginnings of a disciplinary becoming even outside the context of the GWS major or coursework. I use LIHA analyses to first explore a high school assignment on Jordan and Queen Rania before then examining an essay critique of 1950s gendered advertising from one of Fabiola's first-year writing classes. In doing so, I describe how Fabiola's interactions with people and resources, along with changes she made in her texts, supported both her writing development in English and her burgeoning disciplinary identities.

"She Helped Many People:" Exploring Feminist Ideas Through Writing in High School At South Sierra High School, the texts Fabiola wrote were usually in response to topics assigned by the teacher. A prominent exception to this trend occurred in 12th grade. In her humanities class that year, she had to select a country (for which she chose Jordan), decide whether or not it was democratic based on criteria provided by the teacher, and use this information to develop a lengthy multimodal pre-sentation. Such an assignment seemed to provide little explicit space for developing interests in feminism, but Fabiola drew upon the open-endedness of this assignment to do just that.

Interactions Fabiola's interactions with individuals and texts/technologies during this literacy event were particularly influential in the creation of her text. Fabiola explained that her teacher played an important role through providing lists of (English-language) websites that students could use to find information. Fabiola's choice of country for this assignment was also inspired through interactions with others, in that the manager of the convenience store at which she worked was Jordanian. He often made derogatory comments about Mexico, and these critiques, along with Fabiola's understanding of how women were treated in Jordan, inspired her to learn more about his country. In this way, national/cultural identity and gender—made relevant through her interactions with her manager—played key roles in shaping her written text. Fabiola described not receiving any writing instruction or feedback from her teacher, which also had an influence, described later.

Impacts In terms of the impact Fabiola's interactions had on her multimodal text, the conversations with her manager, the open-ended nature of the assignment, and her teacher's list of websites provided inspiration and access to resources that in turn allowed her to pursue her own burgeoning ideas about gender through study of a particular country. For example, she was required to find three secondary sources on current events in the country to assess its level of democracy, and for one of these, shown in slide 1 ("My Research") of Fig. 7.1, she chose an article on Jordan's endorsement of a bill to curb domestic violence in the country.

Fabiola was also required by the assignment to list the natural and human rights that Jordan supports ("Natural/Human Rights"), and two of the five facts she selected for that slide focused on women's rights, in relation to both domestic violence and honor killings. In addition, the mandatory slide "People of Jordan" included a specific mention of the discrepancies in male/female literacy rates, and the person she chose to exemplify support for democracy in that country was Queen Rania of Jordan. Additionally, Fabiola added a non-required slide on "Women/Men from Jordan," describing gender-specific clothing worn in the country.

Even though only 5 of the 14 total slides in her presentation addressed gender directly, almost all of Fabiola's interview comments about this assignment focused on these issues. For example, she described her favorite part of the project as follows:

My research:

- Article #1 from IRIN: "Jordan government moves to curve domestic violence" ~ Endorse Family Protection bill ~ The bill obligates health care staff and teachers to report to the authorities any incident of family violence ~ 11 of 62 courts in Jordan reported 132 domestic violence cases in 06-07

Natural/Human Rights

- Human Rights in Jordan, are the best in the Middle East
- King Hussein fought for peace between Israel and Jordan
- Law: Work is the right of every citizen; 23.5% live below poverty line of US $2.00 per day
- 42% of women has ben victim of physical violence and even higher number endure sexual and verbal abuse at home
- According to the police records every year 20-25 women are killed "In the name of HONOR"

People of Jordan

- Ethnicity: 98% Arabic, 1%Circassian, 1% Armenian
- Religion: 92% Sunni Muslim, 6% Christian, 2% Shia Muslim.
- Language: Arabic, English(understood among middle and upper class)
- Literacy Rate: read and write - female 84.7%, male 95.1%

Queen Rania of Jordan

- My Hero project: Queen Rania of Jordan is the founder of My Hero project
- She serves as the National Early Childhood Development and Family Safety Council
- She is also member of the UNICEF (United Nation Children's Fund) and the Global Leadership Initiative
- Closely involved with Dar Al-Amman, a center for abused and neglected children, the first of its kind in the Middle East
- Involved with the Jordan Cancer Society and other health topics

Women/Men from Jordan

- Women in Jordan: Most of jordanian women use the Hijab which is part of their religion. The purpose of the Hijab is to show respect to your family but specially to your husband.
- Men in Jordan: The Kanduras is a traditional male dress, they can use it at any time, but most men use it for important occasions.

Fig. 7.1 Selected slides from Fabiola's democracy presentation on Jordan, 12th grade

Lo que más me interesó de todo lo que leí fue la princesa Rania, y pues, ha ayudado a mucha gente y está trabajando para que las mujeres tengan más derechos, y para que todo esté en peace. / What interested me most from everything that I read was Princess Rania, and well, she has helped many people and is working for women to have more rights, and for everything to be in peace. (Interview, 11 March 2010)

Although nothing about the assignment itself, the curriculum of the course, or even her teacher's instruction provided direct guidance or support to focus on gender, the openness of the task allowed her to produce a text that demonstrated a clear interest in issues that would later become central to her disciplinary identities.

However, Fabiola expressed frustration with this literacy event, in that she felt her writing did not adequately explain everything she had learned through her research: "*Pienso que no expliqué bien, ni puse cosas importantes que yo aprendí … Como te digo, es que escribir es más difícil.* / I think that I didn't explain it well, or put important things that I learned … Like I told you, writing is really difficult" (Interview, 11 March 2010). In this sense, a lack of interactions with her teacher or others about writing likely had an impact, at least from Fabiola's perspective, on the effectiveness of her text.

Change Over Time Fabiola's simultaneous interest in her topic and frustration with her text are unsurprising because she reported receiving multiple resources for research but no instruction about writing (or, more specifically, writing from sources) or feedback on her writing for the assignment. In fact, she thought that other texts she had written earlier in high school showed greater writing expertise. However, this literacy event still appeared to be an important opportunity to write-to-learn about both the course content (democracy) and women's issues in different countries. In this way, Fabiola began developing knowledge and interactional histories with gender-related writing that were later extended to more explicitly gender-focused literacy events.

Dishwashers and Aprons: Developing Writing Expertise and Stepping into a Discipline As described earlier, upon high school graduation, Fabiola enrolled at WCU, where she took a sequence of writing courses (among other classes) in her first year. The writing course she took in her first semester included three main argumentative writing assignments that were based, respectively, upon a film (*Far from Heaven*, Patton & Haynes, 2002), advertisements (circa 1950), and a book (*1984*, Orwell, 1949), along with other articles and book chapters related to topics raised in those texts. Here I profile Fabiola's experiences with the second writing task, for which she had to analyze an advertisement from the 1950s and relate it to social roles and consumer culture at that time, drawing upon the book *Mechanical Brides: Women and Machines from Home to Office* (Lupton, 1993), excerpts of which were assigned as class readings. Fabiola's essay—for which she analyzed a 1950 advertisement for a HotPoint brand dishwasher—and the processes through which she created it were key to further developing her disciplinary interests. And unlike her high school assignment, this opportunity for exploring gender-related issues was accompanied by writing instruction.

The pedagogical pattern established in the first writing assignment of the semester and followed in this second assignment was a series of in-class activities on the rhetorical techniques being taught—in this case, creating an argument and carrying it through each paragraph, using multiple sources (including visual ones) as evidence, and employing transitional devices effectively—as well as class discussion of ideas and readings students were expected to draw upon in their writing. The professor provided feedback on their first drafts, which were revised again before being submitted for a grade. The essay was later placed in a final portfolio to be externally assessed by the university's writing program instructors.

Interactions In this literacy event, interactions Fabiola had with texts, her instructor, and me strongly influenced the essay she produced. First, the teacher-provided readings and instructional activities placed a much stronger focus on both gender and writing development than did the 12th-grade writing assignment, offering a more explicit opportunity to develop disciplinary interests through writing. Second, Fabiola's interactions with her instructor (who, as mentioned earlier, was rather critical of her writing) and me via the feedback process were influential on her development of argumentative writing more generally. For example, in his feedback on her first draft, Fabiola's instructor emphasized three primary areas for improvement: (1) word meaning (in particular, misuse of the term, "utilitarian"), (2) sentence-level transitions (in particular, misuse of transitions like "moreover" and "in addition"), and (3) using evidence to support arguments in two of her body paragraphs. When she sent me her instructor's comments and asked me to give her feedback on how to revise her essay, Fabiola had already corrected the first two issues. After receiving my interpretation of his feedback about the third area (argument and evidence), Fabiola made further changes. A tracing of the argument-focused feedback and resulting revisions made to one of her paragraphs is presented in Table 7.2, showing how thoroughly Fabiola's changes responded to the feedback she received.

Table 7.2 Fabiola's sample essay revisions, second year of university

First draft	Lupton explains how mechanical devices played a major role in identifying women's cultural work. For example, one mechanical device that can be related to women's work is a dishwasher, iron...etc. She also explicates that advertisements want to encourage women to buy products not only because they are going to be helpful but because they secure their family health. "[I]n achieving health and happiness, advertising and design have encourage women to embrace house work as women's 'natural' calling" (Lupton). The "HotPoint" ad, advices women to care not only about saving her self some time but also, care about her family health. This in return, will cause her to take care of her family in a better way because they are going to be healthier as well as happy	
Feedback	*Instructor:* It is not at all clear what point you want to make about how and why the Hotpoint dishwasher makes a point about the family health. Is the ad really about housework as woman's "natural" calling? If it is, you don't indicate how it is.	*Amanda:* I think some of the confusion with this paragraph is (1) that you talk about health but your second and fourth sentences don't relate to health at all, and (2) you don't give enough evidence from the HotPoint ad to convince the reader that it's appealing to the idea of health.

(continued)

Table 7.2 (continued)

Revision (new text in bold, deleted text crossed-out, description of changes in brackets)	~~Lupton explains how mechanical devices played a major role in identifying women's cultural work. For example, one mechanical device that can be related to women's work is a dishwasher, iron...etc.~~ [removed first sentence] The "HotPoint" ad, advices women to care not only about saving her self some time but also, care about her family's health. This in return, will cause her to take care of her family in a better way because they are going to be healthier as well as happy. [clarified application to health, based in ad, by moving final sentences to the top of the paragraph] The HotPoint ad also states that "[i]t...protects you family's health by doing dishes the sanitary way" (The HotPoint ad). This quote persuades the wife by letting her know that her job is to wash dishes but also to do them the "sanitary way" and maintain her family's health. [added evidence from ad and explanation] Lupton explicates that advertisements want to encourage women to buy products not only because they are going to be helpful but because they secure their family health. "[I]n achieving health and happiness, advertising and design have encourage women to embrace house work as women's 'natural' calling" (Lupton 15, italics added). In this quote, Lupton endorses that is women's responsibility to maintain her family's health. [added italics to link to health and an explanation of the quotation]

These interactions demonstrated Fabiola's significant motivation to address concerns identified by individuals providing her with feedback, as well as ways in which she relied upon additional feedback from me in order to address more complex issues of argument and evidence that her instructor mentioned but did not provide focused suggestions for revising.

Impacts The instructor's comments did not focus on sentence-level corrections, as some others might have done, and although Fabiola's revised writing still demonstrated features of developing English writing, it contained an improved argumentative structure, earned her a passing grade for the assignment, and eventually became part of a writing portfolio that was also judged as "passing" for the course. This assignment was also clearly important for opportunities it provided Fabiola to develop disciplinary ideas and arguments through writing. In fact, she explained in an interview that the mid-twentieth-century context she wrote about in her essay inspired her to look at more recent representations of gender in advertising, explaining that:

> Times have changed a lot since the '50s. … [but] I looked for [current-day] advertisements about electro-domestics and there's still women with kids, or women helping their husbands or things like that. It's like, oh, why don't they put a man with *un mandil* [an apron]? That would make that product appeal to me. (Interview, 16 December 2010)

Fabiola reported that it was these particular questions and ideas that led her to enroll in her first GWS course, which she took that next semester.

Change Over Time Although Fabiola's writing class was situated in a writing program rather than a disciplinary department, the reading and writing opportunities it provided nonetheless helped to further her awareness of gender issues, both historically and contemporarily. It also led to an interest in the GWS program, which she selected as her major shortly after taking and enjoying the first GWS course in which she enrolled. It could be argued that these interests might have developed in any number of ways, and even outside of institutionally provided and defined writing tasks. However, the manner in which this assignment provided Fabiola with influential opportunities to simultaneously build argumentative writing expertise and disciplinary knowledge suggests that for Fabiola, becoming a feminist was firmly grounded in and expressed through the writing she completed and the interactive processes through which she did so.

After the Turning Point: Forging and Sustaining Disciplinary Identities After taking an introductory GWS course in her second semester, Fabiola signed up for the major and took at least one course in the department each semester as well as a fourth-year capstone project, in which she wrote a senior thesis on masculinity and *machismo* among Mexican second-generation immigrant men. Through these courses she had multiple opportunities to use writing to develop and explore varied identities in relation to disciplinary discourses, and her academic performance in her major was strong. At the same time, not all identities enjoyed similar acceptance in her GWS courses, at least from Fabiola's perspective. To better understand this success and its complexities, I use LIHA analyses to explore two literacy events that occurred after her turning point of selecting the GWS major (see Table 7.1) in order to illuminate some of the ways in which Fabiola's writing in her GWS major both facilitated and restricted her disciplinary becoming.

"I Sent It to My Aunt": Negotiating Non-disciplinary Audiences, Communities, and Identities As she began her second year, Fabiola's coursework was dominated by GWS courses: three in total that fall semester. Although all of the writing she completed in those classes contributed to her disciplinary interests in different ways, one particular literacy event provided particularly useful insights into the complex ways that Fabiola was developing unique and intersectional disciplinary identities through GWS writing opportunities. In her Chicana Feminist Writers class (which was housed in Chicano Studies but counted toward the GWS major), Fabiola wrote a final research paper entitled, "Queerness in Society: Religion and The Latino Community," which she described as the text she had strongest memories of out of all the writing she completed that semester.

Interactions The course focus, as well as the freedom students had to choose their own topic for the argumentative research paper, provided obvious venues for Fabiola to explore and enact a range of identities that were relevant to her lived experiences. However, in talking with her about this text I discovered that a specific out-of-class experience motivated her topic choice. She explained:

Fabiola: I don't know if I told you, but I have a gay cousin and my
             aunt called me [before I started writing the paper] … I asked
             about him. She told me that he was living with his boyfriend,
             and [she said], "Well, you know I love my son and every-
             thing, even though I know that he's not going to be accepted
             by God." You know when people tell you those things that
             you just, you just say like, "Wait, wait, what?" … I felt like
             that this is a good inspiration for me to write about queer-
             ness and religion, since we're Latino. So I was like, "Okay,
             well, this is going to be in the paper." I sent it to her.
Amanda: You did?
Fabiola: Yeah. I don't know what she thinks. She hasn't emailed me
             anything back. I hope she's not mad.
             (Interview, 19 December 2011)

This interaction with her aunt not only shaped the key arguments
Fabiola would address in her paper; it also gave her a non-disciplinary
audience for her writing.[6] Interactions with her Chicano Studies professor also played important roles in shaping her text. This professor
provided the assigned course readings upon which Fabiola drew for her
paper and also suggested additional texts for her particular topic,
including *De Colores* (Barbarosa & Lenoir, 2001), a bilingual documentary about Spanish-speaking communities who support lesbian
and gay family members, and *Fish Out of Water* (Dickens, 2009), a
documentary exploring homosexuality and the Bible. Fabiola also
interacted with me during this event, through feedback on her draft, in
ways that both shaped her text and underscored her negotiation of
non-disciplinary audiences, communities, and identities through disciplinary writing.

Impacts Fabiola's interactions with her aunt, textual resources provided
by her professor, and me all served to shape the text she produced. In
terms of the argumentative structure of the paper, it was organized
almost entirely in response to concerns raised by her aunt. She began
her text by introducing the ways in which queerness is (or is not)

accepted in society before focusing in particular on the acceptance of queerness in religion and then analyzing the acceptance of queerness in Latino communities, which she argued are largely defined by their Christian (and often Catholic) religious affiliation. Her professor's assigned and suggested texts also played key roles in providing Fabiola with ideas around which to build her arguments. For example, Fabiola's use of an assigned text, *Borderlands/La Frontera*, written by well-known feminist writer Anzaldua (1987), allowed her to assert the importance of understanding queerness in society more generally, and in Mexican and Latino communities in particular. Her watching of *De Colores*, in contrast, inspired another familial conversation, this time with her mother:

Fabiola: I'd just watched the documentary and I was just shocked, and I called my Mom and I was like, "Oh, how are you going to do this to other people [by rejecting their homosexuality]?"

Amanda: What was your mom's reaction when you started talking about those
ideas?

Fabiola: She was calm. It was mostly I think because I was like, "I can't believe
this!" I was mad. And she was like, "Okay, but … " But, if I would have been calm I think she would have had a different reaction [instead of just trying to calm me down].

Amanda: So you think that if you had been calm that she would have responded—

Fabiola: Disagreed.

Amanda: She would have disagreed?

Fabiola: Yeah. I think she would have disagreed with me.

Amanda: What do you think that her arguments would have been?

Fabiola: That they're not the same as us. That we're NORMAL and you know, a man and a woman gets married. A man with a man or girl with a girl, it's not correct. Yeah. And they shouldn't be doing this, things like that.
(Interview, 19 December 2011)

Such considerations made an impact on Fabiola's text: The notion of "normal" as heterosexual appeared (and was critiqued) four times, and the beginning of the paper's section on religion was framed around ideas of normality.

The other documentary, *Fish Out of Water*, played an important role in shaping the research paper for her aunt as an audience. The film featured many different Christian theologians and leaders commenting upon Biblical passages and their interpretations of them as supporting the inclusion and acceptance of queerness in religious communities and conversations. Fabiola felt that the Bible verses presented in the film would be persuasive to her aunt, explaining that "I hope she finds [those] more convincing" (Interview, 19 December 2011). She referenced them extensively, with quotations from the documentary in which religious leaders commented on biblical passages comprising almost 8 of the 13 pages of the research paper.

Finally, my interactions with Fabiola through the feedback process influenced her text in ways that refined her positionality in relation to the topic of her paper and the linguistic and cultural communities about which she was writing. One such example of this process can be seen in the opening to the third section of her text that appeared as follows in her first draft:

```
The Latino community is a very religious commu-
nity and for them, following the rules of God is
one of their priorities.
```

In my feedback, I asked her "Can you find a statistic to support this?" about the first part of this sentence. In doing so, I intended to elicit some sort of empirical support for her description of levels of religiosity in the Latino community. Instead, she responded by specifying her own positionality in this community, shown in bold below:

```
My experience with the Latino community is that
they are a very religious community and for them,
following the rules of God is one of their
priorities.
```

Through these changes, Fabiola framed herself as both an insider ("My experience with …") and an outsider (using "they" and "them" rather than "we") in relation to these communities.

Fabiola engaged in similar positioning (without my feedback) in the final sentences of her paper, in which she drew upon her cultural and linguistic knowledge to summarize her argument by saying:

```
There is a dicho [saying] in Spanish and it says:
"Dios nos crea a su imagen y semejanza" which
translates into "God creates us in his own image."
This means that God creates us to resemble he/
she, and for the religious people, they should
know this and accept it because is what God wants.
```

Through knowledge of Spanish and the *dicho*, Fabiola placed herself as a bilingual and bicultural insider, but her argument that religious people need to follow this teaching positioned her as a critic of how some members of this community might not always follow the intent of their biblical teachings.

Change Over Time Like the HotPoint advertisement essay, this literacy event provided Fabiola with opportunities to write about gender-related issues, this time within a more explicitly disciplinary community in which the professor's specialized disciplinary expertise provided Fabiola with additional resources for writing. Although teacher feedback while drafting and explicit writing instruction were not a feature of this literacy event, as they were in the previous one, Fabiola's interactions with texts, her family, and me combined to influence her writing and develop her position within not only her disciplinary communities but also her familial, linguistic, and cultural ones. In that sense, this literacy event reflected the ways that Fabiola's growing disciplinary affiliations were also deeply embedded in a range of other identities.

"I'm a Mexican Feminist": Blogging into Multiple but Circumscribed Disciplinary Identities Fabiola continued to take GWS courses alongside her other required courses throughout her time at university, and in the spring semester of her third year, she took a Feminist Research course, in which the primary writing task was a weekly blog. For these literacy events, the instructor asked students to not only respond to ideas raised in their readings and class discussions but also connect them to their personal experiences, much in the way that feminist discourses support the inclusion of the personal as evidentiary (Spigelman, 2001). Fabiola dreaded this assignment at first, she explained, because classmates would be reading her posts, but by the end of the course she described it as the literacy event she found the most rewarding of all those she completed in her various classes that semester. The blog posts also demonstrated how Fabiola both negotiated and contested GWS norms regarding intersectional identities of linguistically minoritized writers and their acceptance in this disciplinary community.

Interactions Fabiola described both the assigned readings and in-class discussions as important for developing her ideas before blogging about them, but perhaps the most influential set of interactions while writing were those Fabiola had with the expectations of the task and the disciplinary discourses they implied. She described her writing process for this task as unique:

> Mostly my blogs have given me some opportunity to discover what I really think because I write a lot ... Sometimes I write and I don't include [everything I write at first] in the blogs. I start writing again and I try to include those ideas and I go on from there and I try to be more academic. Sometimes I write opinions that are not my opinion, but sometimes I'm like, okay, my opinion in this case might be acceptable so I write it. (Interview, 29 April 2013)

This process of negotiation included both a sensitivity to audience and a desire to align with the disciplinary "codes" (Smagorinsky, Cook, & Reed, 2005, p. 74) expected by her instructor and fellow student readers. In this sense, Fabiola's drafting process was shaped by her anticipation of an audience of blog readers and their expectations for "academic" ways of writing even in an assignment that encouraged the inclusion of personal experiences (i.e., "opinions") as legitimate content. Fabiola described these efforts at "try[ing] to be more academic" sometimes leading to performances intended to please the instructors (echoing Goffman's 1981 notion of an "animator") but in others still including her own opinions. An additional disciplinary discourse with which Fabiola interacted—although without explicit instruction to do so from her instructor—was that of intersectionality (Shields, 2008), in that her personal experiences and opinions were recounted through the lenses of multiple identities in her posts over the course of the semester.

Impacts Fabiola's interactions with task expectations and disciplinary discourses were visible in the rhetorical structure of her blog posts, in which she engaged in argumentation that was personal but also closely tied to course readings. In doing so, Fabiola positioned herself in relation to key concepts in feminist theory while also making relevant the intersectionality of several identities: those of an immigrant, a Mexican *and* an American, and a language learner. These posts tended to begin by framing personal connections to the assigned topic before analyzing aspects of the readings through various lenses of identity. For example, in a post written in early March of that year on "Recognition," Fabiola began with a (self-generated) question about marginalization and then responded to that question in relation to her own Mexican identity:

```
How can our identity be recognized/viewed/inter-
preted in countries other then our own? Is this
why many people are marginalized in the Unites
States? I see that the United States is a country
were the world comes together, this is a country
where many ethnicities get together and learn
about one another. But what happens when people
are reluctant to learn about other's culture? We
judge without knowing the real reasons as of why
those ethnicities do certain things. We also
have to take into account their culture and where
they are coming from. For instance, I know that
Mexicans were colonized by Spain and one of the
questions that I am always asking myself is: are
we replicating the Spaniard culture, or do we
```

```
still  have  some  of  our  own  (Mexican)  culture
alive?  First,  Spaniard's  culture  is  very  similar
to  those  of  the  West,  therefore,  to  what  I  have
seen,  we  are  not  criticize  or  viewed  as  radical
as  other  ethnicities  are  viewed  by  the  Westerners.
```

These explicit mentions of Mexican history and culture were followed by Fabiola's analysis of the ways in which Native Americans' cultures were misunderstood and marginalized during the boarding school era in the United States, drawing upon an assigned reading, *Forced to Care* (Glenn, 2012). Through these rhetorical moves, Fabiola integrated what she called her "personal opinion" with "academic" writing in ways that foregrounded both national/cultural and disciplinary identities. In fact, after reading the aforementioned post, I asked Fabiola (by email) if she defined herself as a feminist, and if so, how she would describe her feminism. Her response? "I consider myself a Mexican Feminist =)" (email, 7 March 2013). And while in this post Fabiola identified with her discipline and its values through a lens of national/cultural identity, and her other blog posts made similar rhetorical moves in relation to her Mexican-American, immigrant, and language-learner identities as well.

Only two blog posts varied from the rhetorical structure described earlier, and in each instance such moves uniquely negotiated particular disciplinary discourses. In one entry, which was among her longest posts of the semester, she framed her response around a class discussion but then went on to describe her own opinions rather than analyzing the assigned reading:

April 5, 2013: Theory of the Oppressor and the Oppressed. An important question was raised in my Advanced Feminist Theory class: What is the centralized image of the oppressor in the United States? One person answered: "a white old dude" and many agreed. This made me think about my own image of the oppressor and the oppressed. Since I was not raised in the United States, my image of the oppressor has been male figures, specially masculine and paternalistic figures. When I

> thought a little deeper about the question posted
> in class and the answer received, I realized that
> people cannot see beyond the stereotypes that we
> (everyone) have created.

The post continued, and Fabiola described her own ideas about commonly held stereotypes and how she believed they could be overcome. Perhaps most notable was the last line of her post, where she added: "NOTE: most of what I say here is based on *my personal opinion*." In this sense, Fabiola showed an awareness that her post might have been defying reader expectations for "be[ing] academic." She was therefore "bend[ing] the rules" (Hyland, 2009, p. 29) in a highly self-aware manner, testing the boundaries of disciplinary writing, at least as she understood them. At the same time, she may have also been navigating the extent to which the personal as evidentiary (Spigelman, 2001) was able to stand on its own in her GWS writing without references to other disciplinary texts.

The other post in which Fabiola did not reference assigned readings was also significant, this time because of the ways that it foregrounded an identity—that of a language learner—that she argued has been marginalized in disciplinary discourses. In this last posting of the semester, written in early May, she explicitly addressed the tensions in writing effective posts for an "academic" audience and foregrounded her status as a linguistically minoritized learner of English:

> When I was writing my blogs, I always felt the
> necessity to put something that made me feel mad
> or frustrated; however, I never felt like I
> transmitted my true feelings and I want to share
> why. The reason I believe it was hard for me to
> write my blogs in a way that would have been
> transparent was because of English being my sec-
> ond language. I always knew that my grammar was
> not 100% correct and my thoughts were not clear
> 100% because of the language that I had to use…A
> question that came up in this class often was:
> who is speaking and who is not and why. Prof.

_____ give us the opportunity to validate our-
selves and to say it is ok to think a certain way
because we all come from different places and
once again, we all see through our cultural
lenses; therefore having different ideas and
points of view. Thinking back, when I was in high
school and before, I used to talk, more then anyone could imagine. Teachers used to take me out
of the classroom for some minutes "until I was
ready to come back and pay attention." When I got
to the University, my world changed completely. I
felt isolated I used to cry (a lot) because I
felt that I had just become the dumbest person in
the world. Every piece of writing, until now, is
criticized and the comments are about my grammar
and the flow of my argument or that I did not
interpreted the author's argument correctly.
When I read Butler or Foucault, I think: "why are
my thoughts not validated when I can't understand what these authors are saying? And why do
they say that my writings do not make sense when
for me, Butler and Foucault are the writers that
I have never been able to understand, but yet,
they are authors that have been used in all my
classes and are widely recognized for their work.
Why do I get criticized and the writings of those
two authors are embraced when they are difficult
or almost impossible to understand, especially
for people who do not have "higher education"?

Given my knowledge of how greatly Fabiola's English language and literacy repertoire had grown over the years I had known her, and the many
different (and skillful) ways in which she positioned her disciplinary
identities, this post was particularly striking. In it, Fabiola raised a number of issues relevant to her interactions with disciplinary discourses. She
first described her language-learning identity in terms of the ways she felt
her writing was less clear because she did not have "100% correct" grammar. She then connected those ideas to larger concepts of voice by

explaining how she felt less able to assert her own right to speak (echoing Norton, 2000) after receiving criticism of her writing from university instructors. Fabiola concluded by critiquing members of GWS communities for reifying certain disciplinary discourses that are difficult to interpret but not making an effort to understand hers.

Change Over Time Fabiola's overall success in her courses, particularly in GWS, as well as the development of ideas and argumentation she demonstrated in her essays and blog posts, suggests that she in fact had substantial academic and linguistic expertise and was quite adept at GWS disciplinary writing, despite critical feedback she may have received. However, her final blog of the semester demonstrated a strong sense of identity as a minoritized language learner, which she appeared to have developed at least partially in response to her disciplinary audiences' seeming lack of tolerance for multilingual writers' texts that include features of developing English. Such a student perspective is a useful counterpoint to existing research on disciplinary instructors, such as Leki's (2007) study that found faculty in disciplinary majors were actually more willing to overlook these students' grammatical errors than those of their English-only writers.

Writing Through Disciplinary Contradictions

In many ways, Fabiola's pathway into and through postsecondary education both differed from and resonated with those of the other young people who have appeared so far in this book. In terms of differences, she enrolled in a university rather than a community college program (as Jaime, Chap. 4, and Ana, Chap. 5, did), and she was not placed in the long series of remedial courses experienced by Jaime at community college or Diego (Chap. 6) at university. And although her postsecondary goals changed while at university, Fabiola had access to ideas that were central to her emerging interests as well as a clear pathway toward graduation from her very first semester, unlike Jaime and Diego. At the same time, Fabiola shared several similarities with other youth, particularly Diego. For example, they both benefitted from US citizenship, which provided access to scholarships and funding while also removing the many legal barriers to higher education and future employment faced by youth without authorization/documentation. Both also received rather negative initial assessments of their writing by first-semester instructors, although Fabiola's course was not a remedial one. Such commonalities beg the question: Why was her journey through university so very different from Diego's? Her expertise in school-based reading—developed first in Spanish and then later in English—was notably stronger than Diego's, and it not only helped her complete course assignments but also likely facilitated her writing development over time, given the deep and synergistic relationships between reading and writing. Further, Fabiola (unlike Diego) had multiple years to develop her writing in university settings through repeated and increasingly sophisticated extended writing assignments; she also consistently sought out feedback and engaged in revision, factors that Leki (2007) noted as key to writing improvement for the students in her study. Although Diego reported receiving and acting upon feedback in some cases, these practices were not as frequent or as involved as those of Fabiola. Another notable difference relates to the particular disciplinary path Fabiola chose: Through GWS studies, she saw many of her own minoritized identities (including gender) as legitimated and valued subjects of study. Although Diego's remedial English courses at university included course content (e.g., *Burro Genius*) that showed a measure of relevance to his background as a Mexican-origin youth, it appeared that he instead sought other identities—like that of a business finance expert—to which he did not have access while at university.

In responding to an earlier draft of this chapter, Fabiola told me, "I think I have always been a feminist, but I think writing about it has helped me become a more literate feminist" (21 May 2017). These close relationships between writing and disciplinary becoming developed over time and in diverse contexts through the development of disciplinary knowledge, identities, and negotiation (Stevens et al., 2008). In high school, Fabiola navigated outside of institutional confines, developing knowledge about gender-related issues and an individual sense of feminist identity through school-based writing even without a disciplinarily focused writing assignment, writing feedback, or disciplinary communities of teachers and students. Her first-year writing course provided further institutional supports, including explicit writing instruction and feedback as well as gender-focused course texts and assignments even though it was not a GWS-designated class. These served to deepen her awareness and knowledge of women's historical and contemporary positioning in society and her interest in taking coursework on these topics, which shortly thereafter led to her majoring in GWS.

Once in the GWS major, the literacy events in which Fabiola participated helped her gain both disciplinary knowledge and literacy expertise. Such trends confirm findings from Leki (2007) and Sternglass (1997) regarding the ways in which engagement in the study of a discipline supports literacy development, and vice versa. She also negotiated the disciplinary expectations of her instructors, engaging in the performativity of intersectional identities through writing that followed feminist disciplinary expectations for use of the personal as evidentiary (Spigelman, 2001), but did so in perhaps unexpected ways. For example, interactions she had as a student, a niece, and a daughter while writing her "Queerness and Society" essay influenced the content and structure of the text as well as her sense of audience, which included both disciplinary and non-disciplinary readers. Fabiola's blog also provided opportunities to further explore disciplinary ideas and her own intersectional identities, and she used these spaces to negotiate just how "personal" such writing could be, as well as to contest the discipline's seeming intolerance for the identity category of language learner.

An important contradiction in the literacy events through which Fabiola developed her disciplinary identity as a Mexican feminist is that they largely excluded opportunities for Fabiola to develop legitimate biliterate or language-learning identities in support of her disciplinary or more general writerly identities. In her final blog post, for example, she voiced frustration with her teachers' (and perhaps, by extension, GWS disciplinary communities') celebration of many identities but lack of tolerance for multilingual writers, which she felt prevented rather than enabled the disciplinary "possibilities for selfhood" (Ivanič, 1998, p. 10) she attempted to enact through her writing. Also visible in Fabiola's experiences are the ways in which her bilingual and biliterate resources and expertise were marginalized in disciplinary (and more general university) settings. Her primary opportunities to complete extended school-based writing in Spanish were present at the very beginning of her high school career (and outside of a GWS context), and even then in a setting that prioritized a relatively swift transition to English writing. Fabiola only became comfortable using written Spanish to help her while composing once at university, and even in those instances in limited ways, when institutionally supported opportunities that might have helped her more fully develop her biliterate expertise were no longer accessible. It is also notable that although GWS instructors assigned bilingual texts like *Borderlands/Las Fronteras* by Gloria Anzaldua that embodied fluid uses of language, Fabiola was never invited to employ such techniques in her own GWS writing, and she never attempted to do so except in isolated instances like the *dicho* (saying) presented earlier. Even in her senior thesis—for which she conducted interviews in Spanish—Fabiola's teachers encouraged her to report interview excerpts only in English.

Through such experiences, Fabiola had a range of opportunities to become a "more literate" feminist through writing that reflected her bilingual, Latina, and Mexican identities, particularly in university GWS courses. However, the lack of institutional opportunities to actually write (and learn to write) in Spanish while she was developing her disciplinary identities clearly contributed to Fabiola's sense of becoming an "English writer" at the expense of a "Spanish" or "bilingual" one. In her case, valuable bilingual/biliterate expertise was lost through interactions with institutions and a disciplinary community whose discourses celebrated several minoritized identities but did not appear to tolerate, much less actively support, the development of language-learning or biliterate ones.

Notes

1. Fabiola read English (rather than Spanish) versions of texts in her bilingual humanities class, and I did not observe her extensively in 11th and 12th grades, when she took Spanish-for-Native-Speakers courses. She also did not share writing from the latter classes with me, explaining that they did not write extended texts in either course.
2. This section of the poem can be translated as, "The iris of the eye blinks / when it feels love. / Sometimes that small pupil / remains unblinking / like the heart left without its love."

3. See Chap. 6 for a description of the ways in which this approach could be seen as aligning with current conceptualizations of translanguaging or translingual pedagogies.

4. It is notable that although Fabiola reported being more comfortable using Spanish-language resources while writing, she increasingly spoke with me in English as she progressed through her university studies. As mentioned in the Methodological Appendix, this perhaps reflected a combination of her growing expertise in English as well as the specialized knowledge she was developing in English through her university studies and discussing with me.

5. See Chap. 1 for a further discussion of the reasoning behind the ways in which I use the terms Latino, Latina, and Latinx.

6. Fabiola explained to me that her aunt had a high school education and was able to read a variety of different texts in English. However, I was not able to gather additional details about her aunt's literacy experiences, and so do not know whether or not she would have had sufficient background and expertise to draw meaning from this essay, despite Fabiola's efforts documented elsewhere (see Kibler & Hardigree, 2017) to sometimes use "easier" words in her essays so that readers outside of her university context, like her aunt, could understand and enjoy reading what she had written.

References

Anzaldúa, G. (1987). *Borderlands/La Frontera: The new mestiza.* San Francisco: Aunt Lute Books.

Barbarosa, P. (Producer), & Lenoir, G. (Directors). (2001). *De colores.* San Francisco: EyeBite Productions.

Butler, J. (1990). *Gender trouble: Feminism and the subversion of identity.* New York: Routledge.

Canagarajah, A. S. (Ed.) (2013). *Literacy as translingual practice: Between communities and classrooms.* New York: Routledge.

Davies, P. (2012). 'Me,' 'me,' 'me': The use of the first person in academic writing and some reflections on subjective analyses of personal experiences. *Sociology, 46*(4), 744–752. https://doi.org/10.1177/0038038512437897.

de Courcy, M. (2002). *Learners' experiences of immersion education: Case studies of French and Chinese.* Clevedon, UK: Multilingual Matters.

Dickens, K. (Producer & Director). (2009). *Fish out of water*. US: Yellow Wing Productions.

Foss, K., & Foss, S. (1994). Personal experience as evidence in feminist scholarship. *Western Journal of Communication, 58*(1), 39–43. https://doi.org/10.1080/10570319409374482.

García, O. (2009). *Bilingual education in the 21st century: A global perspective*. Malden, MA: Wiley-Blackwell.

Glenn, E. N. (2012). *Forced to care: Coercion and caregiving in America*. Harvard, MA: Harvard University Press.

Goffman, E. (1981). *Forms of talk*. Philadelphia: University of Pennsylvania Press.

Hyland, K. (2009). Constraint vs. creativity: Identity and disciplinarity in academic writing. In M. Gotti (Ed.), *Commonality and individuality in academic discourse* (pp. 25–52). New York: Peter Lang.

Hyland, K. (2012). *Disciplinary identities: Individuality and community in academic discourse*. Cambridge, UK: Cambridge University Press.

Ivaniĉ, R. (1998). *Writing and identity: The discoursal construction of identity in academic writing*. Amsterdam, The Netherlands: John Benjamins.

Ivaniĉ, R. (2006). Language, learning and identification. In R. Kiely, P. Rea-Dickins, H. Woodfield, & G. Clibbon (Eds.), *British studies in applied linguistics: Language, culture and identity in applied linguistics* (pp. 7–29). Bristol, CT: Equinox.

Kanno, Y., & Grosik, S. A. (2012). Immigrant English learners' transitions to university: Student challenges and institutional policies. In Y. Kanno & L. Harklau (Eds.), *Linguistic minority students go to college: Preparation, access, and persistence* (pp. 130–147). New York: Routledge.

Kibler, A. K. (2014). From high school to the noviciado: An adolescent linguistic minority student's multilingual journey in writing. *The Modern Language Journal, 98*(2), 629–651. https://doi.org/10.1111/modl.12090.

Kibler, A. K. (2016). Promises and limitations of literacy sponsors in resident multilingual youths' transitions to postsecondary schooling. In C. Ortmeier-Hooper & T. Ruecker (Eds.), *Linguistically diverse immigrant and resident writers: Transitions from high school to college* (pp. 99–116). New York: Routledge.

Kibler, A. K. (2017). Becoming a "Mexican feminist": A minoritized bilingual's development of disciplinary identities through writing. *Journal of Second Language Writing, 38*, 26–41. https://doi.org/10.1016/j.jslw.2017.10.011.

Kibler, A. K., & Hardigree, C. (2017). Using evidence in L2 argumentative writing: A longitudinal case study across high school and university. *Language Learning, 67*(1), 75–109. https://doi.org/10.1111/lang.12198.

Kubota, R., & Chiang, L. T. (2012). Gender and race in ESP research. In B. Paltridge & S. Starfield (Eds.), *The handbook of English for specific purposes* (pp. 481–499). Malden, MA: John Wiley & Sons.

Lam, W. S. E. (2009). Multiliteracies on instant messaging in negotiating local, translocal, and transnational affiliations: A case of an adolescent immigrant. *Reading Research Quarterly, 44*(4), 377–397. https://doi.org/10.1598/RRQ.44.4.5.

Leki, I. (2007). *Undergraduates in a second language: Challenges and complexities of academic literacy development.* Mahwah, NJ: Lawrence Erlbaum.

Lupton, E. (1993). *Mechanical brides: Women and machines from home to office.* New York: Cooper-Hewitt.

Martínez, R. A., & Morales, P. Z. (2014). ¿*Puras groserías?*: Rethinking the role of profanity and graphic humor in Latin@ students' bilingual wordplay. *Anthropology and Education Quarterly, 45*(4), 337–354. https://doi.org/10.1111/aeq.12074.

Norton, B. (2000). *Identity and language learning: Gender, ethnicity and educational change.* Harlow, UK: Longman/Pearson Education.

Orwell, G. (1949). *1984.* Orlando, FL: Harcourt.

Patton, J. (Producer), & Haynes, T. (Director). (2002). *Far from heaven* [Motion picture]. New York: Focus Features.

Pavlenko, A., & Piller, I. (2008). Language education and gender. In S. May & N. H. Hornberger (Eds.), *Encyclopedia of language and education* (Vol. 1, 2nd ed., pp. 57–69). New York: Springer.

Prior, P. A. (1998). *Writing/disciplinarity: A sociohistoric account of literate activity in the academy.* Mahwah, NJ: Erlbaum.

Schleppegrell, M. (2004). *The language of schooling: A functional linguistics perspective.* Mahwah, NJ: Erlbaum.

Seloni, L. (2014). "I'm an artist and a scholar who is trying to find a middle point": A textographic analysis of a Colombian art historian's thesis writing. *Journal of Second Language Writing, 25,* 79–99. https://doi.org/10.1016/j.jslw.2014.06.001.

Shields, S. A. (2008). Gender: An intersectionality perspective. *Sex Roles, 59*(5-6), 301–311. https://doi.org/10.1007/s11199-008-9501-8.

Smagorinsky, P., Cook, L. S., & Reed, P. M. (2005). The construction of meaning and identity in the composition and reading of an architectural text. *Reading Research Quarterly, 40*(1), 7–88. https://doi.org/10.1598/RRQ.40.1.4.

Spigelman, C. (2001). Argument and evidence in the case of the personal. *College English, 64*(1), 63–87. Stable URL: http://www.jstor.org/stable/1350110.

Sternglass, M. S. (1997). *Time to know them: A longitudinal study of writing and learning at the college level.* Mahwah, NJ: Lawrence Erlbaum.

Stevens, R., O'Connor, K., Garrison, L., Jocuns, A., & Amos, D. M. (2008). Becoming an engineer: Toward a three dimensional view of engineering learning. *Journal of Engineering Education, 97*(3), 355–368. https://doi.org/10.1002/j.2168-9830.2008.tb00984.x.

8

Using Informal Bilingual Resources, "Jumping" and "Giving Double": Interactional Histories Across School and Religious Communities

Maria—an energetic and social ninth grader when I first met her—was born in the South Sierra community but moved from California to Mexico with her family as a preschooler to be near elderly grandparents. She attended a Spanish-medium elementary school there before returning to the United States in sixth grade, which was her first experience using and learning English in a classroom. Maria completed middle school (grades 6–8) in South Sierra, where she described working diligently, having supportive friends and teachers, and being allowed (and at times encouraged) to submit written work in Spanish. At South Sierra High School, where most classes were in English, Maria participated actively in her various courses, collaborated frequently with classmates, and was seen by teachers as a promising student who was university-bound. She excelled academically in high school, earning a 3.78 weighted GPA and passing the state's standardized high school exit exam on her first attempt. Apart from academics, school was also an important place for Maria to maintain and reinforce friendships with bilingual and English-only classmates through in-person, online, and texted conversations

---

This chapter draws from data first published in Kibler (2014) and Kibler (2016).

© The Author(s) 2019
A. K. Kibler, *Longitudinal Interactional Histories*,
https://doi.org/10.1007/978-3-319-98815-3_8

(which also took place outside of school) that revolved around shared interests like music and her church group, and special events like her *quinceañera*, a coming-of-age celebration for young women that is common in many Latin-American-origin communities.

In the spring of her last year at high school, Maria made an unexpected decision, which is the turning point of her story because of its influence on her language and literacy development. Instead of enrolling in one of the universities to which she had already been accepted, Maria announced she was planning to undertake religious training in a Catholic missionary order. The "Institute," which was affiliated with her local parish and located on the East Coast, was originally established in Argentina and had many Spanish-speaking members and leaders around the world. At the Institute, she would live and engage in religious training full-time with others following a similar path, first in a year-long *noviciado* (novitiate) program, which would be followed by further studies with the eventual goal of becoming a permanent member of this religious order. Starting the summer after high school graduation, she moved to the East Coast and began living and studying at the Institute. Near the beginning of her novitiate program, I attended a bilingual "investiture of habit" ceremony that officially marked Maria's status as a novice, or *novicia*. She was given a new name, changing from Zulema—as I had known her in high school—to Maria. She completed novitiate coursework that first year, taking classes in religion, philosophy, and literature, followed by two years of further study in which religious topics were accompanied by coursework in both Latin and (to a lesser degree) Spanish. After three years at the Institute, Maria was then sent to Rome for an additional and final year of study, including courses in Italian.

I first provide an overview of Maria's language and literacy experiences during high school as well as those at and beyond the Institute to provide general context for her journey. I then use a longitudinal interactional histories approach (LIHA) to analyze two literacy events before and two literacy events after her turning point of entering the Institute (see Table 8.1). I do so in order to explore the interactions influencing her production of texts, how they did so, and patterns of change over time across two distinct literacy contexts: a high school setting, in which relatively few official bilingual resources existed, and the Institute, which was

Table 8.1 Maria's turning point and literacy events presented through LIHA analysis

	Before the turning point		Turning Point: Joining the Institute	After the turning point	
Literacy event	"He knew that I can do it"	"Miguel was sitting back of me"		"Jumping more from one language to the other one"	"You kind of give double"
Year	Grade 9	Grade 12		Grades 13–15	Grades 14–15
Task	Exhibition (narration[a])	Research paper (argumentation)		In-class exams (notes; explanation/ procedure/report)	Bilingual teaching
Institutional context (if applicable)	Untracked high school (bilingual humanities class and school-wide)	Untracked high school humanities class		Catholic Institute	Local Catholic church

Notes: [a]Genre labels in parentheses are aligned with those originally presented in Kibler (2014), as adapted from Schleppegrell (2004)

defined in large part by its bilingual (and multilingual) orientation. In this way, I explore how Maria's journey was influenced by the differing statuses and purposes of bilingual and biliterate practices across settings.

Overview of Maria's Language and Literacy Experiences

During High School In ninth grade Maria was placed in a bilingual humanities course and untracked English-medium classes for all other academic subjects. Teachers did not place her in an ELD course in ninth or tenth grade, however, as they did for Fabiola and Diego, and by eleventh grade it appeared that her school seemed to have lost track of Maria as a state-designed English learner, in that she no longer took standardized English language proficiency assessments even though she was never formally reclassified from English-learner status. (I was never able to determine exactly how or why this occurred.) She took a range of untracked English-medium classes during high school, including subjects such as humanities, math, and science, as well as multiple community college courses. She also completed two Spanish-for-Native-Speakers classes.

Maria engaged in reading a wide variety of texts for her high school courses. In relation to novels and other book-length texts assigned in her classes, she described some of these as "hard." For example, in explaining her experience reading the novel *Nectar in a Sieve* in tenth grade, she said:

> I was reading and flipping pages and I read fast, but my mind is like in other places, like I'm thinking I've got to go back and do that and that and that, or I'm reading something and it reminds me of other things and my mind just go and fly and fly away. (Interview, 15 February 2007)

Despite these concerns, I often observed Maria reading that novel (and a range of other texts in various genres) with great attention during class, using Post-it notes to mark passages of interest and often taking a leading role in small- and whole-group discussions, through which she demonstrated stronger comprehension than did many of her classmates. Similar patterns were visible in her reading of *Senderos Fronterizos* (Jiménez, 2002) in one of her Spanish-for-Native-Speakers classes. In describing that text, she excitedly recounted to me several incidents from the book but also explained sometimes having trouble concentrating while reading and skipping some "boring" chapters. Maria described reading several informational texts in Spanish for that course as well, and finding those resources relatively easy to comprehend.

Maria described herself as a stronger writer in Spanish than English when she began high school. For example, in the "Turning Point" narrative essay she wrote in March of her ninth-grade year, she explained:

```
My middle school it was easy maybe because my
teacher, friend s help me allot and they where
very supported back then my English was not that
good not even know but is better back to busyness
in the school all my big projects I will turn
them in Spanish that is why. I say that because it
was so easy. All my friends where really support-
ive and my teacher helped me to understand
more but it did not help turning my assignments
in Spanish because I did not learn more English.
```

In this instance, Maria portrayed her English (likely encompassing both written and spoken modalities) as "not that good" when this text was written in ninth grade but "better" than it had been in middle school, when she submitted many assignments in Spanish. (I documented this latter trend through reviewing a portfolio of middle school work Maria shared with me.) Of particular interest in understanding Maria's perspectives regarding biliterate development is that she described her middle school teacher's acceptance of Spanish-language writing as unhelpful rather than supportive of the development of her English writing. Such statements likely reflected English-only discourses pervasive through the United States as well as the lack of a formalized bilingual program or curriculum at her middle school due to restrictions in place during Maria's childhood and adolescence.[1] Even the bilingual humanities course in which she was enrolled in ninth grade was strongly focused on transitioning students from Spanish into English (as described later in the chapter and in previous chapters), which also likely informed her perspectives.

By the time she finished high school, Maria described herself as a confident English writer, particularly in terms of the multiple-draft writing tasks that were a common feature of many of her classes. For example, in an interview just before graduation, Maria explained changes in her English writing during high school in the following way:

> Compared to freshman year, it's way better. Because I had gone back to my [ninth grade] Turning Point [text], and I was like, whoa, I'm like, I can see my growth in a way, even a little bit, but I see it. Right now, it's like, I know I have some mistakes, but less since freshman year. (Interview, 15 April 2010)

Maria also saw growth in her abilities to revise her own English writing. In tenth grade she expressed frustration because she could not "see" mistakes in her English texts, but by twelfth grade she was more positive. By that point, she explained, when she reread her papers, "I found things, I didn't find spelling things, because I can't see them, but I found like ideas that were confusing and I had things that I flipped around" (Interview, 15 April 2010).

Maria engaged in a range of literacy practices outside of classes that supported bilingual and biliterate development to different extents. Formal programs in which she participated included Upward Bound, a program supporting students' transitions from high school to postsecondary schooling that took place on weekends and in the summer from grades 9 through 12. Although it served a primarily Spanish-English bilingual student population and was staffed by several bilingual tutors and teachers, the program focused on English reading and writing activities, likely because of the English language and literacy expectations of the US universities for which youth were being prepared. During tenth grade, Maria also participated along with Diego and Fabiola in a Saturday writing program for several months that modeled and gave students opportunities to write a range of traditional and multimodal texts in any language (although she wrote only in English). Maria was also active in her church, attending Spanish-language services and bilingual youth group activities with increasing frequency during high school. Although the only writing she recalled doing for church activities was a single instance of taking notes in English and Spanish in preparation for a retreat she would later help facilitate, she read several Spanish-language texts, including books published by the Institute's press. Finally, outside of institutional settings, Maria composed a poem in Spanish with her mother for her *quinceañera* invitation in tenth grade, wrote diary entries and short pieces of fiction in a personal journal in both languages, and in eleventh grade started her school's first-ever book club, featuring a popular vampire-themed teen book series. Maria also kept in immediate contact with friends, most of whom were bilingual, via texting and her MySpace page, the popular social media platform at the time. For example, in April of her 11th-grade year, her bio as "Mz. GaRcIa" featured flexible and complex discursive languaging practices similar to those described in previous chapters:

Hey my name is Zulema García, I'm 17 years old, b-day _____ . I'm a junior at South Sierra High School. I'm going to graduate in 2010 the best class ever!! oh10 You now!!!. I love my family, and my friends those are the special thing in my heart and I know that I can count on them. I love to have fun with my friends. If you like me as a friend okay thanks, but if you don't ni modo I can continue my life with out you. Thing that I love is when people stand for what they believe also when they don't give up no matter what. People say that soy orgullosa well that is a little true but sometimes you need orgullo to continue, but also you need to be con los pies en la tierra, the only thing that I say if you have orgullo don't let get in the way, cause if you let your orgullo do that then you are going to have problems or even perder great friends. yea if you want to know more just send a message.)[2]

In a post made about a month later, she employed yet a different style:

```
Sometimes people think D@ you are 2faces, but in
reality they dont know that u r sacrificing for
them the only thing d@ you can do is to let time
explain everything.
```

In this entry, Maria used both abbreviations (e.g., "u r" for "you are") typical of texting at the time and keyboard combinations that approximated a feature of African American English ("d@," or "dat," for "that"), which was spoken by some students at her school. Such entries highlighted the varied audiences Maria and other multilingual youth regularly address through digital spaces (Yi, 2007) and the intersectional linguistic and ethnic/racial "networks of self" that Compton-Lilly, Papoi, Venegas, Hamman, and Schwabenbauer (2017) described as important to understanding children's language and literacy practices across settings.

However, by the end of high school, Maria identified growth in her writing solely in terms of English, explaining that her writing in Spanish stayed "the same" since ninth grade. Although Maria spoke proudly of using Spanish in written and oral forms in many different contexts, she described these events in terms of "using" Spanish, not in terms of growth or development of new language or literacy expertise.

At the Institute and Beyond Although Maria often pointed out to me that the Institute she attended after high school provided an "English course of study," it offered a linguistic and cultural setting in which bilingual, multilingual, and international influences were inherent in everyday language and literacy practices. For example, many past and present leaders of the Institute were Spanish speakers from Latin America, and the use of Spanish by these individuals validated it as a language of prestige in the Institute. Maria explained that members of her religious order often visited or studied in Rome, which was in fact where church leaders developed the novitiate program's curriculum, first in Spanish and then in translation in other languages. Even the Institute's official symbol—an ornate crucifix with images and wording that Maria often drew in the margins of her class notes—was bilingual. Maria's peers at the Institute, a group of ten young women who referred to each other as "sisters," came from Australia, New Zealand, Mexico, Tonga, and the United States. Several of these young women came from Spanish-speaking families, and according to Maria, those who did not expressed an interest in learning Spanish. She explained that they all "learned each other's languages" (Interview, 8 February 2011) to some degree.

Apart from a single self-paced Spanish reading course and multiple Latin classes, courses at the Institute were taught and students were assessed in English. Spanish was, however, often present in these experiences. Maria described frequently studying with the help of the library's collection of course texts and institutional documents in both English and Spanish, which I saw when I visited the Institute. This was a striking difference from Maria's high school, where students rarely had institutionally provided, non-English texts available other than in the Spanish-for-Native-Speakers class or on the Internet.

The writing Maria completed for her courses at the Institute was comprised primarily of note-taking and timed in-class exams (or tests, terms that I use interchangeably here), a contrast to the multiple-draft essays that were a common feature of her high school classes. The purpose of this exam-based writing, Maria explained, was to ensure students had mastered specific content rather than particular linguistic or rhetorical forms. Her teachers wanted to know "if we understand it, because we have to go and do apostolic [missionary] work a lot, and pretty much it's like, someone has a question about fate or anything, we have to answer it. And it's really like, we've got to be careful to not say the wrong answer" (Interview, 23 April 2011). These types of conversations with parishioners were an important part of her vocational responsibilities, and given Maria's sociable personality, I had a sense that they would indeed be a frequent part of her daily life. During a visit to the Institute, I saw this happen as I toured a nearby church with Maria and a fellow sister:

> As we walk over to a fresco on the church wall, Maria is approached by a teen-aged young woman, and they start to talk quietly in Spanish. Her fellow sister and I look at the wall and start to talk about the fresco and art

more generally. I look over at Maria in what I think is just a minute or two later, and she's animatedly talking (in Spanish) with at least five teenagers and two different adult couples about the church and an upcoming tour of the catacombs this afternoon. (Fieldnotes, 29 August 2013)

While such a conversation did not delve into the realm of church doctrine, it helped me appreciate the ways in which being able to "understand it" and explain it to others—using resources across languages to do so—was an important element of Maria's experiences. This interaction also helped me understand how the social dynamics of the Institute, including their work to minister to English- and Spanish-speaking parishioners, made her bilingual repertoire more relevant to the goals of that institution than they had been to those of her high school.

Maria's comments on her literacy development during her time at the Institute and in her final year of study in Rome focused primarily on the languages in which she took courses: English, Latin, Italian, and to a lesser extent, Spanish. Specifically, Maria described "getting better" at taking notes and communicating her ideas in written exams in English, although, as described later in the text, there were limits to this success. Her attitudes toward Spanish literacy practices were less positive, however. At the end of her third year, she explained that even though she had taken a short course focused on Spanish reading, she felt her Spanish writing had worsened. Further, studying for her final third-year exams—in English—gave her little time for the Spanish devotional reading she tended to do in the evenings. More of her time, in fact, was devoted to Latin, which she studied during her second and third years. A key literacy practice in those courses was the creation of written translations of religious texts, a process she enjoyed. Describing this experience, she explained both spiritual and literate connections to those texts: "It was really nice to translate because especially with Saint Augustine, with the way he expresses his love for God is really beautiful. That's really wonderful and neat how he writes that" (Interview, 12 June 2013). In Maria's fourth and final year of study, additional languages and literacies also played a role: She was sent to Rome—along with six of the other sisters in her group—to complete her studies and took Italian language classes as well as Italian-medium courses in theology. She also explained that she enjoyed opportunities to meet more Spanish-speaking sisters from other countries while there. Upon her return from Rome, she described herself as "not passionate" about studying or speaking Italian but excited about her ongoing religious studies (Observation, 22 March 2015).

Maria's Longitudinal Interactional Histories

Because of the more formal opportunities provided for bilingual and biliterate practices in the Institute, Maria's language and literacy journey developed quite differently than it might have in other, more common postsecondary contexts for linguistically minoritized students. As a result, I explore her experiences through the turning point of her choice to join the Institute and pursue her studies and undertake vocational responsibilities there. Literacy events demonstrating these trends both before and after this turning point are presented below through LIHA analyses; these events as well as their placement in relation to the turning point are presented in Table 8.1.

Before the Turning Point: Drawing Upon Informal Bilingual Resources Hornberger's (2003) continua of biliteracy model suggests that micro-level, oral, and bilingual events often have less social prestige but are nonetheless important in understanding biliterate development, and in Maria's high school experiences, this was most certainly the case. Bilingual practices were a frequent feature of the literacy events in which she participated, even though most source texts and her final written texts were presented in English. In many ways, both the demographics of the community and the staffing choices made by the school facilitated Maria's use of these informal bilingual resources. For example, at South Sierra High School, the bilingual teachers and homeroom advisors as well as the bilingual humanities course were clustered in ninth (and to a lesser extent tenth) grade, providing Maria with greater access to instructors early in her high school experience with whom she could discuss ideas and her texts using resources across languages. Further, the bilingual and biliterate repertoires she and many of her classmates shared made it natural for them to use these resources, rather than English-only ones, as they engaged in conversations during literacy events at school, a practice tacitly approved by teachers if not actively encouraged by them. LIHA analyses of two sets of literacy events in high school—one in her first year and another in her final year—demonstrate the ways in which Maria's informal bilingual interactions with others (rather than the more frequent and more formalized biliterate textual interactions that she experienced after high school) played key roles in developing her school-based English writing before the turning point of joining the Institute.

"He Knew That I Can Do It": Bilingual Encouragers and Clarifiers As described in previous chapters, a major annual assessment in high school for Maria and her fellow students was an exhibition, in which they submitted a written (or multimodal) text that varied by topic and genre each year and gave an oral presentation. A committee of judges, including teachers, community members, and students, served as the audience for these presentations. For the ninth-grade exhibition, students wrote personal narrative essays about a turning point in their family and school lives (described above), and the primary responsibility for preparing students for the exhibition fell to humanities teachers. Maria's humanities class that year was designated as a bilingual course and taught by Ms. Gutiérrez; in-class preparation for the exhibition included reading and discussing model texts, brainstorming and drafting in-class, and receiving teacher feedback (although Maria also sought feedback from her homeroom advisor). According to the school's curriculum documents, teachers were asked to focus on sensory detail and figurative language in narrative writing, emphases that were evident in classes I observed and texts I gathered.

Interactions Maria's text was shaped by a range of bilingual interactions inside and outside of the classroom. First, Ms. Gutiérrez led discussions about this assignment and the lessons supporting it bilingually. Second, bilingual adults also served as "encouragers" for Maria to produce writing in English, which she had recently begun doing that year. Ms. Gutiérrez, for example, emphasized to students the importance of transitioning into English writing to prepare them for the following year, asking each student to stretch just beyond what they were comfortable with in terms of using English (rather than Spanish) for some or all of their written exhibition. Maria's use of all-English in her exhibition and other writing that year drew admiration from the teacher, who called Maria an "incredibly hard worker" (Interview, 6 May 2007). In the Turning Point narrative itself, Maria explained that in her Upward Bound program the previous summer, Mario, a young immigrant-origin teacher who was a Spanish/English bilingual, had previously played a defining role in encouraging her to write in English.

```
In the study hall Mario helped me to do my work
he told me that he knew that I can do it and he
belive that I could he say to me that I remember
him  when  he  start  and  he  did  not  speak
English before and he knew that I culd too. But that
I put obstgecult to my self and that I give up.
After that talk I decided to not get out of the
program and to give all my energy and not to give
up. In my classes I tried to write all in English
and to do better.
```

As mentioned in the context of Diego's and Fabiola's experiences as well, it is important to consider that while such interactions may have served as important resources in encouraging Maria's engagement in English literacy practices, they nonetheless reflected pressures teachers felt as a result of discourses that highly prized linguistically minoritized students' rapid transitions into English, expectations for which were built into curricula and assessment practices. More broadly, these trends also mirrored broader discourses that have deemed individuals who use non-English languages as less "proficient" in English than those who do not (Canagarajah, 2011, 2013; Kiramba, 2017). Perhaps unsurprisingly, Maria never mentioned being "encouraged" to write in Spanish, other than in her Spanish-for-Native-Speakers class.

A third set of interactions was with bilingual individuals who also served as "clarifiers," providing feedback on the organization and content of drafts of this text. For example, in the first draft of the essay, in which Maria described the impact of separation on her family when her father immigrated to the United States, she included a basic description of her early relationship with her father:

```
My dad and I were so close we may see movies and
we sometime went to Wendy's and ate the good
food, and go t o walk to the park together.
```

Her humanities teacher and homeroom advisor (both of whom were bilingual) provided Maria with feedback on this assignment, using English and Spanish to do so in both oral and written form. Their comments asked her to write introductory and summative sentences, provide specific details, and include figurative language and sensory description.

Impacts Such interactions with bilingual adults serving as teachers, encouragers, and clarifiers influenced her text in several ways. First, she wrote the exhibition text entirely in English, the longest piece she said she had ever written up to that point in time. Second, she engaged actively in the revision process: While students were required to submit their drafts at least once to their humanities teacher, Maria sought out multiple feedback providers and revised many times. Her online version of the document, for example, showed that she revised portions of her text across at least 12 different sessions. This engagement in English writing could be attributed to several factors, among them her overall positive disposition toward doing well at school, of which she often spoke proudly, encouragement from bilingual adults, and the positive regard in which her humanities teacher held her efforts. Third, and as a result of her use of bilingual clarifiers, Maria's final draft was notably more developed than her first one because of feedback she received and her revision efforts. In her final draft, for example, her previous description was revised to become the following:

```
Me and my dad where so close because we play
allot and we spent allot of time together some
times we took lunch to my mom to her work then,
me and my dad went to buy some Ice cream and walk
to the park together or some times he took me and
go to the beach and walk, when we were there we
hear the sound of the water or waves and the
birds sing, the sand between or feet. When me and
```

```
my dad spent so much time together   I was so
Happy like the sun when come out after I week
of  that was rain.
```

Maria's revisions followed closely from the feedback she received, which emphasized adding details and incorporating figurative language, among other issues. Her revisions included the addition of a general statement about playing and spending time together, as well as different and more specific details of what she and her father did: taking lunch to her mother, buying ice cream, and walking on the beach. Maria described this final detail using sensory images related to sound ("the water or waves and the birds sing") and touch ("sand between or feet"). Her final sentence also included a simile about being with her father ("Happy like the sun …"). Of note in this case was that interactions with clarifiers were *not* focused on "fixing" her text. In fact, several grammatical features that might be expected of developing multilingual writers are still visible in this final draft (e.g., unconventional verb forms) as well as features found in many other developing writers' texts (e.g., issues with punctuation, spelling, capitalization). Rather, the feedback she received provided Maria with access to the narrative writing techniques (i.e., sensory detail and figurative language) that all writers at the school were being asked to develop, which at least in part contributed to her earning a "pass with distinction" on her exhibition.

Change Over Time Maria's early transition to English writing, encouraged by bilingual adults, was validated through a high-stakes and public assessment—the exhibition—in ways that supported narrative writing craft and multiple-draft writing in English, which were valued genres and processes, respectively, at her high school. This development continued throughout high school: A narrative Maria completed in 12th grade, for example, demonstrated her ability to produce a first draft that already used sensory details, framed and analyzed the impact of narrative events, and used greater syntactic complexity and variety than were found in her ninth-grade text (Kibler, 2014). However, because Maria did not participate in settings over time that required similar repeated tasks in Spanish, a parallel analysis of change was not possible.

"Miguel Was Sitting Back of Me": Bilingual Idea Shapers By her 12th-grade year, Maria had written in many different genres at South Sierra High School, almost all of which were in English. The processes through which she composed her English-medium texts, however, were almost always bilingual. Such interactions were a consistent feature of her writing process in grades 9 through 12, even as her expertise in English grew. A research paper she completed in her 12th-grade humanities class is representative of the ways that such bilingual interactions, in this case with classmates and religious discourses, shaped ideas for Maria's texts, as well as how she used this particular writing assignment to develop interests that would inform her postsecondary career.

In Maria's humanities class, students had been studying the topic of human rights. For this assignment, they were asked to select and research a current event or topic related to one of the elements of the United Nations Declaration of Human Rights. They then used this research to write an argumentative paper on their topic. In-class activities, Maria explained, included time to brainstorm topics, find sources via the Internet, and draft their texts. According to the school's curriculum documents, instruction was focused on using evidence to support a thesis, but because I did not observe the class during this particular assignment and because Maria did not mention it in her interview, it is difficult to know to what extent this instruction occurred.

Interactions Maria selected abortion as her topic for research, a decision that was influenced by discourses prominent in her church community, which were strongly focused on opposing abortion. Maria explained how learning more about the topic through her school research paper fit into the religious teaching and guidance she had received:

> In church they told us, learn about something that you can defend yourself [on], and put in whatever skill you want into learning more about it. The only topic I can defend myself on would be abortion, because, most of the things that I learned, is like I have been, because of the church placing time [on it]. (Interview, 15 April 2010)

In this way, the church's anti-abortion stance, along with the value placed on defending religious beliefs, provided the motivation to engage with this topic for her research project.

Maria's text was also influenced by a key set of interactions with a bilingual classmate who helped Maria negotiate the tensions between these religious discourses and the expectations for a research paper to provide evidence to support arguments. Throughout high school, I frequently observed Maria chatting bilingually with, soliciting ideas from, and even jointly composing with friends and other students while writing countless texts, and this case was no different. In an interview a few weeks after completing her paper, Maria explained:

> When I was writing it, Miguel was sitting back of me. I guess he could see what I was doing. He was like, "Maria." I'm like, "What?" "You're going to pro- you're going to work on that?" I'm like, "Yeah." He's like, "Which one are you?" I'm like, "I'm pro-life." He's like, "But that's bias because you already stand, you know, you're kind of taking a stand already" ... So I was like, "OK, you're right. I could probably be bias. But most of my information, *te seguro*, I promise you, thanks you and only you, I would try to find information *que es* [that is] medically, like not my opinion—not someone that's pro-choice or pro-life—medical opinion, straight up." (Interview, 15 April 2010)[3]

Maria said that Miguel "kept bringing it up" as they spent time on the assignment in class, and as a result they carried on this conversation across several days. Maria reported that as she researched, however, she became so invested in the topic and in finding information online that she did not have enough time to work on the writing itself. As a result, she did not complete her draft or have other youth or adults to provide her with written feedback, which she almost always did for other texts in high school.

Impacts Maria's final text reflected the influence of both religious discourses and bilingual classmates in shaping ideas while writing. Her church community and its discourses clearly provided the inspiration for her writing, but her conversations with Miguel had a notable impact on her written text in terms of mediating differences between religious and academic purposes for research and writing. As a result of interactions with Miguel, Maria organized her abortion essay into two sections, reviewing medical definitions related to abortion before beginning her primary argument in attempts to avoid the "bias" about which Miguel warned her. At the same time, it was easy to see that Maria's interest in learning about the topic led to having insufficient time to complete the academic task itself. Her introductory paragraph, for example, outlined four areas she would explore—medical definitions of abortion, the history of Roe vs. Wade, and the biological and psychological effects of abortion—but she only addressed the first two and did not include any summative statements at the end of her text.

Change Over Time In considering the ways in which this literacy event fit into Maria's long-term journey, as well as her choice to enter the novitiate (a decision she made just a month after finishing this essay), it appeared that this assignment helped further develop her growing interest in pursuing a religious vocation. Herrington and Curtis (2000) profiled Nam, a first-year university student who planned to attend seminary, and found that he, like Maria, used an open-ended writing prompt to "bridge private concerns with public ones" (p. 127) "as a sort of venue—within a place of secular learning—to affirm the Christian truths" that he valued (p. 86). This purpose appeared to dominate Maria's engagement with this assignment, in that most of her time was spent on reading sources online (and talking with Miguel about her topic) rather than composing her text, and there was little evidence that writing instruction or feedback played a prominent role in her experiences. As such, this literacy event demonstrated the ways in which Maria was able to draw upon informal bilingual resources and navigate multiple communities to further interests that became highly relevant in her postsecondary experiences, much as Fabiola did in her own 12th-grade writing (see Chap. 7), rather than to develop writing expertise in a more traditional sense.

After the Turning Point: Negotiating Formal Bilingual and Biliterate Institutional Resources Once Maria began her training at the Institute, bilingual and biliterate resources played both familiar and new roles in the literacy events in which she engaged. To better understand these practices and the ways that institutional recognition of her bilingual and biliterate communicative repertoire influenced these processes, I use LIHA analyses to explore two recurring literacy events—her preparations for in-class tests and her teaching of religious texts to children—that were key facets of Maria's experiences after her turning point of joining the Institute (see Table 8.1).

"Jumping More From One Language to the Other One": Bilingual Resources to Prepare for In-Class Tests Maria took multiple courses at the Institute simultaneously, all of which were included in a shared curriculum (called the *dispensa*) that every student completed, and courses were taught either in the equivalent of semesters or as intensive short courses. Unlike the multiple-draft essays that were a dominant type of literacy event and key means of assessing student learning in high school, in-class written tests were the key form of assessment in her studies at the Institute. Her preparation for these exams was nearly identical in each course over all her years of study, and likely as a result she tended to speak about the interactions she had during these literacy events in more general terms (e.g., "I usually …"). Maria described the process of preparing for tests as one that began in class: "What we do in class is mainly notes. And like pretty much, our teacher comes each class, they say and talk, and pretty much we take notes of the most important parts" (Interview, 4 November 2010). Teachers would then typically assign study guides for students to complete and sometimes provided students with class-wide feedback on their responses to those guides to discuss common student mistakes. To create her guides, Maria used her notes from class as well as a range of texts available in the Institute library, described later in the chapter.

Interactions The interactions Maria had while preparing for her tests differed dramatically from those she had during high school literacy events in several ways. For example, policies and practices at the Institute related to studying and exam-taking dictated the ways in which Maria was able to access various resources: Silence was expected during individual study time, and so conversations while creating notes or study guides were rare. Rather, she solicited help from fellow sisters during other activities to explore these ideas in conversations—both in English and Spanish—outside of classes or study periods: "We [the sisters] helped each other. Like, all of us explained, like probably we're washing dishes and we're explaining each other what [something] is, and we discuss it a lot" (Interview, 23 April 2011). In some cases, she also consulted her instructors for clarification. In this sense, Maria drew upon expertise in both languages to better understand the information that she would later be tested on through exams.

Textual resources available to Maria as she wrote also shifted at the Institute, reflecting a more substantive institutional recognition of bilingual and biliterate expertise. Maria described two key sources she drew upon when preparing for tests: first, course lectures, books, and institutional documents, from which she created notes and study guides; second, the notes and guides themselves that she used to study. Unlike in high school, when Maria often relied upon online sources while creating research projects, access to the Internet was extremely limited at the Institute. Assigned texts were available in the library in both English and Spanish and, as Maria explained and I noted during a visit to the Institute, some were available only in Spanish. Maria reported reading texts in both languages as needed to prepare for exams:

> So, like, the constitution is translated in English, but it's more difficult for me to read it in English, so I'm reading it in Spanish. So right now it came in handy that I know how to read both of them because if I find a book that's difficult in one of the languages, I just translate to the other one. So, I'm jumping more than I did in [high] school I guess where I did English. I'm jumping more from one language to the other one. (Interview, 23 April 2011)

This trend continued from her time as a novitiate through her later years of study. At the end of her third year, for example, she explained that she often started with Spanish texts when preparing for English exams: "Most of the things that I read are in Spanish first because it's better for me. Then I read them in English and take notes" (Interview, 4 March 2013).

Impacts These interactions had varied results on Maria's exam writing. She completed note-taking in both Spanish and English, although usually more of the latter, but her tests were always written completely in English. In many cases, she demonstrated her knowledge successfully, and teacher assessments focused on the content of her responses rather than linguistic accuracy of written expression. For example, in an in-class philosophy test taken in the spring of her first year, she received full credit for responses, such as the one presented in Fig. 8.1, that had several features that writing teachers would likely identify as incorrect or unconventional.

In Hornberger and Skilton–Sylvester's (2003) sense, these were contextualized texts—with features that might be seen as errors typical of developing multilingual writers—that were nonetheless treated as saying something of importance.

However, as I learned in a visit to Maria's Institute after her third year of study, the range of informal and formal bilingual resources she employed while studying was not always adequate to help her meet the demands of written tests:

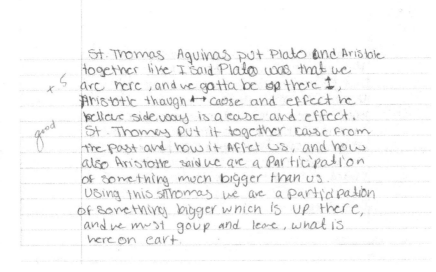

Fig. 8.1 Maria's response on a philosophy exam, first year at the Institute

As I am given a tour of the [Institute] house, off in a corner is a bulletin board that Maria and her fellow sister point out to me. It shows the class schedule as well as notes and photos from sisters who are now posted elsewhere on missionary work. Maria also says that this is where they post all of the test scores, which "teaches humility." Scores from the most recent exams are posted by name for all the sisters living there, across all subjects. Maria's scores are in the 6-8.5 range, with one 3 (a metaphysics class she tells me later she failed), and the other girls in her cohort have scores between 7-10 … Later in the visit we walk around a church rose garden, and Maria talks about the metaphysics test that she failed the previous semester, mostly because she was travelling and didn't have time to study. She says that she studied hard and did well on the re-take this spring. She then says that she takes some of her exams orally (surprise!!) when the teachers allow her, and that's been much better than before. I ask how it helps her, and she says that she likes being able to have the teachers explain the question if she doesn't understand, and that they can often help by "steering" her in the right direction. She says she knows the information but doesn't always know where to start writing or what to write about without that support. (Fieldnotes, 29 August 2013)

I was surprised by what I learned during this visit: first, that Maria struggled with passing written exams (something she had not told me before), and second, that her teachers had modified literacy events to enable Maria to demonstrate her knowledge through English-medium oral assessments. As I thought more about this change, however, I realized it was in keeping with Institute discourses about the precision of ideas, using writing as a means to an end rather than an end in itself. This modification allowed Maria to progress through her studies and gain religious knowledge, regardless of her English-writing expertise. Although English remained the language of assessment—a policy for the Institute, Maria told me—written texts were not the sole means of demonstrating her learning.

Change Over Time Differences in the genres Maria wrote in high school and the Institute made it somewhat difficult to assess change over time, but some trends were visible. For example, Maria at first found postsecondary note-taking experiences to be much more challenging than the teacher-directed note-taking activities in high school (consistent with Harklau, 2001). But by the end of her first year, she reported finding this process to be easier, particularly because of new strategies she employed, like using color-coding and highlighting to "pop out the parts that are more important for me," and revisiting and double-highlighting words and ideas that were difficult to remember (Interview, 1 June 2011). Maria did not send me her earliest notes, but examples from later in the year, once she reported improvement, demonstrated her use of these approaches to note-taking. A representative set of notes, completed mid-year in her Scripture class, is found in Fig. 8.2.

Maria described learning to do this on her own and noticing that it seemed to help her better understand the course material: "Pretty much now I see, I understand more the teachers and more, like, their point[s]" (Interview, 1 June 2011). Trends of self-perceived growth continued through her time at the Institute. In her third year, for example, she explained that "even though my notes were not as clear as I would like them to be, they are making more sense than before" (Interview, 3 September 2013).

In sum, Maria's note-taking and exam-taking in the Institute provided her with opportunities to develop religious expertise through self-study and interactions with peers, teachers, and texts in both English and Spanish. While this focus allowed Maria to develop confidence in her note-taking and supported writing to learn, the development of expertise in learning to write in English was perhaps less pronounced. (See Manchón, 2011 for a discussion of this distinction.) And while Spanish language and literacy practices played key facilitative roles in developing knowledge, English remained the exclusive means to demonstrate this knowledge on assessments, either orally or in writing.

"You Kind of Give Double": Bilingual Teaching in the Institute In reading through my many pages of fieldnotes and interviews, I was repeatedly struck by how enthusiastic Maria was about one particular set of responsibilities at the Institute: teaching duties she was assigned with first, fifth, and seventh graders at a local Catholic church near the Institute. These were weekly classes in which children learned prayers,

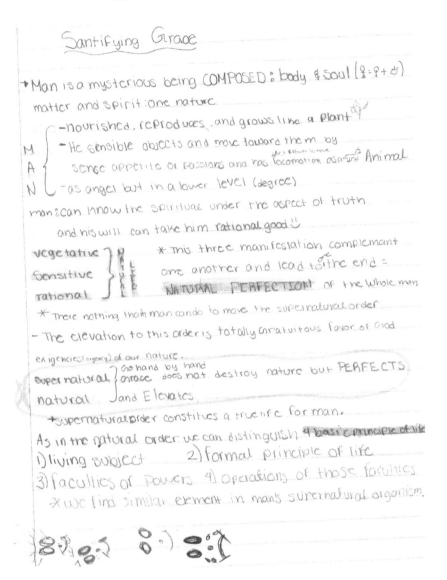

Fig. 8.2 Maria's note-taking, first year at the Institute

religious doctrine, and biblical stories and (for the older students) prepared for their first communion ceremony. Her descriptions of leading these classes were notable not only because of her excitement about the students but also because of the sense of bilingual and biliterate expertise with which she spoke of her teaching. Although the literacy events described in this section diverge from others profiled in this and other chapters in that the creation of written texts was present but not central, these literate practices were absolutely key to understanding how Maria's use of bilingual resources and her own biliterate expertise developed over time and in concert with other experiences at the Institute.

Interactions As Maria engaged in this type of literacy event, her interactions with the children themselves were key to the oral and written texts she created and used. Her students, she explained, lived in homes where primarily Spanish was spoken, but they used both English and Spanish in their everyday and school lives. She also observed that:

> Everything they know that they've learned about the Catholic church they know it in Spanish, so the kids know their prayers in Spanish instead of English ... [but] the language they understand more and they know how to speak, like they know how to express themselves in English. (Interview, 12 December 2012)

Maria explained that in some ways this pattern reflected her own experiences as a child, in that she originally knew all her prayers in Spanish and only learned the English versions after coming to the Institute. These particular nuances in both her own communicative repertoire and those of her students influenced her language use while teaching, described further below.

Also influential on Maria's teaching were the written texts she was given by church leaders to use in her classes, which she described as the only guidance she received in how to teach. Although lesson plan guides were often in English, the copies of prayers and other texts she taught were provided in both English and Spanish, and sometimes even in side-by-side translations on the same page. As Maria explained, in using these texts "you have to teach them both, and try to go back and forth ... you kind of give double, speaking both the languages. So I'm able to switch back and forth" (Interview, 12 December 2012). Maria explained that writing played a supportive, contingent role as she taught. The lesson plans and handouts were typically provided, and so she did not need to create them, but during classes, she said that she sometimes used the board to write "little words to explain what [something] is. But it's not tons of writing I'm doing, it's more like talking" (Interview, 17 December 2011).

Impacts These interactions with texts and her students shaped the particular bilingual and biliterate approach Maria developed and used in her teaching. Maria explained that she differentiated her content and tone for the older and younger students, at least in part because the older ones "are at the age where … they're like way too cool to participate" (Interview, 12 December 2012), but she reported using resources across languages in similar ways with all groups. The following example she gave is representative of how she described engaging in these language and literacy practices:

> For example, our basic day, it will be like as they get there we pray Hail Mary in Spanish, and I have written it down, not on the board but on a piece of paper, for them to read it with me if they get distracted. And then I go to English, and I start asking them, "who is our creator," And it's written down [in English], in the walls of the classroom … And then I have the Our Father in English written down for them to start learning it. (Interview, 17 December 2011)

In this process, Maria drew upon children's oral Spanish knowledge of a common prayer, using the written form alongside it, to begin the class with a familiar experience. She then used English for a more conversational interaction about church doctrine, although still alongside written uses of that language, before starting to learn new prayers in English, both in written and spoken form.

She identified the more conversational portions of the lesson as the most challenging, in that students who could easily converse about other topics in English often did not know how to discuss religious matters in the same way:

Like when I say, "what is the Holy Trinity," they stay quiet. But when I say [the same question in Spanish], "*quién es la Santa Trinidad,*" they will answer ... It's fortunate that my Spanish is so good. So I go with that with them. And it goes much easier, they pay attention more, and it helps them a lot. Little by little I try infiltrate it, like, "the Holy Trinity is *Santa Trinidad.*" Little things, like the Eucharist is "*la Eucaristía,*" "*tabernáculo*" is "tabernacle." (Interview, 17 December 2011)

In this sense, Maria used her own bilingual expertise to elicit her students' knowledge in Spanish and engage them in active participation, while also "infiltrating" these conversations with the English translations to help them learn about church teachings across languages. Key to these pedagogical practices was Maria's own bilingual and biliterate repertoire, in that she could "go with that with them" in ways that responded to students' existing knowledge and communicative repertoires. While it could be argued that Maria's practices had the potential to further shift her students toward uses of English in this religious space, the role of Spanish in both the institution overall and the texts students read seemed to support ongoing bilingual and biliterate practices in church settings.

Change Over Time Because Maria described her teaching in fairly consistent ways over time, and I was not able to observe her teaching, it is difficult to say how her engagement in these literacy events changed over time. Her existing bilingual and biliterate repertoire may have played a role in her being selected for this teaching position, and her teaching provided new opportunities to use her expertise to guide children into language and literacy practices in both English and Spanish. This bilingual teaching may have also supported her students' socialization into specific regional or Latinx communities and identities, as Baquedano-López (2000) found in a Mexican-origin parish in Los Angeles. Such experiences perhaps additionally helped Maria develop her reading expertise, at least in relation to the texts she taught, as she noted getting better at the translation practices such lessons required. Maria's teaching approach provided her students with language and literacy opportunities that were in many ways parallel to her own Institute studies: She helped students draw upon their bilingual and biliterate expertise—as she did in her studying and note-taking—in ways that also supported the development and expression of knowledge in both languages.

Writing Through the Opportunities and Contradictions of Informal and Formal Bilingual/Biliterate Resources

Perhaps more so than any other young person in this study, Maria pursued a pathway in which bilingual and biliterate identities, rather than linguistically minoritized ones, were recognized both institutionally and interactionally. Although in high school she experienced—as did the other youth—discourses that emphasized progress in English over the development of bilingual and biliterate resources, her postsecondary studies did not focus on remediation at the expense of pursuing her interests and goals, as Jaime's and Diego's did (Chaps. 4 and 6). Further, Maria's teachers, rather than critiquing her written expression in English (as Fabiola's instructors sometimes did, Chap. 7), modified their assessment practices so that she could use oral modalities to demonstrate her learning. Maria also enjoyed greater status and recognition of her bilingual and biliterate expertise than did Ana (Chap. 5), whose full communicative repertoire was not institutionally recognized in her vocational program despite its importance to her daily work as a professional. The multilingual character of Maria's postsecondary coursework, which included English, Latin, Italian, and Spanish to varying degrees, was likewise unique among youth in this study and linguistically minoritized students in the United States more generally (García, Pujol-Ferran, & Reddy, 2013).

The nature of Maria's interactions during literacy events varied across contexts in ways that were significant to understanding her experiences over time. The informal bilingual interactions and the discourses with which Maria engaged while writing during high school provided encouragement, clarified her writing, and shaped her ideas in ways that helped her complete school-based writing and further her own future vocational interests through English-medium writing tasks. Specifically, early in high school, a range of bilingual encouragers and clarifiers, alongside bilingual instruction, supported her development of narrative and multiple-draft writing in English. Bilingual classmates also played important roles in her writing throughout high school, with the literacy event in 12th grade suggesting ways in which these interactions were significant to negotiating academic and non-academic discourses in ways that furthered Maria's vocational interests. Once in the Institute, Maria's use of more formal biliterate resources provided venues for her to develop religious expertise through peer, teacher, and textual interactions and to share those understandings with her teachers via oral and written means and with her own students via her bilingual and biliterate teaching approaches. The notion that Maria had moved from a student in a bilingual class—the role in which I first met her in ninth grade—to a bilingual teacher herself further highlights the length and breadth of her language and literacy journey.

In terms of the relationships between macro-, meso-, and micro-level contexts, it is unsurprising that Maria expressed growing confidence in her English but not Spanish writing development in secondary school contexts that privileged monolingual English literacy practices, regardless of their support of some forms of bilingual transition and home language maintenance. Once in the Institute, with its greater official support for and valuing of bilingual and biliterate practices, she quite expectedly tended to draw upon bilingual resources more frequently. However, these macro- and meso-level discourses prevalent at her high school and the Institute did not fully account for the micro-level and situated events through which Maria developed her bilingual and biliterate communicative repertoire. First, even in a high school setting that emphasized English literacy practices, Maria was able to engage in bilingual oral language practices to negotiate writing tasks. Second, despite the importance of bilingual and biliterate practices in Maria's life and work at the Institute, her ongoing reading in Spanish, and bilingual pedagogical practices, she did not develop confidence in what she could accomplish while writing in Spanish. Such trends suggest that biliterate writing development will not necessarily occur in bilingual environments without explicit attention to the development of writing in both languages, regardless of an institution's overall orientation to bilingualism (see also Gentil, 2005). Such practices did not appear to hamper Maria's participation in the activities of the Institute to which she was assigned, but a larger question of empowerment is still relevant. Church leaders, for example, wrote key documents for the Institute in Spanish, only later translating them into English, and many books available through the Institute's press were available only in Spanish. Maria's literacy expertise in Spanish allowed her to consume such texts, but was not developed, at least by the end of this study, to the point where she felt confident in her ability to "author" any texts in Spanish herself. Opportunities of this sort could certainly arise in the future, however, and her bilingual and biliterate repertoire would serve as an important foundation for engaging in those literacy practices.

Notes

1. Proposition 227 was a ballot initiative passed by voters in California in 1998 that dismantled many forms of bilingual education in the state. It was repealed in 2016 through the same ballot initiative process.
2. Relevant translations include: "*ni modo*" (oh, well/it doesn't matter); "*soy orgullosa*" (I'm proud/conceited); "*orgullo*" (pride); "*con los pies en la tierra*" (with your feet on the ground); "*perder*" (to lose).
3. It should be noted that my understanding of Maria and Miguel's conversations as having been bilingual is not based upon Maria's use of Spanish in this interview excerpt. Rather, it is based upon the extensive observations I conducted over time at South Sierra High School, in which Spanish/English bilinguals tended to use both languages with each other in peer classroom conversations regardless of age or levels of English expertise.

References

Baquedano-López, P. (2000). Narrating community in doctrina classes. *Narrative Inquiry, 10*(2), 429–452. https://doi.org/10.1075/ni.10.2.07baq.

Canagarajah, A. S. (2011). Codemeshing in academic writing: Identifying teachable strategies of translanguaging. *The Modern Language Journal, 95*(3), 401–417. https://doi.org/10.1111/j.1540-4781.2011.01207.x.

Canagarajah, A. S. (Ed.) (2013). *Literacy as transligual practice: Between communities and classrooms.* New York: Routledge.

Compton-Lilly, C., Papoi, K., Venegas, P., Hamman, L., & Schwabenbauer, B. (2017). Intersectional identity negotiation: The case of young immigrant children. *Journal of Literacy Research, 49*(1), 115–140. https://doi.org/10.11 77/1086296X16683421.

García, O., Pujol-Ferran, M., & Reddy, P. (2013). Educating international and immigrant students in U.S. higher education: Opportunities and challenges. In A. Doiz, D. Lasagabaster, & J. M. Serra (Eds.), *English-medium instruction at universities: Global challenges* (pp. 174–195). Bristol, UK: Multilingual Matters.

Gentil, G. (2005). Commitments to academic biliteracy: Case studies of francophone university writers. *Written Communication, 22*(4), 421–471. https://doi.org/10.1177/0741088305280350.

Harklau, L. (2001). From high school to college: Student perspectives on literacy practice. *Journal of Literacy Research, 33*(1), 33–70. https://doi.org/10.1080/10862960109548102.

Herrington, A. J., & Curtis, M. (2000). *Persons in process: Four stories of writing and personal development in college.* Urbana, IL: National Council of Teachers of English.

Hornberger, N. H. (2003). Continua of biliteracy. In N. H. Hornberger (Ed.), *Continua of biliteracy: An ecological framework for educational policy, research, and practice in multilingual settings* (pp. 3–34). Bristol, UK: Multilingual Matters.

Hornberger, N. H., & Skilton-Sylvester, E. (2003). Revisiting the continua of biliteracy: International and critical perspectives. In N. H. Hornberger (Ed.), *Continua of biliteracy: An ecological framework for educational policy, research, and practice in multilingual settings* (pp. 35–67). Bristol, UK: Multilingual Matters.

Jiménez, F. (2002). *Senderos fronterizos.* Boston: Houghton Mifflin.

Kibler, A. K. (2014). From high school to the *noviciado*: An adolescent linguistic minority student's multilingual journey in writing. *Modern Language Journal, 98*(2), 629–651. https://doi.org/10.1111/j.1540-4781.2014.12090.x.

Kibler, A. K. (2016). Promises and limitations of literacy sponsors in resident multilingual youths' transitions to postsecondary schooling. In C. Ortmeier-Hooper & T. Ruecker (Eds.), *Linguistically diverse immigrant and resident writers: Transitions from high school to college* (pp. 99–116). New York: Routledge.

Kiramba, L. K. (2017). Translanguaging in the writing of emergent multilinguals. *International Multilingual Research Journal, 11*(2), 115–130. http://dx.doi.org/10.1080/19313152.2016.1239457.

Manchón, R. (2011). Situating the learning-to-write and writing-to-learn dimensions of L2 writing. In R. Manchón (Ed.), *Learning-to-write and writing-to-learn in an additional language* (pp. 3–14). Amsterdam, Netherlands: John Benjamins.

Schleppegrell, M. (2004). *The language of schooling: A functional linguistics perspective*. Mahwah, NJ: Erlbaum.

Yi, Y. (2007). Engaging literacy: A biliterate student's composing practices beyond school. *Journal of Second Language Writing, 16*(1), 23–39. https://doi.org/10.1016/j.jslw.2007.03.001.

9

Building Equitable Futures for Immigrant-Origin Multilingual Youth: Conclusions and Implications of Longitudinal Interactional Histories

This final chapter synthesizes individuals' interactional histories, and in so doing builds a case for the ways in which a better understanding of the language and literacy practices with and through which immigrant-origin multilingual youth develop expertise can be leveraged to create more equitable instructional practices, policies, and research. First, in recognition of the dynamic nature of contexts for language and literacy development, I present a brief overview of the ways that policies and institutions changed both during the study itself and in the three years since its conclusion before turning to updates on youth themselves. Next, I synthesize the cases of Jaime, Ana, Diego, Fabiola, and Maria in order to provide insights into the nature of language and literacy development, or as Compton-Lilly (2014) described it in terms of writing, a "long-term trajectory of becoming" (p. 399) over time. I then analyze the relationships between macro-, meso-, and micro-level factors influencing these processes, and the roles played by bilingual and biliterate practices both inside and outside of formal educational settings. Finally, I address limitations of this study before exploring its implications for educators, policymakers, and researchers.

© The Author(s) 2019   **261**
A. K. Kibler, *Longitudinal Interactional Histories*,
https://doi.org/10.1007/978-3-319-98815-3_9

Bringing Interactional Histories into the Present

In an interview just before Jaime's 2010 high school graduation, he told me about his recent visit to an Apple store, where he first saw what he described as "some great new stuff." I enthusiastically asked, "Oh, the i— what do they call it, the iPad? Is that what it is?" As I look back from the perch of 2018, less than ten years later, my comment seems quaint, almost comical, because of how rapidly such devices have changed since then. Technology is perhaps particularly prone to being outdated, but this moment was poignant for me as I pondered the ways in which studying something (or someone) for longer spans of time makes visible both what endures, and what does not, at larger timescales (Cole, 1996). Such issues are particularly important when considering the historical and cultural situatedness of youth's experiences and the impacts of ongoing changes in individuals' lives, languages, and literacies. What else has changed in relation to the contexts for language and literacy development for Mexican immigrant-origin youth like Jaime, Ana, Diego, Fabiola, and Maria since this study began, now more than a decade ago?

Societal and political debates around immigrant-origin populations are deeply embedded in the history of the United States but are also inherent to global migration more generally and have only become more intense in the current era of globalization (Banks, Suarez-Orozco, & Ben-Peretz, 2016). It is not surprising, then, that immigration policies and discourses have undergone dramatic changes during and after this study. As described in Chap. 4, the late 2000s saw the rise of the DREAMers movement and increased support for legislative solutions for unauthorized/undocumented immigrant youth. Although the DREAM Act was never passed in Congress, despite multiple reintroductions between 2009 and 2011, executive action resulted in the establishment of the more modest DACA program in 2012, which provided protection from deportation and work permission through an executive order. Both Ana and Jaime were among the nearly 700,000 youth, the majority of whom are from Mexico, whose applications were accepted as of January 2018 (Migration Policy Institute, 2018). State-level protections for immigrants and DACA recipients grew notably through this period as well, and of particular relevance to this study, scholarships and state financial aid for higher education were made available to unauthorized/undocumented students. Those funding provisions had little impact on the two such youth in this book, however, because they went into effect in 2012 and 2013, only after Ana's and Jaime's initial postsecondary experiences had ended.

Yet, immigration policies and the discourses that surround them seem destined to change, and change again. In 2017, DACA recipients were thrown into limbo once more, at the mercy of Congress and later the courts. The president who initiated this change campaigned on a promise to "build the wall" between the United States and Mexico and has continued to demonize Mexican immigrants in particular. From the early years of his presidency onward, we have also seen surges in anti-immigrant sentiment and emboldened White supremacist and neo-Nazi extremist activity. This particular moment has been a deeply challenging one for many immigrant families and their advocates, particularly in relation to fears of deportation and anti-immigrant and racial violence. As this book goes to press, the fates of government policies regarding current DREAMers and DACA recipients remain unknown.

The educational institutions through which Jaime, Ana, Diego, Fabiola, and Maria progressed have changed in some respects, while maintaining the status quo in many others. New K-12 content area standards (and corresponding K-12 English language proficiency standards) and assessments, focused on "career and college readiness," were introduced in California and many other states a few years after the youth in this study graduated from high school. These shifts have led to a range of changes in instructional practice that are just now being understood, but the significant emphasis on standardized testing for purposes of accountability—which was already in place when these young people began schooling—has continued. Likewise, serious concerns remain about the effects of poverty, under-resourced schools, and a lack of teacher expertise in providing instruction that supports language and literacy development for minoritized multilingual students (National Academies of Sciences, Engineering, and Medicine, 2017).

There is also evidence that students currently classified as "English learners" in California's K-12 schools are undergoing even more extensive labeling and categorization than in the past. The state education code now requires districts to closely track students who do not meet particular levels of achievement or growth on standardized English language proficiency and English language arts assessments after a certain number of years, labeling them as "long-term English learners" or "at risk" to become one. In this sense, language—as curricularized (Valdés, 2015) through standardized assessments—is creating further categorizations of learners based on time spent in US schools. The manufacturing of such labels, largely undertaken with intentions of better serving this population, is nonetheless problematic in other ways (Kibler & Valdés, 2016; Kibler et al., in press), and it is not yet known how the imposition of such categorizations will impact immigrant-origin multilingual young people and their schooling experiences in the long term.

Official support for bilingualism and biliteracy in K-12 schools, particularly at the state level, has grown in certain ways since this study began. For example, although the students in this study attended schools when California ballot Proposition 227, which restricted many forms of bilingual education, was still in force, this measure was repealed in 2016 through another voter-initiated proposition. Additionally, since 2012, the state (along with several others) has offered high school students the option to earn a Seal of Biliteracy if they complete certain testing and/or coursework requirements in both English and another language. Dual language programs continue to grow both nationwide and in the communities in and around South Sierra, suggesting an interest in multilingualism from both immigrant and non-immigrant communities. When considering the possible impact of such policies, however, it is necessary to recognize that these educational settings are not immune to the larger societal discourses and raciolinguistic ideologies (Flores & Rosa, 2015; Rosa & Flores, 2017) through which the practices of multilingual people of color have been and continue to be marginalized. As a result, dual language and other bilingual programs remain socioculturally, linguistically, and politically complex spaces for minoritized multilingual students and their families (Palmer, 2009; Valdés, 1997), particularly in light of recent trends related to the gentrification of dual language programs (Valdez, Friere, & Delavan, 2016).

Zooming in to the particular secondary and postsecondary institutions that Jaime, Ana, Diego, Fabiola, and Maria attended, they continue much as before. Although South Sierra High School has a new campus, and many of the teachers and administrators at both South Sierra and West Hills High Schools have changed, the curricula at both high schools—and at the postsecondary institutions youth attended—remain largely the same, as do established policies about tracking. However, changes are occurring elsewhere in the state of California. As this book is going to press, a 2017 state executive order is dramatically reshaping remedial programs in the California State University system, which is currently the largest four-year university system in the United States. The impact of such shifts will have significant and as yet unknown implications for the many immigrant-origin linguistically minoritized youth who attend these institutions each year.

An update would not be complete without attention to youth themselves and how their lives today reflect the range of interactional histories developed through their language and literacy journeys. What are they doing now, over three years after the end of the study?

- Jaime still works in food service at the technology company that employed him a few years out of high school, and he now has a second job making medical deliveries. He hopes to earn enough extra income to move out of his family's home soon and rent a place with his long-time girlfriend, who is finishing a nursing program. He enjoys watching movies and hiking when he has the time and still hopes to take a short community college course to help launch him into a new career. He reports using both Spanish and English on a daily basis both at work and with friends.

- Ana continued to work in her home salon until she married her long-time boyfriend, who grew up in a nearby community much like South Sierra, in 2015. My husband and I attended the small outdoor ceremony, officiated in Spanish, where friends and family members both young and old gathered to celebrate the marriage. About a year later,

Ana and her husband had a son. She currently stays home with him and has made it a priority to teach him to speak (and eventually read) in both English and Spanish.

- Although Diego stopped returning my calls and texts before the end of the study, I heard through other youth that he eventually finished an associate's degree at a local community college. My only other interaction with Diego was three years after he left Ocean College, when he texted me to say hello and tell me about his work as a landscaper, as well as his struggles to stay on top of the increasing rents in the South Sierra community, which was gentrifying rapidly.

- Since university graduation, Fabiola has worked as an accounts manager in a small business, where she processes invoice paperwork and communicates extensively (in English) with clients via email and telephone. Inspired by reading the book *Lean In: Women, Work, and the Will to Lead* (Sandberg, 2013), she argued for a raise after about two years with the company and received it. She sent me a copy of the book shortly thereafter, as "a feminist gift." She and her husband live a few towns away from South Sierra but are still close to family and friends there. She also travels to Mexico periodically to visit her mother, siblings, nieces, and nephews.

- After completing her year of study in Rome, Maria was posted to a Catholic parish in Toronto, Canada, that serves both recently arrived Arabic-speaking Syrian refugees and longer-standing Italian- and Spanish-speaking immigrant communities. Her responsibilities at the church include coordinating events for their youth groups and food pantry, alongside other religious duties. Maria uses Spanish frequently with families and youth and enjoys using what she remembers of her Italian with some of the older parishioners, but she is now eager to learn Arabic as well. In late 2017, she took her permanent vows as a member of the Institute and remains posted at the same church.

Such stories are necessarily unique, in that they reflect not only youth's shared backgrounds as members of Mexican immigrant families and the South Sierra community but also their individual aspirations, personalities, goals, and family contexts. Multiple languages and literacies—only some of which were supported through formal schooling—continue to play important roles in their lives as professionals, parents, partners, and family members.

Insights into Longitudinal Language and Literacy Becoming

> Writing is not played against a single opponent with fixed rules on a fixed court, nor performed on a stage before an audience awaiting entertainment. Writing occurs in almost all spheres of action and in many moments, each with separate demands and opportunities. Trajectories of writing development are intertwined with trajectories of intellectual, professional, and personal development, such that writing development contributes to personal uniqueness. (Bazerman et al., 2017, p. 353)

Much as Bazerman et al. (2017) pointed out, these young people's experiences make clear that literacy development is inextricable from the complex and multiple social practices in which they are embedded. To capture these wide-ranging literacy practices, I argue that researchers must attend carefully to three key issues when looking at individuals and their texts across time: the micro-, meso-, and macro-level interactions they have while writing, the ways in which these interactions influence the texts that are created, and changes over time in writers' texts and composing processes. Such explorations provide key insights into the identities they develop through participation in these literacy events. I address these issues below to summarize the insights that a longitudinal interactional histories approach (LIHA) to analysis (see Chap. 3) brought to this particular study.

Exploring the first two elements of LIHA—the interactions youth had with various discourses, governmental and institutional policies and practices, individuals, texts, and technologies while writing, and the impact of those interactions on their texts—underscores how important these histories are when considering language and literacy development over time. For example, Jaime's interactions in varied academic tracks and settings ranged notably, from his lack of engagement in a remedial high school social studies writing task to a lack of opportunity for any meaningful literacy interactions in a SDAIE English class to a remedial community college writing context in which increased writing-focused pedagogical support occurred alongside a new willingness to seek input from others in creating written texts. In Ana's case, when she saw literacy events (and the instructors who initiated them) as relevant to her linguistic and cultural identities and vocational aspirations, she was proactive in seeking and using resources across a range of languages and modalities to support her writing and meet the demands of her varied audiences. Diego interacted with textual resources and other people while reading and writing in ways that depended on in-class and interpersonal interaction to help him negotiate literacy events, a pattern used in high school and university with more or less success depending on the demands and features of the task and the institutional context. As Fabiola engaged in literacy events that required increasingly sophisticated disciplinary competencies, she drew upon a wide range of resources, including her university instructors and me, texts she read, and her knowledge of and engagement with multiple cultural, linguistic, and familial communities. Finally, Maria's shift into exam preparation and teaching-focused literacy events at the Institute was accomplished through ongoing informal (and often bilingual) collaborative interactions with others alongside new and more formal uses of bilingualism and biliteracies.

Such a lens highlights the ways in which change over time—the third element of LIHA—differed for each individual in this study. Fabiola became increasingly adept at drawing upon argumentative and feminist writing traditions through her university experiences, for example, while Jaime's community college writing included more sophisticated texts in genres that were fairly similar to those he originally attempted in high school. Over time and particularly as institutional contexts changed, these young people also took on (and often, although not always, developed expertise in) literacy events that were new, such as Ana's multimodal composing in cosmetology school and work-related bilingual and biliterate practices, Diego's preparation for multiple-choice and short-answer tests, and Maria's bilingual exam preparation and teaching.

It is important to note, however, that developments in literacy expertise did not necessarily ensure successful trajectories through secondary and postsecondary contexts (see also Leki, 2007; Ruecker, 2015). Jaime's success with writing in community college, for example, did not support a successful pathway toward completing his studies at that institution. Such trends underscore the complicated relationships between institutionally based literacy practices, individuals' expertise, and the many factors influencing linguistically minoritized immigrant-origin youth's progress through those institutions.

The changes in literacy expertise during the years of this study make clear the intersectional (Shields, 2008) identities youth developed through their engagement in literacy practices over time. Jaime's identities, developed through both in-school and out-of-school writing, included being someone with a "point of view" in relation to discourses of immigration and achievement. Ana's identities were made visible in relation to her active engagement in literacy practices that supported her as a bilingual/biliterate Latina and professional stylist. Diego demonstrated identities as both a hard-working student and an increasingly competent English user, particularly when he was able to interact with instructors and use oral and visual modalities alongside written ones. Fabiola became a "more literate feminist" through writing about feminist topics in ways that made visible various identities as a feminist, Mexican, Latina, immigrant, bilingual, and language-learner. Finally, Maria's development of bilingual and biliterate identities related closely to the pursuit of her (gendered) religious calling. In this sense, youth's multifaceted identities—in which axes of privilege and discrimination shifted notably depending on the policy-related and institutional contexts for literacy practices—suggest that intersectionality is a particularly fruitful and dynamic lens through which to view adolescent and young adults' development over time, much as Compton-Lilly, Papoi, Venegas, Hamman, and Schwabenbauer (2017) have also found with younger learners.

Such changes underscore both the complexity and the importance of understanding individuals' longitudinal interactional histories in literacy events, particularly for minoritized multilingual writers whose texts are often judged for what they lack rather than what they contain, and whose teachers may not fully recognize the ways in which interactions at multiple levels influence immigrant-origin youth and their texts over time. It is critical, then, to recenter pedagogical and empirical definitions of literacy development, and writing development in particular, on changes in the interactional processes through which texts are developed rather than on texts in isolation. In this sense, researchers and educators are better able to see goodness (Lawrence-Lightfoot & Davis, 1997) in what minoritized multilingual students can (or strive to) do as they create texts.

Insights into Relationships Among Macro-, Meso-, and Micro-Level Factors Influencing Language and Literacy Development

The ways in which longitudinal research can shed light on those factors that have relatively stronger long-term influences on an individual's language and literacy expertise offer both an immense affordance and a substantial challenge. Although the turning points described in this book were often institutionally linked, speaking to the power of formal educational settings to shape individuals' language and literacy journeys, this was not always the case. Rather, the LIHA analyses presented in previous chapters demonstrate the following: Instead of any single interaction or factor, it was the constellation of multiple interactions—at the macro- and meso-levels with policies, practices, discourses, and at the micro-level with individuals, texts, and technologies—that worked in combination to most profoundly influence change over time in language and literacy repertoires.

At the macro-level, immigration-related policies and discourses were clearly influential on youth's school-based opportunities to develop language and literacy expertise. All the participants in this study experienced anti-immigrant discourses in varied ways, but immigration-related policies impacting unauthorized/undocumented populations were an issue that played key roles in Ana's and Jaime's experiences. Although both young people attended postsecondary institutions and Ana completed hers, their overall networks of support in those contexts were notably weaker than those of Fabiola, Maria, and Diego due to more limited financial and employment opportunities. Perhaps just as powerful were the ways in which both of their schooling experiences seemed to be colored by the prospects of limited future career opportunities (see also Gonzales, 2011, 2016). Although it is impossible to know how their experiences would have unfolded differently with citizenship or some other form of authorization/documentation, or even the benefit of state-level programs enacted just a few years after they graduated, one cannot help but wonder to what extent their engagement in school-based literacy events was shaped by these realities.

It is also important to note the potential relevance of other macro-level considerations which were part of youth's intersectional identities, like gender. While the size of this study makes it difficult to draw any firm conclusions, the relative lack of institutional success that the two male youth in the study experienced raises critical questions regarding the ways in which young men from minoritized communities may be particularly vulnerable to discourses that negatively stereotype their experiences and capacities. From another perspective, it can also be argued that Ana, Fabiola, and Maria all entered into academic studies or vocations that are, or at least in the past have been, associated with stereotypically female social roles, such as hair stylist, feminist, and religious sister. Such gender roles and understandings are continuing to evolve in society, and these youth's experiences are clearly not inclusive of the wide span of postsecondary pathways taken by linguistically minoritized young people, but the extent to which institutional support and gendered opportunities may interact with other marginalized social identities is an important concern.

At the meso-level, institutional policies and practices during high school—and the discourses they embodied or promoted—unsurprisingly tended to emphasize youth's development of English-medium language and literacy practices but often fell short in achieving those aims. At the high school level, neither South Sierra nor West Hills was able to fully support students' language and literacy development or their transitions to the postsecondary opportunities to which they aspired. In some cases, instructional shortcomings were dramatic, such as the lack of attention paid to Diego's struggles with reading comprehension, or the racialized "basic skills" discourse found in the SDAIE track at West Hills, which resulted in dramatically restricted opportunities for language and literacy development (in line with other research into similar settings such as Enright & Gilliland, 2011; Fu, 1995). As a result, it can easily be argued that these high schools failed the very students whom they were supposed to serve, leaving Mexican immigrant-origin youth to face the consequences for their high school's instructional shortcomings. Yet, the particular interactional histories that youth built through some high school literacy events add a layer of complexity in understanding the long-term influence of these contexts. At times—though clearly not often enough—high school literacy events seemed to help create positive interactional histories, which in turn supported later engagement and development, if not always immediate success. Those instances were characterized by explicit encouragement for students to assume identities that were aligned to their longer-term goals and aspirations, alongside pedagogical guidance and interactional affordances that enabled them to do so.

At the postsecondary level, institutional experiences likewise seemed more productive for youth when they allowed relatively quick access to content related to their interests (e.g., religion, cosmetology, feminism) as well as a clear institutional pathway allowing them to meet their long-term goals. Such a statement does not imply that Jaime and Diego did not benefit from the literacy-focused instruction they received in postsecondary remedial courses. Rather, when seen from a broader longitudinal perspective, the extent to which these courses prevented young people from progressing more quickly to their postsecondary interests and goals is what seemed to have been most problematic. Ironically, as Ana, Jaime, and Maria left traditional school-based contexts, the bilingual and biliterate expertise that was typically marginalized or ignored in those settings became important keys to their success.

Yet the influence of macro- and meso-level contexts cannot be fully understood without also considering the micro-level interactions in which individuals engaged during any given literacy event. The LIHA analyses suggest that youth were not isolated or lone composers. Rather, a range of fellow youth as well as adults, alongside a range of multimodal resources, played multiple influential roles across languages in the creation of their texts. But while these resources dramatically shaped young people's texts and often supported literacy development in powerful ways, they hardly assured youth's academic or vocational success.

A key insight from this study is that micro-level interactions were true affordances for learning and appeared to facilitate individuals' progress only when the role(s) they played matched larger institutional or vocational demands of the settings in which they were engaged (see also

Kibler, 2016). For example, Maria's writing at the Institute was judged primarily on the accuracy of information rather than written expression per se, and so her interactions with others about better understanding the content they were learning–rather than discussions about how to write about it—were what facilitated her eventual passing of written and oral examinations. In much the same way, Jaime and Fabiola encountered success in postsecondary settings as they interacted with individuals who were knowledgeable in the specific writing genres and conventions that were valued, taught, and assessed in those contexts. In fact, Fabiola's and Jaime's postsecondary trajectories likely varied not because of dramatic differences in literacy expertise, but because Fabiola had far greater institutional and financial resources to support her schooling than did Jaime, as well as positive dispositions toward literacy and schooling and aspirations informed by a clear legal pathway to future employment. For Diego, a match between resources and institutional demands was less consistent. His reliance on teachers while writing—an understandable strategy when faced with instruction that did not recognize his particular needs—provided him a level of success in completing extended writing tasks and passing classroom assessments. It did not, however, support the development of reading comprehension necessary to engage in those writing tasks, the literacy expertise required for his university placement test, or the type of critical reading practices expected by other teachers, who in at least one case interpreted Diego's struggles as simply a lack of effort. In contrast, Ana's choice to pursue a cosmetology degree rather than a traditional postsecondary schooling made available to her a range of different individual and textual resources that were multimodal (and at times bilingual) and thus well-matched to both her interests and the demands of the program.

The complexity of such macro/meso/micro relationships leads to a range of provocative questions when considering the development of school-based languages and literacies for minoritized youth from immigrant backgrounds. For example, what can be said when even concerted individual efforts and well-intentioned institutional practices seem to be overpowered by a range of macro-level policies and discourses? And how can one fully account for the impacts of anti-immigrant, linguistically minoritizing, and racialized discourses and instructional experiences that so often ignore young people's bilingual/biliterate strengths and instructional needs? The cases presented in this book explain some ways in which these tensions played out from a longitudinal perspective and suggest that political, institutional, and instructional responses to linguistically minoritized Mexican and other immigrant-origin multilingual youth must engage with these issues in context rather than in isolation.

Insights into the Bilingual and Biliterate Becoming of Immigrant-Origin Minoritized Youth

Youth in this book successfully navigated a range of bilingual and biliterate communities, both inside and outside of school, highlighting the ways that such practices grow from and are embedded in the varied familial, community, institutional, and societal contexts in which they occur. As youth progressed through adolescence and into adulthood, they were exposed to a range of new academic, social, and employment settings, each of which required different ways of using languages (Hoyle & Adger, 1998). For the young people in this study, responsiveness to new situations required the use and further development of flexible expertise that spanned a broad range of bilingual and biliterate practices.

Bilingual and biliterate interactions played various unofficial and official roles in the multiple communities in which youth participated. During high school, the youth in this study lived in predominantly Latinx and Mexican neighborhoods in which most adults were Spanish-dominant, and most children and young people were bilingual. Their schools reflected this larger community, and their classroom interactions with other students, like their sibling relationships at home, typically drew upon diverse resources across languages. Bilingual classmates frequently played key roles in students' composing processes during school-based literacy events (Kibler, 2010), and teachers who were bilingual/bicultural provided important guidance for students in varied ways. In Maria's case, for example, such teachers offered unique encouragement to begin writing in English, and for Ana, a Mexican-origin

Latina teacher and role model inspired pride in her bilingual and biliterate academic identities. Spanish also had some level of official status in students' high schools, although only as part of a transitional ninth-grade bilingual humanities course and in Spanish classes designed for heritage speakers.

While bilingual and biliterate expertise remained important to social and familial relationships for all youth throughout the study, it took on new and varied roles unique to each individual in relation to their post-secondary studies or professional pursuits. For Jaime and Ana, bilingual expertise allowed them to serve as language brokers with both clients and fellow employees, and English literacy practices played an important role in making those interactions possible. For Fabiola, her family and community relationships provided inspiration and even an audience for her disciplinary writing in GWS at university, even though her Spanish language and literacy practices and her language-learner identity were not overtly recognized or valued institutionally. Maria's uses of Spanish alongside English, to both support her studies and engage in teaching, played central and official roles in her experiences. For Diego, bilingual and biliterate practices were less prominent in his postsecondary institutionally based interactions, but the hardworking student identity that he developed in high school and carried into university had its roots in interactions with bilingual teachers in ninth grade.

However, for all but one of the youth, institutionally provided opportunities to develop bilingual and biliterate expertise at the postsecondary level were even scarcer than those provided in high school. Neither Jaime nor Ana nor Diego nor Fabiola had postsecondary institutional opportunities to read or write in Spanish or instructor-provided opportunities to draw upon their bilingual/biliterate expertise in support of their English writing. For example, Fabiola was exposed to some bilingual texts and began to use Spanish in limited ways in support of her composing processes later in her university studies, but this latter approach was neither initiated nor supported institutionally. Ana's bilingual practices were key to the creation of her English-medium and multimodal texts created in vocational school, but even these were likewise undertaken without instructors' recognition or encouragement. Maria's case was unique in that Spanish had official status and prestige at the Institute she attended through its history, leadership, founding documents, and curriculum.

Such trends highlight some of the institutional mechanisms through which non-English language and literacy resources are marginalized in US educational settings, or at the very least treated as peripheral to individuals' progress, despite the important roles they play in both school-based literacy events and in out-of-school lives. The findings of this study suggest that however normalized this pattern has become, it deserves renewed attention and concern when considering the range of factors that influence language and literacy development across the lifespan.

Limitations

The challenges of longitudinal qualitative research are substantial, and although my data collection was a sustained and extensive undertaking, I was not able to complete in-depth observations or teacher interviews in all contexts or years of the study, nor was I able to observe and interview within the context of students' workplaces. I also did not attempt to gather everything that youth wrote, as a result of logistical realities and a particular interest in what extended texts might reveal about interactional histories. Additional observational, interview, and textual data would have provided evidence and nuance to support, refine, or even challenge the turning points and LIHA analyses presented here. Future studies could also certainly strive to undertake such work with minoritized multilingual youth from a range of different backgrounds and contexts in efforts to build upon the analysis of language and literacy journeys presented here.

Further, selection of the turning points and other literacy events presented in the LIHA analyses was ultimately mine, and so they are inevitably my creation, reflect my positionality as a researcher, and exclude other stories that could have been told. However, the time I spent with youth during ethnographic observations, our ongoing communication, their accounts of literacy events, and the texts themselves guided me toward those moments that appeared to have the largest impact and that were most helpful in understanding young people's complex language and literacy journeys over time (see Chap. 3). Other research could usefully include an even larger voice for study participants in selecting turning points and literacy events, an undertaking that would provide important but necessarily different insights.

Implications

> Indeed, it is long past time for us to accept that embodied, mediated, dialogic, semiotic practice is the matrix of all so-called "modes" and to recognize that semiotic (including literate) development is a ubiquitous cultural process, not the special provenance of school. (Prior, 2017, p. 217)

It is important to situate the implications of this study in a broader perspective, and I find it particularly useful to do so in light of Prior's (2017) argument that writing must be seen as but one of several meaning-making modes and that the development of various literacies takes place in many contexts as part of the cultural practices in which we participate. In the article referenced above, Prior went on to warn that a "just-writing, just-in-school" perspective or agenda (p. 217) is limited if our goal is to better understand writing development across the lifespan. In many ways, this study is an attempt to fulfill that vision, balancing an understanding of youth's full communicative repertoires alongside a recognition that for the school-aged youth in this study, participation in writing and other literacy events was a key cultural practice in the institutions in which they spent many hours of their days. For linguistically minoritized immigrant-origin youth, such a focus has the potential to both broaden our understandings of literacy practices and suggest ways that structural and instructional barriers to equitable schooling can potentially be addressed. The longitudinal interactional histories that youth in this study brought to, employed in, and developed through literacy events have important implications for educators, policymakers, and researchers. Foremost among them is that such stakeholders must respond to this complexity with nuanced and multifaceted efforts, not simplistic solutions, and ones that recognize the value of these young people's histories as well as their futures.

Teaching Implications Despite the powerful influence of institutional and governmental policies and practices on students' long-term trajectories, and the limitation of schooling as but one set of sites for literacy practices, individual educators play key roles in minoritized immigrant-origin multilingual students' language and literacy development. While there are many different pedagogical issues raised in the chapters of this book, here I focus on two broad outlooks that have the potential to harness the power of longitudinal and interactional perspectives to support ambitious instruction, particularly in the context of writing.

A Pedagogy of Building Positive Interactional Histories All texts that students produce are shaped by the interactions they have while writing, which are in turn influenced by their histories of participation in previous literacy events. As a result, teachers' understanding of students' experiences while creating their texts is key to understanding the texts themselves. Teachers can accomplish this by, for example, carefully observing students during classroom-based writing and the lessons that build toward it, looking closely at changes that occur across students' drafts, asking students to submit written or oral reflections about their writing processes, and engaging in teacher self-reflection about interactions with students. Key to this approach is attending to a broad range of texts and interactions that might influence writing; such considerations are particularly important for multilingual students, whose literacy practices will draw upon resources across languages, many of which may be invisible to a teacher without careful attention and observation. Teachers may also find that opening up writing assignments to include a variety of modalities and uses of language, thereby allowing students to use their full communicative repertoires, can provide a more accurate picture of what they know and can accomplish through writing. Finally, this pedagogical outlook also involves careful attention to changes in students' writing processes and texts over time, with the recognition that any single teacher's semester- or year-long perspective is necessarily a very narrow window through which to judge what is a very long-term and complex journey. Using multiyear portfolios or similar collections of writing—something that is perhaps easier to accomplish in K-12 settings rather than at the postsecondary level—can help teachers understand and reflect upon changes over time.

A pedagogy that seeks to build positive interactional histories provides unique opportunities to support students' development of language and literacy expertise. For example, careful observation of students' interactions can make visible certain practices with which they are particularly adept, as well as practices with which they might be struggling. Such observations then allow teachers to build instruction upon students' strengths while also supporting focused needs that students may have within the context of (rather than isolated from) complex and authentic literacy events, practices that align well with other models of ambitious instruction for English-learner-classified students (e.g., Bunch, Kibler, & Pimentel, 2014; Valdés, Kibler, & Walqui, 2014). In this sense, teachers can support students' language and literacy journeys through building successful interactional histories.

A Writing Pedagogy of Multilingual Agency Inextricable from the creation of students' texts is their development of agentive identities through literacy practices. A writing pedagogy of multilingual agency first and foremost strives to seek goodness by recognizing the significant linguistic and cultural expertise that minoritized multilingual students bring to any given literacy event, including transcultural skills and dispositions related to "reading" and flexibly responding to diverse situations (Orellana & D'warte, 2010). Similarly, teachers can better understand and build upon students' expertise if they recognize that students carry into the classroom important and historically situated out-of-school literacy expertise, what Gutiérrez (2008) has called socio-critical literacies.

Such focus requires teachers to provide opportunities to write that somehow matter to students, which is not an easy or predictable task. Youth in this study, for example, often viewed and participated in the same high school writing assignment quite differently, suggesting that effective task design and instructional support are necessary but not sufficient for the development of multilingual agency through writing. Rather, what seemed to make the most difference were those literacy events that allowed students to assume positive, rather than marginalized, identities that were aligned to their longer-term goals and aspirations: Latina professional, DREAMer, hardworking English user, Mexican feminist, and bilingual Catholic spokesperson, among others. While these cannot be the literal focus for an entire curriculum, allowing authentic choice and assignments in which students' ideas are valued above "right answers" has notable potential in developing agentive identities. And because students' interests can span the curriculum, opportunities to engage in literacy events in STEM contexts as well as in humanities and social sciences are important to support the range of identities to which students aspire.

The everyday demands of secondary and postsecondary classrooms can be overwhelming, and such lofty aspirations can seem very distant from those realities. However, without such a perspective—one that consistently reminds us that multilingual youth are skillful, agentive, and future-bound—pedagogical practices can easily become infused with the minoritizing discourses that can preclude students from developing their linguistic and academic potential.

Policy Implications Macro- and meso-level interactions, in particular with governmental and school policies, have an undeniable but not entirely deterministic influence on the language and literacy development of minoritized immigrant-origin multilingual youth. In this sense, socio-institutional mechanisms tend to create contexts that—while not explicitly prohibiting these students from succeeding—do not actively support or respond to their needs and circumstances. The longitudinal interactional histories explored in this book suggest that educational institutions could benefit from recentering their decision-making based on the multifaceted experiences of the minoritized multilingual students who navigate these institutions and whose trajectories are simultaneously influenced by multiple factors, from language and literacy expertise to poverty and immigration status. In this sense, wide-ranging and longitudinal quantitative data should be examined alongside students' and educators' lived experiences in these institutions, which can, in particular, highlight students' literacy strengths across languages in ways that are rarely measured institutionally.

Just as many influences on students' language and literacy development are out of classroom teachers' hands, school-based policies and decisions are often determined by those made by governmental institutions. While the vicissitudes of immigration policy are more likely to provoke fear and anxiety than provide either stability or assurance for Mexican and other immigrant populations in the United States in the near future, the influence of such policies on students' material circumstances and long-term educational aspirations and opportunities underscores how such mechanisms can marginalize immigrant-origin students. Other issues in the hands of governmental institutions—ranging from school evaluation systems to economic and housing policies—likewise tend to systematically work against, rather than for, minoritized multilingual children and youth. Untangling such systemic issues lies at the heart of the larger changes that would be necessary to provide more supportive contexts for language and literacy development across the lifespan.

Research Implications Understanding the ways that language and literacy practices and identities develop over time, particularly for linguistically minoritized multilingual youth from immigrant families, is a multifaceted and multigenerational scholarly endeavor to which I hope this book contributes. Based on my experiences, I would argue that at least three implications from this work have particular potential to meaningfully inform future research. First, researchers can benefit from conceptualizing texts as inextricable from the interactional processes through which they are created and the histories upon which individuals draw while creating those texts, a perspective that calls for both in-depth and longitudinal data collection and analysis. While the particular longitudinal interactional histories approach I employed is obviously not the only means of capturing such phenomena, it served the purposes of this study well and may prove useful to other researchers interested in similar issues.

Second, longitudinal studies in which ecological contexts (Hornberger, 2003; van Lier, 2000) are emphasized can help researchers better understand the complex relationships among interactions that profoundly influence language and literacy practices and expertise over time. In this sense, the development of positive interactional histories can be seen as resulting from a "network of interdependencies" in a given ecology (van Lier, 2010, p. 3). Because longitudinal and ethnographic vantage points provide insight into the various ecological (or as I describe it, interactional) histories that an individual may bring into a network, I argue that such methodologies can be used to provide particularly robust understandings of affordances for bilingual and biliterate learning made possible and taken up in and across settings. At the same time, it is important to acknowledge a unique interplay between longitudinal and ethnographic study: The longer a study is, the more difficult it often becomes to maintain the same intensity of fieldwork, particularly as individuals' geographic and institutional settings shift. For this reason, engaging in ethnographic fieldwork in the early stages of a longitudinal study provides a critically important basis for maintaining relationships over time and interpreting later data that may not have been gathered as frequently or through direct observation.

Third, researchers engaged in classroom-based research of any sort can benefit from understanding the complexity inherent to longitudinal language and literacy journeys and the ways that interactions at multiple levels may influence both short- and long-term outcomes. Such a recognition can help researchers prioritize and contextualize their work in ways that acknowledge both what pedagogical interventions can achieve and what they cannot, at least without larger institutional or political changes. In this sense, research can support the development of more nuanced responses to the educational imperative of improving opportunities for language and literacy development for minoritized multilingual immigrant-origin children and youth.

Looking Forward

The findings from this study critically call into question how well our society and its institutions serve Mexican and other immigrant-origin minoritized multilingual populations in ways that sustain and expand the bilingual and biliterate expertise they actively employ outside of curricularized educational spaces. The experiences of Jaime, Ana, Diego, Fabiola, and Maria suggest that the development of positive interactional histories with literacy practices cannot be assured through any singular instructional or institutional approach. At the same time, however, those that forestalled access to agentive or future-oriented literacy opportunities, or that overlooked young people's genuine language and literacy strengths and needs, clearly mediated against that development. Further, these journeys also tell us that interactional histories have the potential to support strong, multifaceted identities through writing for immigrant-origin multilingual youth, particularly when resources align with goals valued by both the individual and the institutions in which they are studying or working. Such alignment, however, can overlook larger inequitable circumstances, such as the largely monolingual orientation of school settings and the limited institutionally provided opportunities young people typically have to sustain and enrich their existing bilingual and biliterate repertoires. Shifting such paradigms, however, involves far more than bureaucratic or programmatic changes: It requires a fundamental rethinking of the value that multilingualism and multilingual literacies and individuals bring to our society and the investments necessary to realize minoritized multilinguals' immense academic, professional, and civic potential.

References

Banks, J. A., Suárez-Orozco, M. M., & Ben-Peretz, M. (Eds.). (2016). *Global migration, diversity, and civic education: Improving policy and practice.* New York: Teachers College Press.

Bazerman, C., Applebee, A. N., Berninger, V. W., Brandt, D., Graham, S., Matsuda, P. K., Murphy, S., Rowe, D. W., & Schleppegrell, M. (2017). Taking the long view on writing development. *Research in the Teaching of English, 51*(3), 351–360.

Bunch, G. C., Kibler, A. K., & Pimentel, S. (2014). Shared responsibility: Realizing opportunities for English learners in the common core English language arts and disciplinary literacy standards. In L. Minaya-Rowe (Ed.), *Effective educational programs, practices, and policies for English learners* (pp. 1–28). Charlotte, NC: Information Age Publishing.

Cole, M. (1996). *Cultural psychology.* Cambridge, MA: Harvard University Press.

Compton-Lilly, C. (2014). The development of writing habitus: A ten-year case study of a young writer. *Written Communication, 31*(4), 371–403. https:// doi.org/10.1177/0741088314549539.

Compton-Lilly, C., Papoi, K., Venegas, P., Hamman, L., & Schwabenbauer, B. (2017). Intersectional identity negotiation: The case of young immigrant children. *Journal of Literacy Research, 49*(1), 115–140. https://doi.org/10.11 77/1086296X16683421.

Enright, K. A., & Gilliland, B. (2011). Multilingual writing in an age of account-ability: From policy to practice in U.S. high school classrooms. *Journal of Second Language Writing, 20*(3), 182–195. https://doi.org/10.1016/j. jslw.2011.05.006.

Flores, N., & Rosa, J. (2015). Undoing appropriateness: Raciolinguistic ideolo-gies and language diversity in education. *Harvard Educational Review, 85*(2), 149–171. https://doi.org/10.17763/0017-8055.85.2.149.

Fu, D. (1995). *My trouble is my English: Asian students and the American dream.* Portsmouth, NH: Heinemann-Boynton/Cook.

Gonzales, R. G. (2011). Learning to be illegal: Undocumented youth and shift-ing legal contexts in the transition to adulthood. *American Sociological Review, 76*(4), 602–619. https://doi.org/10.1177/0003122411411901.

Gonzales, R. G. (2016). *Lives in limbo: Undocumented and coming of age in America.* Berkeley: University of California Press.

Gutiérrez, K. D. (2008). Developing a sociocritical literacy in the third space. *Reading Research Quarterly, 43*(2), 148–164. https://doi.org/10.1598/ RRQ.43.2.3.

Hornberger, N. H. (2003). Continua of biliteracy. In N. H. Hornberger (Ed.), *Continua of biliteracy: An ecological framework for educational policy, research, and practice in multilingual settings* (pp. 3–34). Bristol, UK: Multilingual Matters.

Hoyle, S. M., & Adger, C. T. (1998). Introduction. In S. M. Hoyle & C. T. Adger (Eds.), *Kids talk: Strategic language use in later childhood* (pp. 3–22). New York: Oxford University Press.

Kibler, A. K. (2010). Writing through two languages: First language expertise in a language minority classroom. *Journal of Second Language Writing, 19*(3), 121–142. https://doi.org/10.1016/j.jslw.2010.04.001.

Kibler, A. K. (2016). Promises and limitations of literacy sponsors in resident multilingual youths' transitions to postsecondary schooling. In C. Ortmeier-Hooper & T. Ruecker (Eds.), *Linguistically diverse immigrant and resident writers: Transitions from high school to college* (pp. 99–116). New York: Routledge.

Kibler, A. K., & Valdés, G. (2016). Conceptualizing language learners: Socio-institutional mechanisms and their consequences. *Modern Language Journal,* *100*(S1), 96–116. https://doi.org/10.1111/modl.12310.

Kibler, A., Karam, F., Futch Ehrlich, V., Bergey, R., Wang, C., & Molloy Elreda, L. (in press). Who are long-term English learners? Deconstructing a manufactured learner label. *Applied Linguistics.* https://doi.org/10.1093/applin/amw039.

Lawrence-Lightfoot, S., & Davis, J. H. (1997). *The art and science of portraiture.* San Francisco: Jossey-Bass Publishers.

Leki, I. (2007). *Undergraduates in a second language: Challenges and complexities of academic literacy development.* Mahwah, NJ: Lawrence Erlbaum.

Migration Policy Institute. (2018). *Deferred Action for Childhood Arrivals (DACA) data tools.* Retrieved from: https://www.migrationpolicy.org/programs/data-hub/deferred-action-childhood-arrivals-daca-profiles

National Academies of Sciences, Engineering, and Medicine. (2017). *Promoting the educational success of children and youth learning English: Promising futures.* Washington, DC: The National Academies Press. https://doi.org/10.17226/24677.

Orellana, M. F., & D'warte, J. (2010). Recognizing different kinds of "head starts". *Educational Researcher, 39*(4), 295–300. https://doi.org/10.3102/0013189X10369829.

Palmer, D. (2009). Middle-class English speakers in a two-way immersion bilingual classroom: "Everybody should be listening to Jonathan right now...". *TESOL Quarterly, 43*(2), 177–202. https://doi.org/10.1002/j.1545-7249.2009.tb00164.x.

Prior, P. (2017). Setting a research agenda for lifespan writing development: The long view from where? *Research in the Teaching of English, 52*(2), 211–219.

Rosa, J., & Flores, N. (2017). Unsettling race and language: Toward a raciolinguistic perspective. *Language in Society, 46*(5), 621–647. https://doi.org/10.1017/S0047404517000562.

Ruecker, T. (2015). *Transiciones: Pathways of Latinas and Latinos writing in high school and college.* Logan, UT: Utah State University Press.

Sandberg, S. (2013). *Lean in: Women, work, and the will to lead.* New York: Knopf.

Shields, S. A. (2008). Gender: An intersectionality perspective. *Sex Roles, 59*(5–6), 301–311. https://doi.org/10.1007/s11199-008-9501-8.

Valdés, G. (1997). Dual language immersion programs: A cautionary note concerning the education of language-minority students. *Harvard Educational Review, 67*(3), 391–429. https://doi.org/10.17763/haer.67.3.n5q175qp86120948.

Valdés, G. (2015). Latin@s and the intergenerational continuity of Spanish: The challenges of curricularizing language. *International Multilingual Research Journal, 9(4)*, 253–273. https://doi.org/10.1080/19313152.2015.1086625.

Valdés, G., Kibler, A. K., & Walqui, A. (2014). *Changes in the expertise of ESL professionals: Knowledge and action in an era of new standards.* Alexandria, VA: TESOL International Association.

Valdez, V. E., Friere, J. A., & Delavan, M. G. (2016). The gentrification of dual language education. *The Urban Review, 48(4)*, 601–627. https://doi.org/10.1007/s11256-016-0370-0.

van Lier, L. (2000). From input to affordance: Social-interactive learning from an ecological perspective. In J. P. Lantolf (Ed.), *Sociocultural theory and second language learning* (pp. 245–260). Oxford, UK: Oxford University Press.

van Lier, L. (2010). The ecology of language learning: Practice to theory, theory to practice. *Procedia – Social and Behavioral Sciences, 3*, 2–6. https://doi.org/10.1016/j.sbspro.2010.07.005.

Methodological Appendix

This appendix provides further details on methodological issues, including my positioning as a researcher, interview guides, transcription, and presentation of youth's writing. A full description of the methodology employed in this study can be found in Chap. 3.

Researcher Positioning

My first introduction to South Sierra High School, and to the young people who would eventually become the focus of this study, happened at the beginning of my second year as a doctoral student, a year before the ethnographic phase of the study would begin. I was initially asked to work with the school to help their teachers of ninth-grade bilingual humanities and English language development (or ELD, the common term at the time for "ESL" or "ESOL" courses in California) develop curricula and incorporate technology into their teaching. My duties at the school over the next two years ranged from providing instructional coaching to helping individual students in class (at teachers' requests) to

© The Author(s) 2019
A. K. Kibler, *Longitudinal Interactional Histories*,
https://doi.org/10.1007/978-3-319-98815-3

developing assessments and compiling data for a related research project. Throughout these activities, I spent a significant amount of time observing, helping out in classrooms, and talking with teachers and students.

Throughout my fieldwork, I strove for what ethnographers call an emic perspective: an insider's view of how informants themselves understand the activities in which they are engaged (Watson-Gegeo, 1988). Yet being an outsider to some degree is, of course, inevitable. As Heath and Street (2008) explained, "our physical features … as well as our own cultural identities and life experiences, prevent our fully participating as the 'other'" (p. 34). Innocence to these differences is naive at best, and contemporary expectations for qualitative research demand a reflexive stance in which critical introspection is used to uncover the ways that a researcher's various social identities, positionalities, and subjectivities influence all phases of research, from study design to publication (Marcus, 1994; see also Berger, 2015; Gough, 2003; Hamden, 2013). Researchers are called upon to seek out and recognize the contributions and limitations of their work in this regard in order to both create improved research accounts (Guillemin & Gillam, 2004) and fulfill ethnical responsibilities to produce research that respects the goodness of those being studied.

Being deeply involved in the life of the school at the time I began the ethnographic phase of the study, I followed the guidance of Emerson, Fretz, and Shaw (2011), who advise researchers to attend carefully to their own positioning as well as how they are seen and treated by others. My responsibilities as an instructional coach at South Sierra High School and as a researcher put me in two different worlds during fieldwork: acting as a colleague with other adults and as someone just "hanging out" with young people. Although I attempted to separate these roles to some degree by, for example, avoiding conversations with teachers when I was collecting data, they inevitably overlapped. In the early weeks of my study, students would often look my way when a note was thrown across the classroom or a particularly colorful curse word was uttered, waiting to see what I would do and if I would take on the teacherly task of classroom management. A conspiratorial smile, a look of feigned innocence, or an assurance that I'd "heard those words before" were my most common responses to these meaningful looks, and eventually these incidents subsided, although they never disappeared altogether. Students called me by my first name, as I suggested they could, and of the two young people profiled in this book who spoke to me primarily in Spanish during the ethnographic phase, one used the more formal *usted* form of address, while the other employed *tú*, the more familiar form.

A range of other complexities related to these schooling contexts followed me and my relationships with youth throughout the study. Even after I was no longer observing or coaching regularly at their high school, the young people in this study nonetheless knew me as a doctoral student, and later a university professor, roles that were clearly linked to insider status in the world of formal education. And even though our relationships were less classroom-based later in the study, they inevitably bore the marks of the school setting in which we first met. For example, youth often did not describe to me the literacy practices in which they engaged outside of specific academic or educational spaces as "real" reading and writing. Although this outlook is likely shared by many young people, it is possible that the initiation of this study in the school context and my professional positioning made such a perspective more prominent in their eyes. Youth might have also understood me as a reminder of the schooling opportunities they took (or did not take) after high school (see Chap. 3). While no methodological decision could erase this dynamic, I tried to begin and end our interviews with questions that were unrelated to school and instead drew upon my knowledge of their strengths and the positive identities they had developed through hobbies and interests or relationships with family and friends. I also tried to position myself as someone who was happy to use what I knew to assist youth when they needed it. During classroom observations, for example, I always helped students with classwork when they asked me to, and in youth's transitions into postsecondary settings I let them know I was always available if they wanted someone to look at their assignments or help them navigate new institutions. Fabiola was the only youth to take me up on this offer at the postsecondary level (see Chap. 7).

Our joint experiences over time helped build a "shared sensitivity" (Okano, 2009, p. 271) and trust that helped us to talk about some of the more difficult challenges young people faced, although our long-term relationships were not immune to tensions arising from our different social positionalities and identities. Further, although they spoke to me openly about discrimination they experienced inside and outside of schools as Mexican and immigrant-origin individuals, such conversations would have clearly had a different tenor and dynamic if I had been a member of those communities. (See Chap. 1 for further reflections on issues of background and privilege as well as their implications for this study.) It is also important to acknowledge the ways in which I responded to other of youth's positionalities that were quite different from each other's and my own. For example, Maria knew that I was not Catholic, and this outsider status was clear to us both, even though I never spoke with her about my own religious beliefs and she never asked me about them. She very willingly taught me about the Institute and her religious practices, and I sought out a range of information that could inform me about her setting, but my positioning as a non-Catholic and non-member of her religious order certainly could have influenced not only what information or perspectives Maria shared with me but also my understanding of her situated literacy practices (see Kibler, 2014). Fabiola's feminist writing occupied conceptual territory that was at times directly opposed to Maria's, but I attempted to use a similar relational approach in my interactions with her. I had never formally studied feminism before this research project, and much of my early disciplinary learning in this field I attribute to Fabiola, her texts, and our discussions. Although I also read more widely on feminism, in my conversations with Fabiola and my written feedback, I attempted to position myself as a "student" of hers in GWS matters, deferring to the expertise she had gained through her major but also asking questions to help me better understand (and in writing, to help her more clearly explain) her ideas and arguments and those of others in the field. At the same time, our shared identities as women, as well as my support of feminist ideas, might have encouraged Fabiola to share ideas about feminism more openly, or perhaps just differently, than if we had not had this in common (see Kibler, 2017).

It is also relevant to comment upon myself as an L2 user of Spanish and how my language use impacted how I presented myself and was likely viewed by others in this setting. I grew up in family and community settings in which various social and regional varieties of English were used, but I developed Spanish language and literacy expertise through university-level foreign language classes, travel in Spain and Latin

America, and on-the-job interaction with Spanish-speaking students and their families when working as an ESL teacher and a researcher. During fieldwork, my strong listening comprehension allowed me access to most of youth's conversations with other Spanish speakers. My Spanish-language production allowed me to interact with them on a variety of topics, although it clearly marked me as an L2 user and therefore an outsider in their Spanish-dominant and bilingual communities. In those instances in which I was not sure I had understood the explicit or implied meanings of Spanish-language interactions as they occurred, I would later ask youth about the conversation and also review available audio or video recordings of the situation soon afterward to clarify the interaction. Additionally, I prepared bilingual versions of interview prompts ahead of time so that I could discuss relevant topics with precision in individuals' language of choice. To further ensure as authentic a representation and interpretation of young people's language use as possible, at the analysis stage of the study I relied upon assistance from a bilingual and bicultural adult member of the South Sierra community and a Mexican-origin bilingual/bicultural advanced graduate student in Spanish linguistics to assist me in creating and refining transcripts.

Language use in the settings I observed was complex, and for the most part I followed the norms of language choice that applied to each particular context in which I found myself. In South Sierra High School classrooms, I abided by teachers' language preferences, using mostly English in ELD, science, math, and English-medium humanities classes, but using Spanish exclusively in the Spanish-for-Native-Speakers class and both languages in the bilingual humanities course that Maria, Fabiola, and Diego took in ninth grade. At West Hills High School, which Jaime attended, I was a visitor to those classes without any history with teachers or students, and as a result they rarely addressed me during class. When they did, it was always in English, a language choice I maintained throughout those interactions. Outside of school contexts and in interviews, I spoke with youth and others in those settings in the languages in which they addressed me. Two of the five young people in this study (Diego and Fabiola) almost always used Spanish with me during initial years of the study. This balance shifted, in that they gradually spoke to me using more English over time, perhaps reflecting the increasingly

English-medium contexts in which they studied and worked as well as their growing expertise.

An additional element of reflexivity that I would be remiss not to mention is the influence that my own beliefs about language development and teaching inevitably had on this study. Owing to my experiences as a teacher and researcher, I believe that although language and literacy development is nonlinear, unpredictable, and complex, formal instructional experiences nonetheless have the potential to influence such trajectories in meaningful ways. As a result, I focused this study (at least in part) on the work of teachers and the opportunities they provided in classrooms. In relation to teaching, I consider promising those classrooms in which elements such as high expectations, conceptually and linguistically rich curricula that are relevant to students' lives, informative assessments, and interactive and multimodal tasks, to name a few, are combined with an attention to language in the service of (rather than separate from) meaning-making. While these pedagogical beliefs often shaped my initial responses to the instruction I observed or heard about from youth, in both the data analysis and the writing of this book I worked to understand and describe instructional activities and assignments on their own terms and in relation to the goals of teachers and their institutions rather than in comparison to my own vision of instruction. I also endeavored to ground any critiques of pedagogical practices in relation to evidence arising from the data. In terms of the teaching profession more generally, my own secondary and university teaching experiences have also nurtured a deep understanding of the immense dedication and commitment involved in teaching adolescents and the ways in which even the most prepared and practiced teachers are constantly developing and improving their craft. As a result, I strove to present teaching and learning situations in ways that highlight the complex ecological contexts in which educators work and their genuine efforts to support youth, even as they might have been engaged in practices that in the long term sometimes did not serve the youth in this study well.

At the same time, my experiences have also taught me that teachers are far from the only influence on an individual's engagement in language and literacy practices. A range of fellow young people and other adults also play important but often unrecognized roles in literacy events, and for this reason I chose to examine their presence and impact on the experiences of youth in this study. I also purposefully attended to language and literacy practices outside of school, in recognition that formal educational experiences alone often provide a limited picture of individuals' expertise and potential, particularly for minoritized multilingual students.

Finally, and perhaps most significantly, my work is influenced by a commitment to social justice and the creation of more equitable educational opportunities for linguistically minoritized populations through efforts to give voice to youth and their experiences. For this reason, although the study relies upon a broad range of data, it purposefully foregrounds youth's perspectives and seeks goodness (Lawrence-Lightfoot & Davis, 1997) in their varied experiences inside and outside of schools. Not only was I genuinely "rooting" for all of the youth in this study; it is also my hope that the stories of Jaime, Ana, Diego, Fabiola, and Maria bring insight into the processes of language and literacy development while also suggesting new directions for educators, policymakers, and researchers to pursue in improving educational, vocational, and civic opportunities for immigrant-origin multilingual youth.

Interview Guides

I conducted audio-recorded, semi-structured interviews with the five young people in this study and a selected number of their teachers using prepared interview guides (Lofland, Snow, Anderson, & Lofland, 2006). Interviews moved in unpredictable (and fruitful) directions, and the flexibility of the interview guides allowed me to respond to the emerging comments, concerns, and perspectives of interviewees. Youth's guides were prepared bilingually because I invited them to use either or both of their languages in the interview and offered the questions in either or both languages, according to their preference. During interviews, I took notes of key words and phrases—what Lofland et al. (2006) called "sparse notes" (p. 106)—rather than taking detailed notes so that I could more effectively manage the conversations. In addition to these semi-structured interviews, I also engaged in innumerable informal conversations with youth and teachers throughout data collection that were not structured but instead responded to immediate events.

Youth Interview Guide 1: Personal, Linguistic, and Academic Histories

For this initial interview, which was conducted early in the ethnographic phase of this study, I invited young people to help me create "maps" of their lives so far, putting on them what they considered to be the most important events they had experienced in and out of school. I began by saying "I know you've had a very interesting life so far, and I want to make sure I understand it better. If I draw a map of your life, starting here, what should I put first?" I then used an interview guide, which was structured around a list of key concepts and ideas that I wanted to address along with general prompts that could be used to probe topics raised (or omitted) by interviewees:

Self:
Birth/age
Coming to the United States, when, and why
Schools
Communities in which you lived
Friends
Work
Goals

Family/Home:
Siblings and ages
Parents and other relatives
Occupations
Languages that family members use

Language and Literacy Uses:
When and where you speak/listen/read/write in English
When and where you speak/listen/read/write in Spanish

Prompts:
Tell me more about…
You didn't say anything about…
How would you describe…
What are your memories about…
What did you do when…
How did you feel when…

Youth Interview Guide 2: Interactional Histories of Literacy Events

Throughout the study, I conducted stimulated elicitation interviews (Prior, 2004) about writing that individuals completed either in or out of school and shared with me on a regular basis (see Chap. 3). Youth were asked to look back at the artifacts related to a text they had written (including drafts, teacher handouts, and feedback they received, if available) as they answered questions about the text and the processes through which it was created. The semi-structured guide for these interviews included specific questions rather than the more general topics used in the aforementioned interview.

In interviews conducted after the ethnographic phase of the study, youth chose which of the two or three texts they had shared with me they most wanted to discuss, but during the ethnographic phase of the study, I selected particular texts as the focus for each of the interviews. Although youth completed three major writing tasks at South Sierra High School during ethnographic fieldwork, argumentative essays (humanities class) and lab reports (biology class) were chosen as the focus for interviews because they were the only two pieces of writing that met the requirements I set for "extended writing" (see Chap. 3) and for which I was able to obtain copies of drafts for all youth in the study. I also interviewed Maria, Fabiola, and Diego about their writing at the Saturday program they attended. As a result of Jaime's move to West Hills, he did not complete the same assignments that the others did, although he did complete a partial first draft of the humanities writing task. Instead, in his interviews during the ethnographic phase, we spoke about the social studies research paper he completed at his new school, which was one of two major extended writing tasks he completed and the only one for which I was able to obtain a copy of multiple drafts, including the final one.

Questions for interviews typically included the following, with some variations depending on the particular event:

General:

Tell me about [the text].

(If school-based) Tell me about the assignment and the class you wrote it for.

Process:

Tell me about the steps you took to create it.

As you were planning to write or while you were writing, what conversations did you have with other people about the ideas you were writing about? About the writing itself?

What helped you write it? What resources did you use? (If outside sources: Where did you find them? Once you got them, how did you use them?)

Did anyone else help you write it? How did they help you?

How did you decide to organize it? Why?

(Questions specific to the particular text, such as asking youth to look at feedback from teachers and/or changes they made between drafts and to explain what they changed or not, and why.)

Purpose:

What were your goals in writing it? What were you trying to achieve?

Did you enjoy anything about writing it? If so, what? Why?

Did you dislike anything about writing it? If so, what? Why?

Audience:

Who will (or has) read this? Did this influence how you wrote? If so, how?

Who will (or has) evaluate(d) or grade(d) it, and what do you think they are (or were) looking for? Did this influence how you wrote? If so, how?

Summary:
What do you like best about what you wrote? (in general, and in terms of the writing)
Would you do anything differently if you could write this over again? If so, what would you change? Why?
How does this compare to other things you've written?

Prompts:
Tell me more about…
Can you give me an example of…
You didn't say anything about…
How would you describe…
What did you do when…

Youth Interview Guide 3: Longitudinal Follow-Up

During all years following the period of ethnographic study, the interactional histories of literacy events interviews (above) also included a more general set of questions about youth's experiences since I had seen them last. This allowed me to better understand the broader context of individuals' language and literacy journeys throughout the study, since we no longer saw each other on a daily or weekly basis; it also encouraged them to reflect on their past experiences. Questions typically included the following but were also personalized based on a review of previous interview transcripts I would undertake in preparation for each new interview, which allowed me to integrate ideas or events discussed in our earlier conversations:

Catching Up:
How are you?
(Questions about particular family, friends, recent events, celebrations, hobbies, etc.)
What does a typical day at work/school look like for you now?
What do you usually do when you get home?

School (If Applicable):

How is school?

What classes are you taking?

For particular classes: How is it going? What is a typical day like? What are you learning? What kinds of reading are you doing for the class? What kinds of writing are you doing for the class? What kinds of tests or assignments have you had, and what are they like? Have you gotten feedback from your teacher on any of the work you've completed? If so, what was it? How did you respond?

What are you enjoying most?

What is most challenging for you?

Work (If Applicable):

How is work?

How many hours per week are you working?

What are your responsibilities?

What are you enjoying most?

What is most challenging for you?

How do you use English and Spanish in your job?

How do you use reading in your job?

How do you use writing in your job?

At the Beginning of a New Experience (e.g., Starting a New School or Job):

What do you think __ will be like? (in general, and in relation to languages and literacies)

Has [previous experience] prepared you for this next step? If so, how?

Are there things you think [previous experience] has not prepared you for? If so, how?

How is it going so far?

Is it what you expected? How so, or why not?

What are the people/students/teachers/co-workers/customers like?

Does it feel different from [previous experience]? If so, how?

At the End of an Experience (e.g., Finishing a Semester/Year, Graduating, Leaving School/Work):

What did you enjoy most? Least? Why?

How have you grown, and what have you learned? (in general, and in relation to languages and literacies)

What were your greatest successes there? (in general, and with languages and literacies)

What were your greatest challenges there? (in general, and with languages and literacies)

What will you remember most about [experience]?

How do you feel about the next steps you're taking?

What are your plans for the next few years?

Literacy Experiences Outside of School/Work:

What kinds of reading have you been doing outside of school/work? In what languages? (including computer/phone use and specific social media)

What kinds of writing have you been doing outside of school/work? In what languages? (including computer/phone use and specific social media)

Reflective Questions on Language and Literacy Journeys:

What roles do English and Spanish play in your life right now? How has that changed over time? How do you feel about the ways you use language or languages?

What have you learned about language since I saw or talked to you last?

Do you feel you have certain strengths as a language user right now? If so, what are they?

Do you feel you have certain weaknesses as a language user right now? If so, what are they?

(Repeat the last three questions for writing/being a writer and reading/being a reader.)

Prompts:
Tell me more about…
Can you give me an example of…
You didn't say anything about…
How would you describe…
What are your memories about…
What did you do when…

Teacher Interview Guides Focused on Literacy Events

During the ethnographic phase of the study, I conducted two interviews with each teacher whose students had engaged in extended writing tasks. Interview questions focused on their curriculum in general, the extended writing tasks students completed for their respective classes, and their reactions to the writing that Jaime, Ana, Diego, Fabiola, and Maria completed. The first interview occurred around the time that students completed their final drafts, and the second interview occurred shortly after teachers had finished their assessments of those drafts. The interview guides typically included the following questions:

Interview 1
Introduction:
How would you describe this class and its curriculum to someone who is not already familiar with it?
How would you explain this writing task to someone who is not familiar with the class?

Purpose:
Why did you assign this task?
What do you hope students will get out of completing the task?
What is important to you in terms of students' writing? (in general, and in term of this particular assignment)
In your opinion, what would a successful student text look like? (in general, and in term of this particular assignment)

Process:

Please describe the steps you and students took to create these texts.

Tell me about how you structured in-class time for students to work on this task. Why did you choose to do it that way?

Tell me about how you approached providing students with ongoing feedback. Why did you choose to do it that way? What were your goals?

How are you planning to approach assessment of the final drafts? What are your goals for that assessment?

Interview 2

Introduction:

How did you end up assessing students' final drafts?

Did you learn anything new about students in your class from having them complete this task? If so, what?

Did you learn anything new from it in relation to teaching writing? If so, what?

Did you learn anything new from it in relation to teaching more generally? If so, what?

Focus on Study Participants:

(Give copies of students' assignments to teacher.) Tell me about ___'s text. What were your expectations about the writing this student would produce? How would you describe the student's writing? How would you describe the process through which it was created?

(Repeat for each student in the study.)

Prompts:

Tell me more about…

Can you give me an example of…

You didn't say anything about…

How would you describe…

What did you do when…

Transcriptions of Observed Interactions and Interviews

My approach to transcription conventions developed over time and in response to the complete body of data included in this book. As a result, sections of data that originally appeared in earlier publications may have been presented in those contexts through slightly differing conventions than those employed here. Here, I describe the consistent approaches I used across chapters for transcribing observed interactions, semi-structured interviews, and more informal conversations.

Transcriptions of data from audio-recorded observations were created using particular conventions intended to provide readers with an accessible but thorough understanding of the interactions being analyzed. For observed interactions, the following conventions were used, modified from Atkinson and Heritage (1984), Bunch (2004), and Jørgensen (1998):

[	Beginning of overlapping utterances, including those that start simultaneously, placed in both lines
]	End of overlapping utterances, placed in both lines
=	Latching of speakers' utterances, in which there is no interval between adjacent utterances
(.)	Brief pause
(2)	Precise number of seconds for pause
-	Truncated word or momentary pause
:	Lengthened segment or syllable
.	Stopping fall in tone*
,	Continuing intonation*
?	Rising intonation*
" "	Tone indicates reading aloud, suggesting wording for writing, vocalizing while writing, or reported speech
CAPS	Emphatic stress
xxx	Unclear utterance for which a good guess can be made as to numbers of syllables uttered; each x equals one syllable
italics	Spoken in non-English languages

('did')   Translation of non-English language, located beneath or
           after original utterance

(( ))   Non-lexical phenomena, vocal or nonvocal, that overlap with or
           interrupt the flow of speech

           Note. Conventions with an * were used to mark intonation units
           (Du Bois, Schuetze-Coburn, Cumming, & Paolino, 1993).

Because observed interactions were analyzed on a fine-grained level, each intonation unit was placed on its own numbered line to allow easy reference to smaller sections of the data.

I employed a slightly different set of transcription conventions for semi-structured interviews and recorded informal conversations, given that those data were included in order to explore individuals' perceptions and ideas rather than to analyze the interactional features of the interviews or conversations themselves. I still retained the aforementioned conventions to show lengthening, truncation, emphatic stress, pauses, intonational contours, and language choice, all of which were still relevant to the purposes for which I used interview data. However, I did not place intonation units on separate lines or mark overlaps and latching because they were less relevant to my use of interview data. To increase readability of interviews, I made several additional modifications, which included: capitalizing the beginning of intonational units either at the beginning of an utterance or after a stopping fall or rising tone, removing most fillers and false starts, using standardized orthography, and placing English translations directly after or within excerpts as needed. I also endeavored to keep interview excerpts as continuous blocks of data, but at times I employed ellipses (…) when interruptions or temporary topic shifts occurred and were not relevant to the data presented, or added brackets [ ] to provide additional information to clarify what was being said.

In both interview and classroom interaction transcripts, non-conventional language features were not marked or otherwise notated unless they obscured meaning. For uses of Spanish—which may be relatively less familiar to some readers—I explained some of the non-conventional features in footnotes to provide relevant context for the translations.

Presentation of Youth's Writing

In all instances, I present the writing youth completed verbatim, without any modifications other than standardizing the font and size so that their texts are easily recognizable as such throughout the book. I did not change spacing, punctuation, capitalization, or any other features of their writing.

References

Atkinson, J., & Heritage, J. (Eds.). (1984). *Structures of social action: Studies in conversation analysis.* Cambridge, UK: Cambridge University Press.

Berger, R. (2015). Now I see it, now I don't: Researcher's position and reflexivity in qualitative research. *Qualitative Research, 15*(2), 219–234. https://doi.org/10.1177/1468794112468475.

Bunch, G. C. (2004). *"But how do we say that?": Reconceptualizing academic language in linguistically diverse mainstream classrooms* (Doctoral dissertation). In *Retrieved from Dissertations & Theses @ Stanford University database Publication No. AAT 3145478.*

Du Bois, J. W., Schuetze-Coburn, S., Cumming, S., & Paolino, D. (1993). Outline of discourse transcription. In J. A. Edwards & M. D. Lampert (Eds.), *Talking data: Transcription and coding in discourse research* (pp. 45–90). Hillsdale, NJ: Erlbaum.

Emerson, R. M., Fretz, R. I., & Shaw, L. L. (2011). *Writing ethnographic fieldnotes* (2nd ed.). Chicago: University of Chicago Press.

Gough, B. (2003). Deconstructing reflexivity. In L. Finlay & B. Gough (Eds.), *Reflexivity: A practical guide for researchers in health and social sciences* (pp. 21–36). Oxford: Blackwell.

Guillemin, M., & Gillam, L. (2004). Ethics, reflexivity and 'ethically important moments' in research. *Qualitative Inquiry, 10*(2), 261–280. https://doi.org/10.1177/1077800403262360.

© The Author(s) 2019
A. K. Kibler, *Longitudinal Interactional Histories,*
https://doi.org/10.1007/978-3-319-98815-3

Hamden, A. K. (2013). Reflexivity of discomfort in insider-outside educational research. *McGill Journal of Education, 44*(3), 377–404. https://doi.org/10.7202/039946ar.

Heath, S. B., & Street, B. V. (2008). *On ethnography: Approaches to language and literacy research.* New York: Teachers College Press.

Jørgensen, J. N. (1998). Children's acquisition of code-switching for power wielding. In P. Auer (Ed.), *Code-switching in conversation: Language, interaction, and identity* (pp. 237–261). New York: Routledge.

Kibler, A. K. (2014). From high school to the *noviciado*: An adolescent linguistic minority student's multilingual journey in writing. *Modern Language Journal, 98*(2), 629–651. https://doi.org/10.1111/j.1540-4781.2014.12090.x.

Kibler, A. K. (2017). Becoming a "Mexican feminist": A minoritized bilingual's development of disciplinary identities through writing. *Journal of Second Language Writing, 38*, 26–41. https://doi.org/10.1016/j.jslw.2017.10.011.

Lawrence-Lightfoot, S., & Davis, J. H. (1997). *The art and science of portraiture.* San Francisco: Jossey-Bass Publishers.

Lofland, J., Snow, D., Anderson, L., & Lofland, L. H. (2006). *Analyzing social settings: A guide to qualitative observation and analysis* (4th ed.). Belmont, CA: Wadsworth.

Marcus, G. E. (1994). What comes (just) after "post"? The case of ethnography. In N. K. Denzin & Y. S. Lincoln (Eds.), *Handbook of qualitative research* (pp. 563–574). Thousand Oaks, CA: Sage.

Okano, K. H. (2009). *Young women in Japan: Transitions to adulthood.* New York: Routledge.

Prior, P. (2004). Tracing process: How texts come into being. In C. Bazerman & P. Prior (Eds.), *What writing does and how it does it: An introduction to analyzing texts and textual practice* (pp. 167–200). Mahwah, NJ: Erlbaum.

Watson-Gegeo, K. A. (1988). Ethnography in ESL: Defining the essentials. *TESOL Quarterly, 22*(4), 575–592. https://doi.org/10.2307/3587257.

Index[1]

---

[1] Note: Page numbers followed by 'n' refer to notes.

© The Author(s) 2019
A. K. Kibler, *Longitudinal Interactional Histories*,
https://doi.org/10.1007/978-3-319-98815-3

CPSIA information can be obtained
at www.ICGtesting.com
Printed in the USA
LVHW011430041118
595899LV00011B/175/P